Born in Lancashire, **MICHAEL HENDERSON** has written for the *Guardian*, *Observer*, *The Times* and *Daily Mail*, and was cricket correspondent for the *Daily Telegraph*. He writes regularly about the arts for the *Spectator* and *New Statesman*, and about cricket for *The Cricketer*. He lives in London.

Praise for *That Will Be England Gone*

'Absolutely and completely loved this book by Michael Henderson - love letter, memoir, lament, polemic. Read, in place of cricket' — Marina Hyde

'Michael Henderson is one of the most knowledgeable writers there is about the summer game. In this vibrant chronicle of the 2019 cricket season, he travels around England taking the temperature of the sport he loves. The result is pure gold . . . The book is also a love poem to an England fast disappearing . . . For those who fear the worst for the sport they love, this is like cool, clear water for a man dying of thirst. It's barnstorming, coruscating stuff, and as fine a book about the game as you'll read for years' — Michael Simkins, *Mail on Sunday*

'Philip Larkin's line "that will be England gone" is the premise of this fascinating book which is about music, literature, poetry and films as well as cricket. Henderson is that rare bird, a reporter with a fine grasp of time and place, but also a stylist of enviable quality and perception' — Michael Parkinson

'Charming . . . a threnody for a vanished and possibly mythical England' — Sebastian Faulks, *Sunday Times*

'Lyrical . . . [Henderson's] pen is filled with the romantic spirit of the great Neville Cardus . . . This book is an extended love letter, a beautifully written one, to a world that he is desperate to keep alive for others to discover and share. Not just his love of cricket, either, but of poetry and classical music and fine cinema . . . A book that started out as an elegy for a changing game seems more poignant now' — Patrick Kidd, *The Times*

'To those who love both cricket and the context in which it is played, the book is rather wonderful, and moving' — Simon Heffer, *Daily Telegraph*

'It is about cricket but also about much more: landscape, place, poetry, music, national mythology . . . This is the book's authentic register, and it is haunted by loss' — Jason Cowley, *New Statesman*

'Englishness itself, as much as cricket, is the main theme of Michael Henderson's genre-melding *That Will Be England Gone* . . . extremely readable . . . often amusing . . . *That Will be England Gone* is part memoir, part sports book, part essay . . . Given that this may be a summer without leather and willow, and that coughing has become taboo, Henderson's book provides a much-needed literary-cricketing alternative: a beautiful clearing of the throat' — Daniel Ray, *Spectator*

'In a work that now seems improbably prescient, that same sense of gazing at a disappearing world has been articulated with great skill and, most of all, great affection by Michael Henderson . . . The book – a paean to the sub-culture of county cricket, its supporters, its players, its observers, its writers, its pubs and its arenas – was completed before the coronavirus crisis struck but its premise seems more pertinent than ever' — Oliver Holt, *Mail on Sunday*

'A travelogue and a love letter to the festival and spa towns of England and in particular to the places where county cricket is played . . . Henderson writes beautifully about Cheltenham and Chesterfield and Trent Bridge in Nottingham, his favourite Test ground. You do not need to love cricket to feel the point' — Philip Collins, *The Times*

'Beautifully written piece of work . . . wonderful book – not just a sports book, which is why it is so good – is to be reminded, or even educated, of what it means to be English and of England's history' — *Yorkshire Post*

'All good sports books are about more than just sport, and this anti-modern elegy to an old rural England takes in countless bypaths from Vienna to Ken Dodd . . . Erudite and occasionally beautiful' — *Financial Times*

'Erudite . . . genuinely beautiful' — *Wisden Cricket Monthly*

'Wonderful elegy to a game that, way more than any other, defines our shared identity . . . a timely reminder of what is missing from our lives in cricket's absence' — Jim White, *The Oldie*

That Will Be England Gone

The Last Summer of Cricket

Michael Henderson

CONSTABLE

CONSTABLE

First published in Great Britain in 2020 by Constable

This paperback edition published in 2021 by Constable

1 3 5 7 9 10 8 6 4 2

A CIP catalogue record for this book
is available from the British Library.

ISBN: 978-1-47213-287-1

Typeset in Minion Pro by SX Composing DTP, Rayleigh, Essex
Printed and bound in Great Britain by Clays Ltd, Elcograf S.p.A.

Papers used by Constable are from well-managed forests
and other responsible sources.

MIX
Paper from
responsible sources
FSC® C104740

Constable
An imprint of
Little, Brown Book Group
Carmelite House
50 Victoria Embankment
London EC4Y 0DZ

An Hachette UK Company
www.hachette.co.uk

www.littlebrown.co.uk

For Giles Phillips
Cricket-lover, wine drinker, gentleman
'We've got to have some music on the new frontier'

And in memory of Bob Willis, and all the blessed days we
shared with our friends

CONTENTS

Prelude

Cricket's rope of destiny was woven by many hands, and not all the weavers wore cream flannels and striped caps. Those who shaped their innings with words also played a part.

'There can be no summer in England without cricket,' wrote Neville Cardus after watching one of his heroes, Frank Woolley of Kent, make a century at Dover. Allowing for romantic embellishment, which came so naturally to Cardus, all who love the game know what he meant. An English landscape without cricketers on the green between April and September is inconceivable.

Cardus created a mythology of cricket. He may not always have been realistic in his presentation of events, but he was truthful to the game's spirit. Marcel Proust, who spent two decades of hard writing ordering a life of leisure, showed how much the imagination owes to memory. From that palette of mixed tones, 'the colourings of an unsuspected world', comes art.

I have never been a cricket fan. The word 'fan' implies fanaticism, which is a step towards tribalism, of which the world has always had enough. I have been a cricket lover, however, since the day in September 1965 that I saw Fred Trueman bowling for Yorkshire against Derbyshire at Scarborough. His purposeful approach and high arm, an alliance of physical power and cunning, were my ludic equivalent of Proust's twin steeples at Martinville. Through half-closed eyes I can see him now, running in from the Trafalgar Road end. Those early memories – one's first bag of chips, for example – are the most vivid.

That love took another two years to ripen. When it did, in the pivotal summer of 1967, I was stubbornly unparochial. I wanted Lancashire to prosper. I hoped England would do well. Yet those attachments never occluded my love for the game, which meant more than winning and losing. The notion of 'postcode' support never occurred. As Yeats wrote of the stage, and those who fill it with illusions more truthful than real life, 'the dream itself enchanted me'.

John Arlott's commentary on *Test Match Special* opened a window to the wider world. Few voices in post-war Britain were so familiar, or so imitated. What made Arlott unique was that he never pressed his claims upon the listener, as do so many modern broadcasters, obsessed by the cult of personality. There was no striving for effect, no rhetoric for its own sake. He meant so much to the generation that had come through a war because he understood that cricket and sport in general mattered less than some zealots would have people believe.

'Of all the pleasures lower than the arts,' he told me one evening in November 1985, 'cricket is the highest.' This, from a man who as a poetry producer at the BBC had known E. M. Forster, George Orwell and Louis MacNeice. His favourite companion in those convivial days was the maker of verses and taker of purses Dylan Thomas, 'the only man I ever kissed on the lips'. He wrote a poem, 'Cricket at Swansea', as a tribute to the notorious sponger.

Arlott was pouring wines from Spain at the Vines, his house in Alderney, and talking about the players who had given him the greatest pleasure, from Jack Hobbs, 'The Master', to Ian Botham, whom he loved like a son. 'What relish for the game, and for life. If you gave him a pair of gloves, and put him in a ring, I reckon you'd find out he was a pretty good boxer, too.'

He understood that cricket yields its pleasures slowly. It is a game of languorous hours and sudden, occasionally violent shifts of fortune. More than any other sport it has an aesthetic sense. A day's cricket, whether it is watched at Lord's, Cheltenham or Ramsbottom, involves much more than the notching of runs. Every minute there are opportunities for digression and diversion.

'A footballer plays his game for ninety minutes,' said Arlott, 'and leaves an impression of skill, or finesse, or violence. A cricketer is showing you his character all the time.' One may say as much of the cricket watcher. The game draws out something in the spectator that other sports, being shorter and more explosive, cannot.

Terence Rattigan thought it was 'beautifully inconclusive'. In his screenplay for *The Final Test*, a peculiar film of 1954 which features members of the England XI in subsidiary parts uttering unlikely things, Rattigan has Robert Morley say that 'to go to cricket for excitement is like going to a Chekhov play for melodrama'.

It is no coincidence that so many writers, interested in plot and character, have been drawn to cricket. Two, Samuel Beckett and Harold Pinter, were Nobel Prize winners. Pinter used to send a draft of his plays to Beckett, who in his early days in Paris served as amanuensis to James Joyce, another cricket lover. As Pinter kept a copy of *Ulysses* by his bed it was almost an apostolic succession.

Pinter's friend, Tom Stoppard, wrote a speech in *The Real Thing* that used the well-sprung cricket bat as a metaphor for the well-written sentence. 'What we're trying to do is write cricket bats,' says Henry, the playwright, to a sceptical lady who believes that political commitment trumps all. Occasionally members of the audience applauded the line. One evening, in the West End, a theatregoer booed: an act which suggested, more than the clapping, that Stoppard was right.

Uniquely, cricket is shaped by forces of nature. The season starts in spring, a time of renewal, and ends in September, with conkers on the ground and woodsmoke in the air. It charts an emotional course from hope to melancholy.

Although they play cricket in other lands, often more attractively than in England, cricket in our island is unique. The game is played on softer pitches, in milder weather, when the most common words are 'rain stopped play'. A sudden shower, or the appearance of the sun, can have an important influence on the outcome of a match.

It is cricket's emotional weather, as much as the climatic conditions, that sets it apart. A game that takes six hours to unfold each day, for five days at a stretch in Test cricket, offers plenty of scope for reflection. Conversations tend to meander, way leading on to way.

Those ruminative pleasures run counter to the spirit of our triumphantly demotic age. Sometimes it seems that unless everything is immediately understood by everybody there has been an assault on democracy. The popular, however vulgar or trivial, is venerated above the accumulated wisdom of the years.

Cricket has not been untouched. The sport that matured over a century of gradual change has altered almost out of recognition since the introduction in 2003 of 20-over cricket, a bowdlerisation aimed specifically at younger spectators. The atmosphere at grounds is coarser and occasionally, when strong drink has taken hold, unpleasant. The clubs are not concerned because it means people are spending money, and cricket is a poor game.

One consequence of this cultural shift has been the creation of strong loyalties that were not apparent before. Spectators beyond Lord's have become more vocal, and less tolerant of good play by England's opponents. The common law of applauding boundaries, or maiden overs, is observed less strictly. Matches have become contests of 'us' against 'them'.

In 2008 Graeme Smith, the South Africa captain, made a century of exceptional fortitude in the fourth innings of a well-contested match at Edgbaston to give his side victory.

His innings was barely recognised. The crowd stood to him as he departed but while he was at the crease, defying England's bowlers over by over, thousands of spectators preferred to demonstrate rituals of football-style loyalty to the cause. When I was growing up that cause was cricket.

A friend who spent that afternoon in the Eric Hollies Stand, the rowdiest part of the ground, said that hardly anybody around him could identify an England player, or the county he played for. It was a modern crowd, full of big-event attenders enjoying a day's revelry. In the subsequent decade the ground, anointed 'Fortress Edgbaston', has become even rowdier.

An experience shortly afterwards, at a T20 match between Lancashire and Yorkshire at Old Trafford, was revealing. Spectators had not gathered in the expectation of watching an evening's sport. They had consented to take part in a form of light entertainment. When pop songs blared out on the speakers, which they did three times an over, young and old joined in, word perfect. There was some sharp cricket that night, and for 18,000 people it meant not a thing.

At such times the cricket lover brought up in more tranquil times can feel lonely. We must recognise, however, there are reasons for cricket's eagerness to flaunt its knickers. Fewer children play the game, at school or among themselves for fun. In the parks of west London, where I live, it is rare to see cricket played, except by Asians.

The clubs, who do so much to compensate for the schools' lack of interest, face their own problems. In an age of limitless leisure opportunities the old loyalties cannot be taken for granted. It was always asking a great deal of club cricketers to give up every Saturday between April and September. Many big-hearted souls are still prepared to do so. Some cannot make that commitment, and so each summer cricket loses dozens of clubs, and hundreds of players.

By far the greatest change is the absence of cricket on terrestrial television. No sooner had England reclaimed the Ashes in the summer of 2005, in a series covered by Channel 4, than the England and Wales Cricket Board (ECB) hitched its wagon to the riches supplied by Sky. The broadcaster's commitment to cricket is outstanding. But the effects have been brutal. English cricket is richer in money, and immeasurably poorer in spirit. The sport's public profile has been diminished.

Amid the clamour 'to do something about it' the ECB, through the cahooting of chairman Colin Graves and chief executive Tom Harrison, came up with a competition called 'The Hundred'. Starting in 2020, bankrolled to the tune of £1.7 billion by television, this new-fangled game of 100 balls a side will bring in £1.3 million a year for all 18 first-class counties for the five seasons up to 2024.

The fact that the eight teams set up for the event are city-based, rather than rooted in the traditional clubs, mattered little to these pioneers, who simply rolled up the map like Frederick the Great of Prussia. The counties, forever short of cash, held out their begging bowls like peasants craving a boon. Privately there were doubts. Publicly, with the exception of Surrey, they acquiesced.

Nobody could explain why we needed to invent a game of 100 balls, or how counties with different traditions (Somerset

7

and Glamorgan being the most peculiar compound as the new 'Welsh Fire') could work together. It was enough to know it would soon be here; a commercial palliative designed for the school holidays, between July and September, to soothe the fevered brow of every bean counter.

To the evident concern of Graves, the founder of Costcutter, the Yorkshire-based grocers, and Harrison, a former Derbyshire bowler who had moved successfully into sports marketing, the public responded with scorn. Media coverage, almost without exception, was withering. What exactly was the purpose of this new game? Did T20, only twenty balls longer, not thrive? Full houses all over the country suggested it did.

Furthermore the new competition would be played alongside the 50-over competition at the height of summer, taking players away from their parent counties. Graves was unrepentant. Young people, he pronounced like a prophet who brooks no doubt, are not attracted to cricket, which is too complicated and not sufficiently diverse. It is a game of the shires in a world that thinks increasingly in urban terms.

It comes down to this stark, astonishing fact. For the first time in the history of professional sport a game is being changed by the people who run it for the notional benefit of those who are not interested. The Hundred is a cozening of the counting house, passed off as a necessity.

Meanwhile those odd people who do love the game, and cannot understand that necessity, are painted as reactionaries. As many of them have not been slow to respond, there's quite a lot to react against.

Something else happened on that day at Edgbaston, when

the noisy 'patriots' in the Hollies Stand ignored Smith's match-winning innings. A friend in the press box asked an overwhelming question: 'Is cricket part of your sporting life, or your other life?'

I had always known the answer. Yet it was the first time anybody had put it in such a straightforward way. Cricket has always been part of that other life, if not from the day I saw Trueman running in at Scarborough, then certainly from the moment I saw his great comrade, Brian Statham, playing his last match for Lancashire – against Trueman and Yorkshire, as it happens – three years later at Old Trafford.

Football belonged to my sporting life. It still does, even if the club I grew up supporting at Maine Road has been taken away from me. Cricket occupied another place, in the realm of the imagination. In the decades since I saw Trueman and Statham, as I have taken a greater interest in literature and music, cricket has kept me company. It fits naturally into that world.

Our tastes, whether low, middle or high, adjust to circumstance and company but some things are undeniably better than others. We are not supposed to say that in an age that favours subjective opinion over objective reflection but it happens to be true. The history of humankind tells us so.

It is possible to enjoy *Carry On Up the Khyber* as well as *La Grande Illusion*, though not in the same way. It's easy to love *Pet Sounds* but the person bold enough to suggest Brian Wilson ranks alongside Johann Sebastian Bach has not been born. 'Caroline, No' may be two minutes of pop magic. It is not the B minor Mass. Bernard Levin called this process of separation 'the sieve of history', and nobody can escape the shaker.

So it is with cricket. You can love Test matches and also enjoy the one-day game, which performs a different function. The old Gillette Cup, played over 60 overs a side, was a marvellous competition, and is much missed. But it never had the amplitude of Test cricket.

I am not the kind of person likely to be attracted to the Hundred. I buy hardback books, think of Wigmore Hall as a second home, and take my holidays in European cities that have great art galleries. I have no interest in social media, have never bought a lottery ticket, and wouldn't watch a 'reality' show on television if I were granted the keys to the Exchequer. It is a generational thing, and age helps to determine taste. As much as I would like to visit 'the cloud-capp'd towers, the gorgeous palaces', I don't expect to find them where teams of unknown provenance play games of mock cricket over 100 balls.

There are more small-c conservatives about, of left and right, than modern tastemakers suppose. The sort of people who find 'diversity' an unjustified imposition, designed to assuage the guilt of those who shouldn't have to bear it for the dubious benefit of those who are capable of finding their own way; who consider 'accessibility' to be an intellectual fraud that excuses ignorance, and sometimes exalts it.

These people would recognise the spirit of conservatism defined in 1956 by the philosopher, Michael Oakeshott, in 'On Being Conservative'. They prefer 'the familiar to the unknown, the tried to the untried, fact to mystery, the actual to the possible, the limited to the unbounded, the near to the distant, the sufficient to the superabundant, the convenient to the perfect, present laughter to utopian bliss'.

That seems a reasonable way of looking at the world. Surely it is wiser to base judgements on observation and experience rather than the flying of ideological kites.

Cricket lovers of that temperament know they are swimming against the tide. Told that the Hundred has been planned with the game's best interests at heart, they share that 'present laughter'. When they heard, as they did repeatedly before the 2019 season, that a World Cup followed by a Test series against Australia represented the summer of their lives, they kept bat and pad together.

It seemed an appropriate time to saddle up Rocinante. Time to revisit some of the places where I learned to love cricket, and see whether the game still speaks of summer, and England, in the way previous generations would recognise. There were bound to be diversions along the way because six months on the road opens up vistas, scenic and emotional. This book is principally about cricket. It is also about things I have shared with friends in the course of a life. Cricket does not exist in an intellectual vacuum.

How easy it is to deride those who grew up watching a less hectic game. Resist the urge. Whether nodding off in deckchairs at Hove, or lolling under the limes at Chesterfield, those old-timers may be dreaming of summers when the world seemed happier, less contentious. On lazy afternoons the scents of those days come back, unbidden.

Beautiful hours they were, of cricketers and 'laughter learnt of friends'. As Hermione Gingold, the Countess in Stephen Sondheim's *A Little Night Music*, used to ponder each night, recalling certain aspects of her far from innocent past, 'Now, where was I . . .?'

I

Here

The View from Malvern

No single view speaks for a nation. But some landscapes, coloured by geography and history, have an emotional clarity that defines us. All peoples share a blood memory, rooted in places and events, which helps to establish a national mythology.

Whenever the English are asked to nominate their favourite views the answers usually include dawn on the Cotswolds and twilight at Buttermere, the white cliffs of Dover, the coastlines of Cornwall and Suffolk, shadows in Dorset lanes, and snow in the Yorkshire Dales: all are much-loved images. Stonehenge, Lincoln Cathedral standing proud on its hill, even the Houses of Parliament seen from Westminster Bridge. Each says something about England, and the English.

If you were looking for a view that is representative, as opposed to beautiful or dramatic, you may head for the

Worcestershire spa town of Malvern, in the spirit of A. E. Housman, who would 'climb the beacon that looked to Wales away'. He was not, despite the title of his famous volume, a Shropshire lad at all. He was born in Bournheath, near Bromsgrove, and 'the blue remembered hills' in his much-anthologised poem about 'the land of lost content' were the Malverns, nine miles long, running south to north, and 680 million years old.

Let's climb that beacon. What do we see?

A dream of England; both the physical entity rooted in native soil, and that land which animates our national imagination. It would be a dull soul who did not stand on this hill, no more than a mound by Alpine standards, let the mind's eye wander, and ponder what kind of country England is.

Directly north is Coalbrookdale in neighbouring Shropshire, where Abraham Darby christened the Industrial Revolution by smelting iron with coke, and creating iron ore. In 1781 the world's first cast-iron bridge opened, and a new age dawned before the nightwatchman had sounded his horn. Within half a century England was the first industrial nation and, spared the revolutions that convulsed the continent, it became the major European power.

As the eye moves east it spies Birmingham which, as a direct consequence of that revolution, became 'the workshop to the world'. Just beyond England's second city, to the north-east, is Lichfield, the birthplace of Samuel Johnson, compiler of the celebrated dictionary and, in the estimation of his comrade, James Boswell of Edinburgh, the world's greatest wit. It was also the birthplace of his friend David Garrick, the

13

leading actor of the day, with whom he set off for London and immortality.

Moving closer the eye takes in Warwick, where William the Conqueror began the building of a great castle in 1068, two years after the Norman invasion. Worcester, down the hill from Malvern, was the scene of the battle in 1651 between Charles II's Royalists, eager to regain the father's crown for the son, and the forces of Oliver Cromwell's New Model Army, which prevailed. Charles fled the scene to hide in an oak tree in Boscobel House, Shropshire, to avoid capture, hence the 'Royal Oak'.

Near Warwick lies Stratford-upon-Avon, where William Shakespeare was born. He is not only the greatest writer in the English language. He is acknowledged in every culture to be the greatest of writers. '*Unser Shakespeare*' – 'our Shakespeare' – the Germans liked to call him. We may have given Shakespeare to the world, and the world has not withheld its thanks, but he was above all an Englishman, from Warwickshire.

Ken Tynan, the cricket-loving drama critic, and a Birmingham man, wrote of *Henry V* that 'the play drives straight to those emotions of soil, birth and breeding which we all profess to have outgrown'. Shakespeare, the Swan of the Avon, is one of the central figures in our national mythology, even if he played fast and loose (to borrow one of his own phrases) with historical facts. A mythology is not necessarily rooted in veracity.

On to Oxford, and its great university. The city 'of lost causes' and 'dreaming spires' has become a global synonym for intellectual distinction. Oxford was also where, in 1555, the

'Oxford Martyrs', Thomas Cranmer, Hugh Latimer and Nicholas Ridley, were burned at the stake outside Balliol College for heresy during the blood-soaked reign of the Catholic Queen Mary. In the nineteenth century it was again the centre of a religious schism when Edward Pusey and Cardinal Newman founded the Oxford Movement of Anglo-Catholic dissenters. Augustus Pugin, the architect who redesigned the Palace of Westminster, and Gerard Manley Hopkins, the poet and Jesuit priest, were well-known adherents, though it was Newman himself who led the way. In February 2019 he was canonised by the Pope, and raised to sainthood.

More recently Oxford is where Colin Dexter set his Morse mysteries, tales taken around the world on television by John Thaw's ale-supping, opera-loving and defiantly agnostic detective. When Dexter began the Morse sequence in 1975 with *Last Bus to Woodstock* he cannot have imagined that so unlikely a detective would find so wide an audience. But the world loves English detectives, the more unlikely the better.

To the west there is the abbey at Tewkesbury where, in 1471, in the last battle of the 'Wars of the Roses', Edward IV led the Yorkists to victory over the House of Lancaster. Each May, enthusiasts re-enact the events at the town's medieval festival. Looking further west, following Housman, one sees the rich pasture land of Herefordshire, which has sustained the county's russet-coloured cattle for centuries. Beef, sheep, pigs, apples, pears: this is the national larder. The county town is Hereford, where the cathedral owns the Mappa Mundi, the most famous medieval map of the world in the world. Beyond lies Offa's Dyke, the Anglo-Saxon earthwork that separates England from Wales.

Hereford is one of the cathedrals that stage the Three Choirs Festival, a celebration of music that dates back to 1715. The others are Worcester and Gloucester. It was at Gloucester in 1910 that an audience first heard a piece of music that has come to represent Englishness. In *Fantasia on a Theme of Thomas Tallis*, scored for string orchestra, Ralph Vaughan Williams took a melody by the composer, written in 1567, and threw a rope across the centuries. The music, refracted through the genius of Vaughan Williams, sounds Elizabethan and modern at the same time. It is an aural trick akin to magic. If England disappeared in a puff of smoke, leaving behind only this, it would be possible to discern something of the national spirit.

Simply by standing on these hills, and turning round slowly, the discerning peeper can take in a significant slice of the social, political, religious, industrial and cultural history of England. It is not a grand landscape. There is nothing spectacular, as there is in the Lake District or the Dales. But nowhere else in England can you feel so many of the forces that have made the English who they are.

This is not an urban world. There are no major cities between Bristol and Birmingham. The towns, in the plains of the rivers Avon and Severn, which wind their way through this part of England, are small and tidy. They are reasonably well-off but not conspicuously prosperous, for this is where the gentry have made their homes. There is no industrial working class here, nor are there many aristocratic families.

In folk memory the old shires are intact. The Local Government Act of 1974, which introduced 'Hereford and Worcester' and 'West Midlands', means little to the people who live here. They know that Warwickshire, Worcestershire and Herefordshire are counties with different histories and traditions. Housman, who imagined the Roman soldiery 'when Uricon the city stood', knew them well: 'The blood that warms an English yeoman, the thoughts that hurt him, they were there.'

Those thoughts are still here, in towns such as Ledbury, Cleobury Mortimer, Tenbury Wells and Evesham. This is Middle England, a place of meadows and streams, and a thousand voluntary activities followed by men and women whose lives are untouched by urban rhythms. It is small-c conservative, and often Conservative in its politics. Stanley Baldwin, the prime minister who is generally held to represent Middle England conservatism, was the MP for Bewdley. Villagers here still count in shillings, measure in pounds, rely on Fahrenheit to tell them how warm it is, and walk a country mile, not a kilometre. Old-fashioned they may be but country folk are not the 'woolly-backs' of metropolitan mockery. They understand that 'heartless, witless nature', as Housman put it, is less innocent than it appears to be in the imaginations of city types who choose to live among them. People who observe the cycle of life at first hand are neither easily deceived nor impressed.

Step off the train at Great Malvern, and one half expects to be greeted by another Stanley, Holloway, whose friendly face lit up so many well-worn films of the 1940s and 1950s. There are hanging baskets, a bookshop, a florist that sells honey, and the 'award-winning' Lady Foley's Tea Room. The town up the slope is full of small shops that sell useful things. The tourists who visit the local theatres, the Three Counties Showground, and the famous schools for boys and girls bring £120 million a year to the local economy, so there are plenty of well-appointed guesthouses. 'Respectable' is the word.

Yet Middle England, however convenient a phrase for outsiders who may never set foot there, will never be a satisfactory definition. Places, like people, have a habit of eluding observers who think in terms of easy categories. Malvern, cosy as it appears, was the place where Bernard Shaw liked to stage the premieres of his plays, and Shaw was no Middle Englander.

It was on the hills above Malvern that Langland's fourteenth-century dreamer saw his vision in *Piers Plowman*, one of the first great English poems. C. S. Lewis was moved to create the imaginary kingdom of Narnia after bumping into one of the town's 116 gas lamps upon leaving the Unicorn pub on a foggy night. Lewis, who attended Malvern College, frequently returned there with his Oxford colleague, J. R. R. Tolkien, whose own contribution to local folklore is no less significant. Middle Earth was what he imagined when he looked out from the beacon. Culturally speaking, Malvern has conquered the world.

Greater writers than Lewis and Tolkien also spent time here. Evelyn Waugh stayed regularly at Madresfield Court, two miles away, as a guest of the Lygon family. In 1932 he used Madresfield, a moated manor house of Tudor, Jacobean and Victorian provenance, as a bolthole to write *Black Mischief*. The house became his model for *Brideshead Revisited*, his best-known if not necessarily best novel, which was published in 1945.

There was another visitor – and yet another Oxonian – in 1932. Wystan Auden had spent two years in Berlin after leaving Oxford, where he had attended lectures by Tolkien, the university's Professor of Anglo-Saxon. In September 1932 he took up a teaching post at the Downs prep school, Colwall, at the southern end of the Malvern Hills. 'Uncle Wiz', as the boys called him, enjoyed three happy years at the Downs. He taught English and French, lent a hand in arithmetic and biology, and, somewhat perplexingly given his unathletic nature, supervised games.

It was at the Downs, where he enjoyed walking along the hills declaiming Langland, driving friends around the countryside and often sleeping outdoors, that Auden found his poetic voice. One evening in June 1933, sitting on the grass after dinner with three friends, he felt 'invaded by a power', 'a mystical vision' which they also felt. 'So long as I was possessed by this spirit,' he wrote, 'it would be literally impossible for me deliberately to injure another human being.'

This 'Plowman' moment produced one of his first great poems, the lyric 'Out on the lawn I lie in bed', which Benjamin Britten, his first musical collaborator, set in the Spring Symphony of 1949. It's worth quoting some of the lines, to get a flavour of life at the Downs in those three years,

> where the sexy airs of summer,
> the bathing hours and the bare arms,
> the leisured drives through a land of farms,
> are good to the newcomer.

Auden was never conventional, as a poet, teacher, Christian or public figure. He loved nothing more than proscribing for the lives of his friends. Britten, a cold fish, could not tolerate such interference. Yet it was in Colwall, far away from Berlin or New York, where he was to live most of his adult life, or Austria, where he died in September 1973, that Auden experienced the moment of rapture that transformed him.

His parting gift to the 'land of farms', in June 1935, was to wed Erika Mann, daughter of Thomas, the great German novelist. Surely this was the oddest literary marriage of all, between an English homosexual and a German lesbian, in a registry office in Ledbury. How easy it is to represent Middle England – and misrepresent it.

When people think of the Malverns, one name crops up time and again. Edward Elgar was not born here but the composer could see the hills from his childhood home in Broadheath, just off the road from Worcester to Leominster, and those hills have come to form the landscape for his music. When Ken Russell made his film about Elgar for the BBC in 1962 he showed him riding a white horse over the Malverns to the accompaniment of one of his great works, the *Introduction and Allegro for Strings*.

Elgar was regarded as an old-fashioned composer when the film was screened. He had been dead 27 years when Russell accepted Huw Wheldon's invitation to hear the music with fresh ears. Thanks to Russell and Michael Kennedy, whose *Portrait of Elgar* was published in 1968, we now understand more about this troubled man whose music, far from proclaiming imperial certainty, is full of self-doubt. 'I couldn't understand how others did not hear it,' said Kennedy. 'His unhappiness seemed so obvious.'

Unlike Vaughan Williams, who loved the great Tudor composers, and collected folk songs, Elgar had little use for English music. He looked towards Germany for his models: Brahms, Schumann and 'the Master of Bayreuth', Richard Wagner. He quotes directly from *Götterdämmerung*, the last of the four operas that constitute the *Ring* cycle, in the closing bars of his second symphony. 'Nimrod', the best-loved of his *Enigma Variations*, the symphonic work that made his name, was a musical portrait of his friend Alfred Jaeger, who was German. It was another German, Richard Strauss, the most famous composer of the day, who acknowledged Elgar to be a master before the English musical world realised there was a genius in their midst.

Whatever Elgar was, he was never a little Englishman. Yet this self-taught, lower middle-class, provincial Catholic, an outsider four times over in an age of rigid social distinctions, composed music that establishes a sense of England as convincingly as any composer has conceived of a national identity in sound. The two symphonies, the *Enigma Variations*, the concertos for violin and cello, and the piano quintet stand supreme in our national music.

Not all musicians warmed to Elgar. Sir Thomas Beecham, the most famous conductor of his day, and a noted wit, thought his work was the musical equivalent of St Pancras railway station. After Elgar's death it became customary to patronise his music as old-fashioned in character and often dull in performance. He was certainly no modernist, in the spirit of Béla Bartók or Igor Stravinsky.

Art will have its revenge. Anthony Burgess, the author of

21

A Clockwork Orange and *Earthly Powers*, who spent much of his life living abroad, confessed in his autobiography that whatever England meant to him, he could find in Elgar's music. These days we pay more attention to Burgess than to Beecham. Thanks to conductors such as Bernard Haitink and Daniel Barenboim, foreigners who understand English culture, his music has found its way into the concert halls of Europe.

Why shouldn't it? Elgar sounds English in the way that Ravel sounds French, or Prokofiev Russian, or Sibelius Finnish, and their work travels. All composers of the first rank are shaped by their cultural inheritance, and in Elgar's case that meant the banks of the Severn and Teme, where as a child he dreamed of composing something great.

Looking over the Vale of Evesham, towards the wool town of Chipping Campden, it can be difficult not to hear echoes of Elgar or Vaughan Williams, who was born a little further away, in the Gloucestershire village of Down Ampney. Their music speaks, in different ways, of England. It may bear little relation to the country passed down to us, but that is what imaginations are for. We are transformed by music, as we are by words and images.

There's the rub. Although we are an urban society, and have been for 200 years, the English imagination has remained defiantly rural. That may not be realistic. It is, however, emotionally truthful, even if the truth is lost on some city dwellers who wish to reorder our lives so that our attitudes accord with theirs.

Many of our favourite pieces of music are rural. Think of Vaughan Williams's *The Lark Ascending*, or his arrangement of 'Greensleeves', which was originally attributed to the young Henry VIII. Our best-loved poems are about nightingales, skylarks, hawks, daffodils and country churchyards, and our unofficial national anthem 'Jerusalem', written by William Blake and later set to music by Hubert Parry, speaks boldly of 'England's green and pleasant land'. Blake, a Londoner, understood this national mythology as clearly as Hardy of Dorset, Wordsworth of Grasmere or Britten of Aldeburgh.

It was at Adlestrop, near Chipping Norton, where Edward Thomas was a passenger in a train that stopped 'unwontedly'. In that brief minute he heard 'mistier and mistier, all the birds of Oxfordshire and Gloucestershire'. The poem is lent emotional weight by the knowledge that Thomas perished at Arras just as he was beginning to find his voice.

G. K. Chesterton, summoning the national spirit, wrote of the rolling English road 'that rambles round the shire'. The parson, sexton and squire are there, as they are in hundreds of stories by Agatha Christie and Dorothy Sayers. Behind it all is a sense of loss, or fear of loss, expressed by Gerard Manley Hopkins in 'Binsey Poplars', when he reflects on the felling of his favourite riverside trees: 'After-comers cannot guess the beauty been.' In this prelapsarian world we are all carried back to an England that was without sin.

Then there are the *Four Quartets* of T. S. Eliot, described by Roger Scruton as the 'greatest poem of homecoming' in our language. Three of the quartets mark specific places: Burnt Norton, a country house in Gloucestershire; East Coker, the Somerset village where Eliot's ancestors lived; and Little Gidding, the Anglican retreat in Huntingdonshire where

Charles I took refuge in the English Civil War, and where another great poet, George Herbert, served as parson.

Our national painters are John Constable, the son of a Suffolk miller, Thomas Gainsborough and J. M. W. Turner. Their canvases abound with mills, streams, horses, open skies and landscapes altered little by time. As children we read books about Toad of Toad Hall, Winnie the Pooh, and Beatrix Potter's friendly creatures from the riverbank. *The Railway Children* was set among the meadows of the West Riding. *Cider with Rosie* belongs to the valleys of Gloucestershire. The *Swallows and Amazons* frolicked in the Lake District. We learned about Robin Hood and his merry band in Sherwood Forest, and the oak-crested Green Man, that love-child born of paganism and Christianity.

Our pubs, those unbreakable symbols of popular culture, bear the names of long-established customs and trades: the Coach and Horses, the Horse and Farrier, the Plough and Harrow, the Royal Oak, the Bull's Head, the Dog and Partridge, the White Hart, the Stag's Head, the Woolpack, the Ring o'Bells, the Holly Bush, the Bay Tree, the Carters Arms. They often have handsome signs outside, indicating the kinds of crafts that were once practised in the area, and the ales they serve evoke another world: Landlord, Pedigree, 6X, Lakeland Gold, Black Sheep, washed down with Scotch eggs, cheese cobs and pork pies. In Malvern there is a classic local, the Nag's Head, which has 14 ales on tap, and where at 5 p.m. they put sandwiches on the bar for all-comers.

The three Johns loom large: Bull, Peel and Barleycorn. Bull is the embodiment of England, a red-faced chap in a scarlet jacket, striding forth. Peel is the huntsman, gadding about the land to the sound of the horn. Barleycorn was treated 'most barbarously', and ground into stones, yet he had the last word as his spirit is renewed each year to bring us cheer.

We are not alone in having a rural imagination. In France there is 'La France Profonde', wherein the soul of the nation may be found. The Germans are proud of their glorious forests, where the Brothers Grimm uncovered so many tales for children of all ages. Every Italian village hides a hundred secrets. Russians, as we know from all those plays and novels, cry at the sight of a birch tree. Every national imagination, one might argue, is essentially rural.

Cricket belongs to this world. First played in the Weald of Kent by shepherds who used their crooks for bats, it spread to the Downs of Sussex and Hampshire, and has always been associated with that England of the imagination. Along with the pub and the church, the cricket field with white figures set against the village green fits neatly into the timeless idyll of country life.

It was never quite so innocent. Those early matches on the uplands of southern England were played for purses, eagerly advanced and reluctantly surrendered. The players' behaviour was not always decorous. There has always been jiggery-pokery in cricket, however nimble the players and administrators have been to reflect the sport in a favourable light. 'It's not cricket', we say, or used to, when our sense of propriety is offended. It never was. Bernard Levin said of romantic Ireland that the Celtic twilight was invented for a good reason. In England we created a game that has too often been asked to serve as an indicator of moral rectitude. In 1611 two men in Sidlesham, near Chichester, were prosecuted for playing cricket instead of attending church.

As the decades slipped by the game played by shepherds for a hatful of coins mutated into one designed to show colonial people the spirit of fair play. In England it was played until 1962 by county teams composed of amateurs as well as professionals, who shared different dressing rooms. Not until 1954 was an England team captained by a man who was paid openly for playing cricket.

The first thing you notice about English cricket is that it is rooted in the old map. The Test matches may be played in London, Birmingham, Nottingham, Manchester and Leeds, but the professional clubs take their identity from the old shires of Essex, Middlesex, Surrey and Sussex. The cricketers play at Taunton, Hove and Worcester. When the play switches to the festival grounds it's off to Tunbridge Wells, Arundel and Kidderminster. A stranger could learn a lot about English history by following the cricketers around for a summer.

It is the right place to come, Malvern, in the first week of April, to take in once more the view from the Worcestershire Beacon, and think of those who lived and worked here. On this hill some remarkable people have helped to shape our national story.

One catches in particular that melancholy expressed by those tormented Victorians, Elgar and Housman, born within two years and a handful of miles of each other. Here, on the ridge that divides Worcestershire and Herefordshire, one may savour a feast for the ravenous eye and get an inkling of what makes the English truly English. If you are not touched by what you see, check your pulse.

Looking a bit further north one reaches the water meadows of the Trent, the third major river in Middle England. It was there, to the southern stretch of Derbyshire, that I headed in April 1967; to Foremarke Hall preparatory school, the 'preparation' being for life at Repton, the parent public school.

It was a bit of a shock for an eight-year-old, coming from Bolton, a post-industrial town in Lancashire far removed from the codes and rituals of private education. The dislocation lasted no longer than a month. Children adjust to prep-school life, however odd or even hostile it may initially appear, with a facility that often confounds those who never experienced it. In time they may come to enjoy it.

Social historians look back at the summer of 1967 with wonder, like 'stout Cortez' coming upon the Pacific. How completely the world changed in those months of liberation! The old order gave way to the new, and the young inherited everything they were owed, simply by being young.

Some notable things did happen. Homosexuality was decriminalised for consenting adults in England and Wales, when Parliament passed the Sexual Offences Act on 27 July. The Beatles released *Sgt Pepper's Lonely Hearts Club Band* to a chorus of joyous voices that included the ever-groovy Tynan and Cyril Connolly. It was never the best Beatles record (*Revolver* breasts the tape, ahead of *Rubber Soul*) but it was an event, or a 'happening', as we were encouraged to say.

It was a good year for Hollywood. *Bonnie and Clyde*, *The Graduate* and *In the Heat of the Night* revealed a shifting of the generational tide that could not be arrested. There was heady talk, which seems absurd from this distance, of an alternative society, which would blow away the *ancien régime* of 'fools in old-style hats and coats'.

Yet how much ground was really broken in the fabled 'summer of love'? In April, when I was preparing for the adventure of boarding school, the 18-year-old Steve Winwood was assembling Traffic in a Berkshire cottage to record that manifesto of hippiedom, 'Dear Mr Fantasy', with its plea to 'play us a tune, something to make us all happy'. Like most things that fell from the mouths of hippies, it was nonsense. But it was a belting song, which scrubs up fresh today. Winwood's vocal performance and guitar solo give it classic status.

That was the year of Cream and Jimi Hendrix, as well as Traffic. In San Francisco, we learned, in a song that has aged less well, they put flowers in their hair. Not everybody joined in these daisy-laden larks. The pop charts, as those historians do not always let on, were dominated by smarmy Engelbert Humperdinck, jolly Harry Secombe and cuddly Vince Hill. If this was an alternative society the custodians clearly took a tolerant attitude towards those who wished to join.

Later that year the ghastly Frankie Vaughan, using hat and cane as props, joined the throng of light entertainers jostling for space on *Top of the Pops*, and neither he nor the lovely Pet Clark skipped the light fandango. This was a very bourgeois revolution, which left little trace in Derbyshire DE6 6EJ, though Mr Turnbull, the English teacher, wore some snazzy shirts.

Prep-school life in the late 1960s was pretty much as it has been portrayed in countless memoirs. Orwell's essay, 'Such, Such Were the Joys', which recalled his own schooldays in Sussex half a century earlier, could have done service as a primer for life at Foremarke.

A Palladian house built for the Burdett family, it had been transformed into a school after the Second World War, and memories of that conflict remained fresh. The four houses were named after heroes of the services: Alexander and Wavell, both field marshals; Mountbatten, admiral of the fleet; and Tedder, marshal of the Royal Air Force. Three earls and a baron, whose pen-and-ink portraits hung in the main corridor, near the servants' quarters. I was in Mountbatten House, numbered 102 in the school.

This was a world of petty snobbery and punishments for minor infractions; of Airfix models and silly nicknames; of 'keeping *cave*' (Latin for 'beware', pronounced KV) to announce the arrival of an interfering master; of biscuit-bagging raids on the pantry after lights out, and pillow fights in the bedders; of lumpy porridge six mornings a week, and inedible curry.

There were 'excellents' for good work, and 'order marks' when a boy fell short of the level required, in or out of the classroom. One boy, Brown N, was awarded a double order mark 'for taking far too much custard'. Note that signifier, 'far'. Jones W, who wailed when he fluffed a Latin test, was told: 'It's high time you had a jolly good blub.'

If you let the side down, or failed to pull your socks up, you would be for the high jump, which often led to the headmaster's study, where the cane might be produced. Usually it wasn't.

In four and a half years at Foremarke I was beaten only once, for being in the woods at night, when they were out of bounds, and compounding the offence by being rude to the master who found us there.

Many of the boys lived overseas, where their fathers were servicemen or in business, oiling the machinery of the old Empire. There was little evidence of great wealth. Several members of staff had lived abroad, too, and not all had adjusted to life in post-war Britain, where the old certainties were suddenly less certain. The boys, from Jamaica, Ceylon, Malaya, Singapore and even Persia, brought an air of mystery to the school. But there was no overt prejudice along racial or ethnic lines. It was a happy school overseen by Tom Davies, 'T. D.', a headmaster of sympathy and tact.

You can't keep secrets in an enclosed world. The masters knew full well what we got up to when they toddled off to the Swan at Milton for pints of Bass they had fully earned. As John Osborne has noted, schoolmasters are overpaid as educators and underpaid as child-minders. We didn't always behave well, and sometimes behaved very badly. But the fun was usually innocent. Every prep-school boy of that era recalls the midnight feasts. We had ours on the roof, where we scoffed chocolate digestives, Jaffa Cakes and fig rolls under 'a cavernous, wind-picked sky'.

We built dens in the woods, cast boats on a murky lake, and strolled along the tree-lined path to St Saviour's, the Foremark (no 'e') church. There was an abundance of parkland for games of cricket, rugby and football, and an outdoor swimming pool. Such a sense of space! Foremarke was a world unto itself, with fields that rolled out of sight and, always, that canopy of sky. It was almost blissfully happy.

Until I went there cricket had played little part in my life, other than that day at Scarborough in 1965. We were regulars at Burnden Park, where Bolton Wanderers played football. Francis Lee, the star striker, was my hero. Yet in the summer of 1966, when England won the World Cup, beating West Germany 4–2 at Wembley, I was unaware that the West Indian cricketers, with Garfield Sobers in the form of his life, had played five Test matches. Old Trafford, twelve miles from our home, was terra incognita.

It was on a playing field by the lake at Foremarke that I picked up a cricket bat for the first time. Even before I did I was taken by the sight of the cut strip and the two sets of stumps pitched 22 yards apart. There is something just-so about wickets being pitched that ought to give every cricket lover a shiver of delight. It's only a ritual, but we are all loyal to habits developed in our youth.

At first the cricket was supervised by Mr Hoare, a partially deaf geography teacher, whose kindly manner was disrupted by occasional spasms of irascible behaviour. When this mood descended, with steam never far from his ears, the only time I have ever seen that much-quoted phenomenon, he would beat boys in his designated den, 'the Roundhouse', with a gym plimsoll. Those who received 'six of the best' let on that he took a short run-up to administer the strokes.

For those first three summers, before he was appointed head of a prep school in Somerset, he coached us in the basic disciplines of defensive play – pick the bat up straight, keep

31

your head over the ball – and drilled us in cover drives that did not persuade him our numbers contained an embryonic Tom Graveney. When it rained we retired to the Roundhouse, where he would read to us from A. G. Macdonell's *England, Their England*, with many returns – every other week, it seemed – to that well-known village cricket match.

In 1969, his final summer, the Under 11s won all five matches against other schools. We bowled out St Chad's of Lichfield for four, and sent packing Emscote Lawn, St Anselm's, Bramcote Lodge and Grace Dieu, with M. R. P. Henderson keeping wicket. To each member of the team the departing master presented a copy of *The Great All Rounders*, a collection of essays edited by John Arlott, with the inscription: 'Played 5, Won 5. Congratulations on a fine season.'

I had devoured some cricket books in the school library, taking particular interest for some reason in *Cricket in the Sun*, a history of West Indian cricket, by J. S. Barker. Now I had a book of my own, which featured essays by writers such as Neville Cardus, C. L. R. James and Alan Ross on Learie Constantine, Keith Miller and Sobers.

Each morning, as soon as the daily papers arrived, I would scour the sports pages to look at the averages of the leading batsmen and bowlers, and study the scores in the county championship. In no time I was familiar with R. T. Virgin of Somerset, B. E. A. Edmeades of Essex, J. S. E. Price of Middlesex and D. W. 'Butch' White of Hampshire, the latter pair prompting great curiosity because *Playfair*, the cricket annual, marked them RF, right arm fast, one distinct grade above the more familiar RFM, right arm fast medium.

Note those initials. Cricketers, uniquely, have always been identified by their given names. No cricket lover needs to be reminded which England players answer to F. S., E. R., P. B. H., D. C. S., A. P. E., I. T. and R. G. D. It's a small matter, though not an insignificant one. Initials indicate formality, and a certain respect.

By the time R. E. J. Chambers succeeded the kindly Hoare as our cricket master in the summer of 1970, cricket had become as important a part of my life as football. Bobby Chambers proved to be an odd one, too. A fine cricketer at Forest School, he had won a Blue at Cambridge, where he opened the batting against the West Indians at Fenner's. It was clear, when he knocked up, he was a stylish player.

When rain stopped play he did not read from Macdonell or talk about Cardus. Instead he would tell us how terrifying it was to face Wes Hall, pounding in from the sightscreen, 'and ending up in his follow-through no more than six yards away from the batsman'. This was Hall, the great Barbadian fast bowler I had read about in those dispatches from the tour of 1963, being described in alarming detail by somebody who had faced him and lived to tell the tale; a man who taught us history!

Chambers had his moods. He took us on day trips to watch county matches at Derby and Nottingham but when England played the Rest of the World at Trent Bridge in 1970, in one of five matches later robbed of Test status, I found myself deselected from the school party after he had succumbed to one of his funks. So I never got to see R. G. Pollock of South Africa in the flesh, on the ground where in 1965 he had made his reputation with a Test century of savage brilliance. In the language of the classroom, it was a bit of a swizz.

That life-changing summer was notable in another respect. My father eventually took me to Old Trafford, for Lancashire's championship matches with Derbyshire and Middlesex, and a Gillette Cup tie against Somerset.

Harry Pilling provided the clearest memory, running out T. J. Barwell with a direct hit from the midwicket boundary in the Gillette tie, which Lancashire lost. Lancastrians of a certain age will never forget little Harry. Never quite good enough to play for England, he was the kind of county pro all teams relied on. Underpaid, not always valued by those who draw up contracts at the end of the year, and cherished by those who love their county.

The mind's eye can also see T. J. P. Eyre, the Derbyshire medium-pace bowler, losing his hairpiece as he approached the crease, and the rigid correctness of C. T. Radley's forward defensive stroke, as he took a full stride towards the bowler, when Middlesex batted. 'That's more like it,' Mr Hoare would have said.

From this distance it was a pretty grim summer. Geoffrey Boycott was dropped by England for slow scoring after making an unbeaten 246 against India at Headingley, and much of the cricket was played in a turgid, get-past-that-bat manner, which is why the Rothman's Cavaliers stood out. Brought together as an international pick-up team, the Cavaliers made lively viewing on Sunday afternoons when the BBC covered their matches.

Among their number was Farokh Engineer, touring that summer with India. The moment I saw him keeping wicket with a grace that could be described as feline, and plundering runs with rather more enterprise than Boycott, I had found a cricketing hero to accompany Franny Lee, the Trotters' goal-hound.

Engineer, a Parsee from Bombay, joined Lancashire in 1968. The team's transformation from a rag-tag-and-bobtail set-up to one-day marvels is usually attributed to Jack Bond's captaincy and the arrival of Clive Lloyd, the Guyanese batsman, in 1969. Lloyd's thrilling strokeplay, and his electric fielding at cover point, certainly raised spirits. But it was Engineer's presence behind the stumps that supplied the prod Lancashire needed.

Years later, he told me that many counties were interested in signing him. 'But when I played for the Cavaliers against Lancashire at Southport, and kept hooking Brian Statham for six, they realised they had to get a move on.' Rot, of course. Nobody hooked Statham for six. But wonderful rot. Engineer played for my club. His triumphs were mine.

Although he never made the runs he should have done, his vivid manner loosened the stays of a rigid club undermined by multiple sackings and walkouts. In 1964 the mutinous atmosphere had led to a special general meeting of members, and the subsequent overthrow of the club committee by a local businessman called Cedric Rhoades. As is often the case, he turned out to be a bigger problem than the old-timers his rebellion had dislodged. Thankfully there were some good years before the wheel turned.

Old Trafford was never a handsome ground. It had developed in a higgledy-piggledy way over a century, and needed an overhaul. To my unformed intelligence it was a demi-Eden.

Seated at mid-off, where the ladies' pavilion was built later, I felt like 'some watcher of the skies'. Throughout those early years, as a junior subscriber, the red-brick pavilion represented a mysterious and impenetrable citadel of adult life. When I finally got there it was to discover the members lived in a fog of pipe smoke and permanent bafflement, much of it alcohol induced.

One regular quaffer took up squatter's rights in the bar shortly before midday, and left his post only occasionally to look at the scoreboard and shout 'Marshal your men!' at whoever happened to be the captain. After one lively afternoon, when members tore into Lancashire's opponents, the man from the *Mirror* dubbed the seats in front of the pavilion 'the pit of hate', a reputation the groundlings did their best to honour.

Engineer rose above this, though with a bat in his mitts he rarely rose above a well-made 30. 'To think he gets upset when he's out,' my great uncle Harry Birtwistle said one day when my hero had failed in a match at Stanley Park, Blackpool. 'He's the best wicketkeeper in the world. Every run he makes is a bonus.'

Uncle Harry, who managed a cotton mill in Pendlebury that Lowry painted, sat on that reconstituted club committee and passed on my tidy green autograph book to every team that visited Old Trafford, Blackpool or Southport. Proper signatures they were, not the printed sheets of names that football clubs used to send back to beseeching boys. Cricketers were much closer to the people who watched them, and most still are. In those days, a handful of summers after the distinction between amateurs and professionals had been rescinded, many were glorified club cricketers.

In the late 1960s I caught the last knockings of some great players. My first Test match, England against Australia at Old Trafford in 1968, brought the sight of Colin Cowdrey practising in the nets. How hard he struck the ball! Here was 'Kipper', the maker of beautiful strokes, hitting with no less power than the blacksmith in *England, Their England*.

That summer also brought Brian Statham's farewell when the great fast bowler scattered the stumps of six Yorkshire batsmen at Old Trafford before taking his sweater for the last time. His friend and England bowling partner, Fred Trueman, bowled in that match, rekindling memories of our day trip to Scarborough. Yorkshire took the county championship in 1968, for the third successive year. Even with Statham pointing the way, those were grim days for Lancastrians.

I saw Ted Dexter, who smacked the ball with a headmaster's severity, and Tom Graveney, the most gracious of batsmen, but it was Engineer I longed to see triumph. In July 1971, on the club ground at Buxton, where Derbyshire played occasional matches, he granted me that fervently held wish. Joining forces with Bond when Lancashire were five wickets down, he made 141 on an afternoon of joy. Time and again he pulled Alan Ward, who was bowling briskly, into the rhododendron bushes at midwicket. It was the only century I saw him make.

Later that month Engineer was out hit wicket in the Gillette Cup semi-final against Gloucestershire, which finished shortly before 9 p.m., with Old Trafford plunged into darkness. His right foot slipped as he set off for a run, and dislodged a bail. That was the night David Hughes, in the team for his slow left-arm bowling, plundered 24 runs from an over by

John Mortimore. They were proper strokes, not slogs. It was a Noah's Ark of an over: two sixes, two fours, two twos.

In September, when they beat Kent in the final on my first visit to Lord's, my cup was brim-full. That match brought another golden moment when Bond, who was 39 and looked ten years older, took off to his right at extra cover to intercept an off-drive by Asif Iqbal, the Pakistan batsman, that was travelling like a rocket. It remains the catch of my life.

It was a classic year in the pop charts. 'I'm Still Waiting', 'Just My Imagination', 'It's Too Late' and 'Heaven Must Have Sent You' hogged the airwaves that summer, and autumn brought 'Maggie May' and 'Life's a Long Song'. Ah, as Noël Coward wrote, 'Extraordinary how potent cheap music is.' David Hepworth wrote an excellent book about pop in 1971 but I'm not sure his memories are sharper than those of the lad who began the year with the Partridge Family and saw it out with King Crimson. In the months between 'I Think I Love You' and 'Islands' the team of Engineer, Hughes and Bond gave me the most memorable summer holiday of all.

When I left Foremarke that December I was immersed in cricket, and not just the kind played by men with the red rose on their caps, though their success in the Gillette Cup and Sunday League brought joy to the tens of thousands who flocked to Old Trafford. I had attended my first Test match, been to Lord's and, thanks to the efforts of two schoolmasters, been acquainted with the great players of the past. John Arlott on the radio and Cardus in print had supplied two strong voices to guide me.

My young eyes could see that cricket, with its gradual revelation of character, offered a pleasure more usually found beyond the world of flannelled fools. There was joy in the sight of white figures on the green, the improbable reversions of fortune, and the balance that apportioned equal weight to young and old, left and right, impulse and restraint, assertion and reception, classical and romantic.

The pleasure could be dramatic, intellectual or, even for one on the cusp of his teenage years, who knew little of such matters, aesthetic. Simple gestures counted: the tipping of a cap or the raising of a bat when a batsman acknowledged the crowd's applause. They revealed the unspoken relationship between performer and watcher.

At Foremarke the curtain parted, and I was enchanted by what I saw. At Old Trafford the stage was occupied by men who had grown up in mill towns, and spoke different lines in another tongue. As introductions to cricket go, mine was as good as anybody's. I still see those men; as real now as they were then, undiminished by time or memory.

In 2019, an hour's idling on the hills above Malvern has not brought an Audenesque revelation. The trees may be coming into leaf, the songbirds at their leisure, and summer ready to march in. Yet, as the cricketers of England prepare to open the season, the sky is full of brooding clouds.

It is supposed to be a time of affirmation. In June and July the grounds of England will stage a World Cup; seven weeks of 50-over cricket the hosts have set their hearts on winning since they departed, abjectly, the previous tournament in Australia four years ago. Every month, it seems, a member of the England set-up has paraphrased Helenio Herrera, the manager who brought the European Cup to Internazionale of Milan in the 1960s: 'The World Cup, we shall have it!' Having invested so much hope and money in the enterprise, England cannot afford not to win it.

Then, when the World Cup caravan leaves Lord's on 14 July, the country will be gripped by 'Ashes fever', as England engage their oldest rivals in five Tests. Apparently the cricket lovers of England have never had it so good.

Everybody wants cricket to prosper. As Cardus wrote, it is an indispensable part of the English summer. Nevertheless there is a touch of desperation about this drum-banging. It calls to mind those Soviet apparatchiks of old, clapped in the chains of party discipline, whose job was to declare, for the benefit of waverers, 'Our business is rejoicing!'

The game is not in a healthy condition. In state schools cricket is almost a dirty word, regarded as a pastime for children whose parents can afford the fees that private schools demand. Fewer school leavers are playing recreational cricket, and so clubs are losing players, and fixtures. Even established old boys' teams at the well-known public schools are finding it harder to get players to turn out.

Away from the Tests, which remain well-attended, particularly when Australia or India are the tourists, cricket can seem invisible. The newspapers that used to offer readers extensive coverage of championship cricket are happy to rely on agency reports, if they carry reports at all. There are big-name columnists, wheeled out to provide comment on major matches. Otherwise, silence. To the modern sports desk obsessed with big events, county cricket, the traditional bedrock of the sport, seems desperately old-fashioned.

The most significant change in the presentation of cricket to the wider public has been the game's absence from terrestrial television. However well Sky have covered the game since they took over from Channel 4 in 2006, the year after that beguiling summer when England regained the Ashes under the captaincy of Michael Vaughan, with Andrew Flintoff writing his own headlines, cricket has ceased to be the sport of summer in the way it once was. A generation of young people, robbed of the chance to watch the game on daytime television and wallow in the achievements of the best players, has grown up knowing next to nothing of cricket.

Flintoff and Vaughan were national figures, like Ian Botham and Bob Willis, and Fred Trueman and Colin Cowdrey, going all the way back to W. G. Grace. The leading England cricketers may now walk down any street in the kingdom unnoticed. A survey of sporting habits in 2018 revealed that more teenagers recognised an American wrestler than Alastair Cook, a knight of the realm, who has played more Tests (161) and made more Test runs (12,472) than any other Englishman.

James Anderson, who has taken more Test wickets than any other English bowler, is hardly more recognisable. To followers of cricket he stands out, of course, but they are fewer in number; hundreds of thousands fewer since the England and Wales Cricket Board opted to take Sky's millions. Joe Root and Stuart Broad are outstanding cricketers, comparable with the greats of the past. They too are less familiar than many members of the approved cast of prominent sportsmen held up for public inspection.

This invisibility is a recent thing. In 1975, when David Steele was lifted out of county cricket to face the mighty Australians and responded with batting of grim-faced defiance, he was voted BBC Sports Personality of the Year. That wider audience of viewers no longer exists. Such is the power of free-to-air television to tell tales and create heroes.

In 1967, when cricket fired my imagination, the *Carry On* company of jesters made a film, *Follow that Camel*, featuring Phil Silvers, the American star of *Bilko*. The film was bookended by scenes on a cricket field, and a running joke was the way the foppish aristocrat, played by Jim Dale, carried his bat with him when he went off to join the French Foreign Legion.

Dale defended Fort Soixante-Neuf in the desert by using that bat to strike grenades over the wall, as though he were pulling balls over the ropes at midwicket. When the film played at the Bolton Lido one wag shouted, to whoops of laughter, 'Sign him up, Lancasheer!' Who, these days, would make a film with cricket granted such a central part?

It is increasingly seen by the restless young as a slow-moving sport, which takes too much time to play or watch. It's hard to contest the fact that, in a world that values instant gratification, cricket favours the longer view, and young people do not. They want everything, and they want it now.

Hence the desire, expressed in almost lascivious terms by the ECB's prime movers, that the Hundred is introduced to save the game, even if, at the time of writing, nobody knows what form this competition will take, or even what the teams, which are effectively city franchises, will be called.

We have come a long way from the days when Alan Ross, the *Observer*'s cricket correspondent, and editor of the *London Magazine*, could write of a day at Lord's: 'You can pick up unobtrusively all you could ever want to know about wildfowling, duck-shooting, rose-growing, trout-fishing, troop movements, club finances, wines, tailors, etc.' A cricket match, he thought, was 'a storehouse of thought, of thought occasioned by the game itself'.

All gone, like Imperial Rome. Now the game is what Hitchcock called a McGuffin, a device to set the tale in motion. It is a spectacle in which the spectators are every bit as important as the performers. We must all be 'entertained'. We must never be bored. And so, as the last summer of cricket some of us will recognise as proper cricket prepares to surprise and charm, thoughts turn to the national poet of elegant disappointment.

Philip Larkin wrote 'Going, Going' in 1971, to a commission from the Department of the Environment for a paper called 'How do you want to live?' It was published in January 1972, and the poet didn't appear to think much of it. 'Thin ranting conventional gruel', he described it in a letter to a friend, though two years later he included it in *High Windows*, his final volume of verse.

Rummaging one afternoon in the much-missed Slightly Foxed bookshop in Gloucester Road, I came across a second edition of *The Whitsun Weddings*, inscribed by Alan Bennett to Nora Nicholson, who had appeared in *Forty Years On*, Bennett's first stage play. 'I hope you like these poems,' he had written. 'They are what I wanted the play to be – very English and full of affection and dissatisfaction.' No comma after 'English', by the way. And Bennett is an Oxford man.

Like many of Larkin's poems, 'Going, Going' has enjoyed a busy life in the subsequent decades because he had the habit of knocking certain nails firmly on the head.

It begins with the plaintive line, 'I thought it would last my time', and proceeds to describe the damage done to the countryside and our provincial towns by planners and other agents of destruction. Is it simply my age, he asks, or is some profound change taking place? It's a profound change. Through indifference England is becoming the

> First slum of Europe: a role
> It won't be so hard to win,
> With a cast of crooks and tarts.

Then, like a romantic symphony, the themes converge in a final movement of regret no less sad for being so lyrical:

> And that will be England gone,
> The shadows, the meadows, the lanes,
> The guildhalls, the carved choirs.
> There'll be books; it will linger on
> In galleries; but all that remains
> For us will be concrete and tyres.

Most things are never meant, he goes on,

> but greeds
> And garbage are too thick-strewn
> To be swept up now, or invent
> Excuses that make them all needs.

Despair is rarely rendered with such precision. 'Excuses that make them all needs': a phrase that rings with a truth Larkin, a cricket lover, cannot have foreseen. The Hundred springs to mind in all its squalid 'necessity'.

England will not be gone completely, and nor will cricket. There will be pockets of resistance on the village greens and the fields of the public schools, though it has disappeared from the parks and streets, where children once improvised pick-up matches with coats and satchels. The England team will still play Test matches, and most county clubs will limp along arthritically, sustained by the funds that international cricket provides. You can't banish entirely something that has played so important a part in the nation's social history.

But the game as many have known it, like the guildhalls, will not come back. A younger generation will not share this sense of loss, for they never knew what was there, for so long. They take their pleasures in more immediate ways, and an air of distraction suits them. As Larkin wrote in another poem, all we can hope to leave them now is money.

Down from the beacon there is time for a pitstop in the Nag's Head. In one of the town's excellent second-hand bookshops the winking of an Arnold Bennett on the fiction shelf becomes unignorable, and into the bag it goes. Then it is a jog to the station, where the iron horse approaches from Hereford, bringing a breeze from the west and a rumour of summer.

II

New Eyes Each Year

Trent Bridge

People, like nations, have a mythology. As we clear time's fences we see 'into the life of things', as Wordsworth wrote in those lines composed above Tintern Abbey. Because we absorb these things without conscious thought, over decades of assimilation, they acquire unsuspected force. Looked back on from middle age they can appear inevitable.

Vienna, therefore, is 'my' city in a way Paris is not. Paris is a masterpiece known to all. It's the centre of civilisation, as the French will tell you. The Eiffel Tower, the Louvre, the cafés in St Germain-des-Prés and the tarts in Montmartre. Along with London (Big Ben, Beefeaters, red buses), it is the most recognisable city in the world.

The Imperial City is mine because I have created it in my image. On every visit there are certain places I feel compelled to see again, often at the same times of day, to respect the rituals stored up through the years. I take a morning coffee in the Kleines Café, which is exactly what it says it is, a small café in Franziskanerplatz, a square so typically Viennese you wouldn't be surprised to hear Stefan Zweig discussing last night's performance at the Staatsoper with Karl Kraus. And I wind down in Alt Wien, a café by day and the closest thing Vienna has to a pub by night. The hours between are devoted to the other great coffee houses: Prückel, Hawelka, Sperl, Landtmann, Braunerhof. There is no finer place to watch the world turn than a Viennese coffee house, preferably on a winter's afternoon when the light is fading.

'Vienna 1900', that detonation of secular Jewish genius, will always draw people to this city of strange dreams. It means Gustav Mahler and Alban Berg, Arthur Schnitzler and Sigmund Freud, Gustav Klimt and Egon Schiele, Adolf Loos and Josef Hoffmann. These men – and it was a world of men – changed the ways in which we see, hear and think. It also means Kraus, the satirist and author of *The Last Days of Mankind*, whose essays goaded polite society. 'I have devastating news for aesthetes everywhere,' he announced one day. 'Old Vienna was once young.'

In the Musikverein I trace echoes of the great performances I have heard in that golden hall: Mitsuko Uchida performing Beethoven's last three piano sonatas, and András Schiff playing Schubert's G major sonata, the one before the last three; Simon Rattle conducting the Vienna Philharmonic for the first time, in Mahler's ninth symphony; Maxim Vengerov raising the Sibelius fiddle concerto to the level of Beethoven; the orchestras of Amsterdam, Leipzig and St Petersburg honouring their reputations in the most famous musical city of all.

I caught the last performance given by that great pianist, Alfred Brendel, in December 2008. Although he made his home in London in 1970, and liked to say 'I belong to no tribe', Brendel is almost a human definition of *Mitteleuropa* culture and chose Vienna, where he grew up musically, as the place where an audience should hear his final notes. They were by Liszt, a slightly unusual choice.

Then there is Schubert.

For the past 20 years I have boarded the 71 tram at Schwarzenbergplatz, bought a red rose at the gates of the southern cemetery, and placed it on the grave of Blessed Franz, who left us in 1828 at the age of 31. On each visit I quote Auden's hymn to the patron saint of music, 'Anthem for St Cecilia's Day':

> Blessed Cecilia, appear in visions
> To all musicians, appear and inspire:
> Translated Daughter, come down and startle
> Composing mortals with immortal fire.

Like Auden's words, Schubert's music is beautiful, and never ornamental; tragic, and never overbearing; sorrowful, and never sentimental. There may be greater composers – Bach and Beethoven – but not one explores more deeply the crooked timber of humanity. As Maxim Gorky said somewhat resentfully of Chekhov, who is Schubert's emotional kinsman: 'whenever somebody mentions Anton Pavlovich, it is as though a baby deer has just wandered into the room'.

Today we would describe Schubert as bipolar. His fluctuations of mood are sudden, and occasionally troubling. Yet, for all the anguish, there is no anger. For all the joy there is no affirmation, at least not in the way that Beethoven, his great contemporary, sought affirmation. In Schubert's music everything is provisional, an emotional state that reflects more truthfully the balance of our own imperfect lives.

Brendel, with his mastery of the classical and romantic styles, is often considered to be the greatest Schubert pianist. 'The better we know a masterpiece,' he once said, 'the more it surprises us.' Of nobody is that truer than Schubert. Harold Schonberg, the American critic, likened his chamber music to the appearance of the moon on a cloudy night. You know it is there yet every time it appears you are startled, as if struck for the first time.

No composer moves so easily from joy to melancholy without a trace of artifice or manipulation. Because he never strives for rhetorical effects, or hectors the listener, not one is more dearly loved than '*heilige Franz*', whose death was the greatest loss of all. Mozart, who died at 35, had written enough music for a lifetime. Schubert, in that final year of extraordinary fecundity, was beginning to hear and therefore write music in an entirely different way. Granted 30 more years of life, some musicologists have suggested, he might have dissolved tonality half a century before Schoenberg.

'Let us drink to the memory of a great man,' he told fellow mourners after the funeral of Beethoven in March 1827. 'And to the one who shall follow.' In November 1828, after 18 months of composition unparalleled in the history of music, he fulfilled that augury. And to think there was only one public concert of his music in his life.

Vienna also means great paintings, by the score, in the Upper Belvedere Palace, the Academy of Fine Arts, the Leopold Collection, the Albertina and, standing sternly over this Alpine range of delights, the Kunsthistorisches Museum. To walk up that marble staircase, no matter how many times you have made the ascent, brings a smile of recognition. Old friends, we have come to see you once more!

Titian comes first, in a room of such splendour jaws have been known to bounce from the floor. Then it's Tintoretto, and Veronese, through Raphael, Perugino and del Sarto to the famous Velázquez portraits of Philip IV of Spain and his family. On the other side of the gallery, if you have not drowned in this flood of beauty, there are the rooms devoted to Dürer, Rembrandt and Pieter Brueghel the elder. *Hunters in the Snow*! *The Homecoming of the Herd*! *Children's Games*! They're all here.

So many masterpieces jostle for attention: Caravaggio's *Madonna of the Rosary*, the *Holy Family under an Apple Tree* by Rubens, and *The Feast of the Bean King* by his pupil, Jacob Jordaens. In one room, hanging on the same wall, are Vermeer's *Allegory of Painting* and *The Great Forest* by Jacob van Ruisdael.

Alan Bennett said one of the great boons of his life was to serve as a trustee of the National Gallery because he was able to walk through the rooms at night, with only the paintings for company. One Thursday evening, when they keep the KHM open until 10 p.m., I had the Vermeer and van Ruisdael to myself, almost, for the better part of an hour. But if I could sneak one of the paintings out of the gallery and live with it for the rest of my days, it would probably be Rembrandt's portrait of Titus, the son who predeceased him.

There are beautiful churches in every street. The Franciscan and Dominican; St Peter's and St Michael's; the Votivkirche and Karlskirche; and the Jesuit church hidden behind the great cathedral of St Stephen's, 'Steffl', the favourite symbol of this beguiling, sinister city. Vienna is part of my mythology, for these reasons and more, but it will never be a place where a well-balanced Englishman feels entirely settled.

The Mask of Gold, Michael Frayn called his superb television portrait of Vienna. Behind the gaiety, the waltzes, the balls, there is the *weltschmerz* that covers this city like a layer of marzipan. And the appalling antisemitism, defined by one of its most infamous mayors, Karl Lueger, who pronounced 'I decide who is Jewish.' This is a city set in aspic, which doesn't really want to mend its ways, but I cannot renounce it.

Vienna is also the city where Auden died, on 28 September 1973. Wherever in the world he lived he could never be too far away from an opera house, and his last years were spent at Kirchstetten, a hamlet in Lower Austria just beyond the Vienna Woods. He is buried in the churchyard there. On the most perfect late summer morning on 28 September 2001, I visited his resting place, and quoted his lines about William Butler Yeats, the ones that encourage us to 'teach the free man how to praise'.

Berlin is also prominent in my mythology. This is not a city set in aspic! Since the Wall came down, chunk by chunk, it has become, after London, the most dynamic metropolis in Europe, as the most powerful nation in Europe has sought to overcome tragic divisions of history and geography. This is a bracing city-state, whose citizens have never been deceived. Berliners, with their ancestral memory, black humour and robust tolerance, make fine companions.

Zwiebelfisch, 'Onion Fish', a bar on the north-western corner of Savignyplatz, proves that taverns can play a part in a personal mythology. This is a German *kneipe* rather than an English pub, and as such places go it is unsurpassable. To stand outside 'the Fish', in the heart of west Berlin, and watch the trains approach the Zoo Station as the light fades, and the lights go on in the restaurants around the square, is to feel close to the heart of things. It always reminds me of Manhattan, where the West Village meets Chelsea. Here, as there, you may hear the humming of a great city.

Kay's in the new town of Edinburgh, the Lion's Head in Greenwich Village, Andechser am Dom in Munich, the Holly Bush in Makeney, Derbyshire and the Grenadier in Belgravia have all claimed more of my time than is strictly wise. The Fish, run by Hartmut Volmerhaus, born in Osnabrück, but every inch a Berliner, remains *primus inter pares*, as long as you are fully prepared. One night, on the other side of Savignyplatz, I shared a few glasses with an actor ('I was in six of Fassbinder's films') who drained 16 beers. Supping with the Hun is not for amateurs.

Every visit to Berlin includes a walk through the streets of east Berlin, from Prenzlauer Berg down the only hill in this flat city to Hackescher Markt. The old streets of ragged, war-torn buildings have given way in recent years to smart apartments in pastel colours but the area retains a vivid sense of old Berlin.

It isn't only the handsome parts of famous cities that claim our interest. When it comes to music and art, Berlin has given me as much as Vienna. In terms of friendship it has given me more. It is a wonderful place, and it belongs to me.

They coalesce, all those loves that constitute a mythology. Schubert and Beethoven; Bach's music for the piano; the songs of Lorenz Hart and Johnny Mercer; Sinatra in his Capitol years, when he loosened his tie and found his 'cello' voice; Bill Evans, with or without Tony Bennett; the Ellington band, with Johnny Hodges on alto; the operas of Wagner and Janáček; the symphonies of Bruckner and Sibelius; the plays of Chekhov – and the stories, too; the novels of Turgenev, Evelyn Waugh and William Trevor; the verse of Hardy and Housman; the still lifes of Chardin and Cézanne; Pieter de Hooch's Dutch interiors; Rothko's bars of red and black; Kandinsky's explosions of colour; the films of Billy Wilder; the ales of Timothy Taylor; Manchester City in 1968; Roxy Music in 1973. These are more than enthusiasms. They have come to define me.

The Hochbrücke at Salzburg, where you can almost touch the mountains; the Residenz gardens in Munich, looking towards the Theatinerkirche; the Thames at Hammersmith in winter; the first glimpse of Chipping Campden as you turn off the Stow road; Eggardon Hill, which seems to offer the whole of Dorset for admiration; the A591 from Grasmere to Keswick, and the A515 between Ashbourne and Buxton. Views can also forge a personality.

Trent Bridge is there, too. It is the cricket ground I love most.

* * *

Why Trent Bridge? Lord's has a richer history, and a grander stage. I have spent more hours there, and many of my most cherished friendships have been forged in the pavilion and the Coronation Garden. Yet, offered the chance to watch a day's play anywhere in the world, I would go to Nottingham. There is no friendlier ground, nor one more handsome. If any ground can be said to represent the soul of English cricket this is it.

When people say Trent Bridge is a club ground, which happens to be the home of Nottinghamshire, they are not withholding respect. They are offering the highest praise. The other five traditional Test match grounds are urban in character as well as location. Other than Lord's, which is a world unto itself, there has been a transformation over the past decade. The Oval, Edgbaston and Old Trafford have become stadiums, and Headingley would like to join the club. Trent Bridge, on the county side of the river from the city of Nottingham, feels like a cricket ground. Its pavilion looks like a clubhouse, and the people who work there welcome spectators as friends they have known all their lives.

It's quite a trick to pull off, feeling old-fashioned when the ground has undergone a transformation no less obvious than the other Test match venues, and it's greatly to the credit of everybody at Trent Bridge that they have done it with such dexterity. Every part of the ground, other than the pavilion, has been altered in the last 20 years, yet time-travellers going all the way back to William Clarke, the grand old man of Notts cricket, would recognise the spirit of the place were they to return. The development, while thorough, has been organic, so the changes appear natural.

Trent Bridge remains what it was, a village green by a river crossing, where the white stands enhance the greenness. Even the Radcliffe Road Stand, where Rapunzel would happily let down her hair from its towers, feels part of the piece. It is a small ground. At times, when the stumps are pitched on strips at the edge of the square, the cover or midwicket boundaries are barely of first-class status. But Trent Bridge feels right. It has a dignity that endears it to a certain kind of cricket lover, who feels protective towards it. Here, more than anywhere in England, the spectator can see how the modern game has emerged from the past, and appreciate the benign forces of tradition.

We can begin with that grand old man, who was also, in the finest traditions of cricket, a bit of a tartar. William Clarke was a noted local cricketer and publican who ran the Bell Inn, a pub that still prospers in the centre of the city. In 1838 he moved in with Mary Chapman, a widow who owned the Trent Bridge Inn, on the coaching route across the bridge, where the roads now diverge to Grantham and Leicester. For eight guineas Clarke bought the meadow behind the pub, enclosed land that he turned over for cricket, and in 1840 it became the place where Nottinghamshire began to stage matches.

Local folk were suspicious at first, because they had been able to watch the cricketers, without paying a penny, on the old Foresters ground. So Clarke took himself off to Lord's, where his round-arm slow bowling made him indispensable. In 1846, at the age of 48, he founded the All-England XI, a travelling band that sauntered north to play matches against the 22-player team of Sheffield, the 18 of Manchester, and the 18 of

Yorkshire. He was the great pioneer of his day, and was not a poor man when he died in 1850. Every cricketer should tip his cap to this troubadour, for he was the first man to make sure they got paid.

The William Clarke Stand will always be there, in front of the Trent Bridge Inn, which likes to call itself 'world-renowned'. It is, but not for its ale. It was the home of the man who established a major cricket ground, a bricklayer who helped to develop the game before W. G. Grace carried it more fully into the public consciousness. Clarke was the first professional.

That bridge over the Trent, flowing behind the ground where Nottingham Forest play football, may be said to mark the point where south becomes north. There is no way of resolving this matter satisfactorily, but if you wanted to divide England strictly, then Nottinghamshire is clearly in the north and Leicestershire is no less clearly in the south. Nottingham, though geographically in the Midlands, feels like a northern city.

D. H. Lawrence, the son of a miner, and Alan Sillitoe certainly revealed a northern sensibility in their books, even if they lived elsewhere. Lawrence, who is regarded with some suspicion in these parts ('not half the man his father was', a disapproving miner told a scholar on the hunt for Lawrentia), spent much of his adult life in Europe, Australia, Mexico and America, and Sillitoe decamped early to Majorca. 'Write about what you know,' Robert Graves told him. Acting upon the poet's advice, Sillitoe wrote *Saturday Night and Sunday Morning*, a fine novel which produced a film that made a star of the young Albert Finney.

In the pavilion there is a map of the county that reveals the birthplace of the club's best-loved cricketers. Harold Larwood, the most-celebrated Notts man of all, on account of his fearsome fast bowling, came from Nuncargate in the Nottinghamshire coalfield, as did Joe Hardstaff Jr. Bill Voce, Larwood's new-ball partner for club and country, was born not far away, at Annesley. Arthur Shrewsbury, the great batsman of the Golden Age, was a Nottingham man but most Notts men came from other parts of the county: Holbeck, Welbeck, Edwinstowe, Ossington, Bulwell, Burton Joyce, Syerston. Derek Randall, the best-loved of modern Notts players, was a Retford lad.

Randall's bat, the one that brought him 174 runs in the Centenary Test at Melbourne in 1977, is in this collection of memorabilia. So is Larwood's MCC sweater from the Australian tour of 1932/3, the Bodyline tour under the captaincy of Douglas Jardine that caused all the fuss. This small room, tucked away in the pavilion, says a lot about Trent Bridge. We're proud of these men, it seems to say. They played their part in our story. But our heads are not big.

My first year here was 1968. It was also the first season that Garry, later Sir Garfield, Sobers spent by the Trent. He crowned that inaugural summer at Swansea in August, striking Malcolm Nash, Glamorgan's left-arm spinner, for six sixes in an over. To do that as an act of will was a feat only the Elect can achieve. 'The greatest pianist, living or dead,' Neville Cardus wrote of Vladimir Horowitz. Sobers, who could bowl as fast as anybody when the mood took him, and batted like a prince, was the greatest cricketer of all.

'Drunk and Sobers', locals liked to call Jim Baxter and the star all-rounder when they caroused in the pubs of Nottingham. I had seen Baxter twice in 1967, wearing Forest's colours in matches at the City Ground against Burnley and West Ham United. The Scot was an elegant left half, to use a term that has fallen from fashion. Later that season, in which Forest finished second to Manchester United in the old First Division, he dazzled for Scotland, who beat England, the World Cup champions, 3–2 at Wembley.

He couldn't handle the booze, and his general indiscipline undermined a club that recovered only when Brian Clough took charge in early 1975. Sobers, by contrast, took the view that if anybody saw him carousing beyond the witching hour his best answer was to make a century or take a fistful of wickets. Steve Camacho, who played Test cricket alongside Sobers, said of him: 'I never saw Garry without a drink in his hand. And I never saw him drunk.' If we can apply the word genius to sport then Sobers was a cricketer of genius.

He had gone to Trent Bridge to a fanfare of trumpets, as the world's greatest player, and the first star overseas signing of the modern game. When he left after seven summers Notts had not won anything, but that was hardly his fault. He joined a team of modest talent, led by Brian Bolus, once of Yorkshire and briefly, in 1963, of England; a blocker batsman who enjoyed kicking the ball away with his pads. Basharat 'Basher' Hassan, from Nairobi, liked to give the ball a clatter down the order. Otherwise it was thin fare.

On that first visit to Trent Bridge our scattering of school-boys endured an innings by Mike Smedley that ground on all day, like John Coltrane in one of his denser moods. Smedley was a valued member of that side, along with Mike 'Pasty' Harris, Norman Hill, Carlton Forbes, Barry Stead and Bob 'Knocker' White. There was some ordinary cricket played in the 1960s, even when Sobers was around to lighten the mood, and Notts played their share.

The days of plenty came later, when Richard Hadlee, the New Zealand seamer, joined Clive Rice, the all-rounder denied a Test career by the banishment of South Africa from the international game. Along with the local lads, Randall, Bruce French and Tim Robinson, and with Chris Broad joining from Gloucestershire, those men shaped a colourful team that won two championships and a Lord's final. It was a joy to go to Trent Bridge when Hadlee was bowling from the pavilion end. Like Shrewsbury, Larwood and Sobers before him, he was one of the great cricketers.

All days at Trent Bridge are golden. Even when Smedley was at the crease, ploughing his lonely furrow, my impressionable mind was never bored. There were always other batsmen to watch. In 1969, Clive Lloyd's first year with Lancashire, he pulled Sobers over midwicket and out of the ground. 'Hubert' made a point of hitting sixes early in his innings. Once, at The Oval, he pulled Robin Jackman into the playground of Archbishop Tenison's School. To treat Sobers that way, though, really was something.

If one memory stands out it is David Gower's whip-crack-away century against Allan Border's Australians in 1985. That was a marvellous year for Robinson, the Notts opener, who made two centuries in the series. Everything he touched turned to gold. It was also the season, *mirabile visu*, when Gower plucked his lyre like Orpheus.

I went to Nottingham for the first day of the third Test with two great friends, Bob Madge and Barrie Atherton. Sitting in the top tier of the stand underneath the old press box, wine cooling in a bucket, we caught Gower in the midsummer of life. Never again did he bat with such freedom. A jolly fine batsman he was.

That's what it says in the bar that honours George Parr, another of the great Notts men: 'a jolly fine batsman he was!' There is the authentic voice of Trent Bridge; a gentle voice, shaded by humour. Even on Test match days, when the ground is full, and the beer begins to sing, there is nothing unpleasant about the atmosphere. That is why so many of us put such a high value on a day here, trying to catch the *moments fugitives* from years that have fled.

Trent Bridge has also found fame in the literary world. James Joyce smuggled cricket into *Ulysses*, his novel of 1922 that is held up as a benchmark of literary modernism. *Ulysses* is set on 'Bloomsday', 16 June 1904, when Leopold Bloom wanders round Dublin meeting the kind of people you are likely to meet in that city of talk. Joyce, a lover of cricket, like Samuel Beckett, his comrade, refers in the book to 'cricket weather' and 'leg before', but it is James Iremonger who is mentioned by name: 'Iremonger having made a hundred and something second wicket not out for Notts.'

A bit more than a hundred, in fact. Iremonger made the highest score of his career, 272, in that match against Kent. Joyce was spot on. He made the first hundred of them on

Bloomsday. Joyceans have investigated every aspect of that baffling book – the Judaism, the Hellenism, the Irishness, the linguistic and musical richness – and largely overlooked the cricketing element. It may not be a significant part of *Ulysses*, but it is there by design.

Iremonger, a Yorkshireman by birth, enjoyed a notable sporting life. He never played for England at cricket but, as a full back for Forest, he represented his country three times at football. In retirement he coached the young Larwood, so he played his part as batsman and as mentor for Notts, the great club that plays on William Clarke's lovely meadow by the Trent.

Arriving at the ground shortly after nine o'clock on an April morning of pale sunlight, to watch Notts play Yorkshire in the first championship match of the season, I don't have to wait long for the traditional greeting. 'Come in, me duck,' says a steward, opening the gate by the Trent Bridge Inn. It may sound like a cliché, the sort of thing that adds colour to a poor comic sketch, but they really do talk like that in Nottingham.

Out on the square a man stoops to study the pitch, to tease out the tricks it has in store. On closer inspection it turns out to be Dickie Bird. The umpire, 86 years old, and retired for 24 of them, can usually be found at a cricket ground every day between April and September. It still comes as a bit of a shock to see him poking the pitch on the first morning before the umpires have had so much as a peep.

The mown grass holds the promised kiss of springtime. Harold Pinter thought that English grass smelled like nothing

61

else in the world. Is this mere sentiment? No. The cutting of grass, and the mowing of the outfield, are part of the rituals of cricket. The olfactory receptors cannot fail to miss it, particularly on the first morning of the season.

Catching Bird in the middle is another of cricket's rituals, unchanging from year to year. Other things have changed. There is now a 'craft ale' bar at midwicket, and the spirit dips a little at the prospect of earnest young men in beards congregating there to discuss 'citrus flavours' of unremarkable brews.

In the pavilion, where a knot of members has assembled, spirits are restored. 'Reg Simpson,' says one man, ready to wander down Memory Lane. 'Now he was a classical batsman. He opened with Len Hutton, you know. A lovely batsman. I don't suppose he's with us now.'

'I'll be here tomorrow as well,' says his friend, gazing at the blue empyrean.

A Yorkshire follower is getting his eye in. 'Look at the boundary, how short it is.'

'There ought to be plenty of sixes.'

'Even I could hit a six.'

In they wander, men and women glad to have survived another winter, in some cases recalling those who have not. There is talk of funerals and bus times, of chance meetings in pubs, and worries that Notts County, one of the founder members of the Football League, will leave it within the month, relegated from what these people would call the Fourth Division.

'You don't follow that lot?'

'Man and boy.'

'Daft bugger.'

In the tearoom, staffed by two friendly black girls, another Yorkshireman is drinking tea and finishing off a bacon cob. Not a roll, bap or barmcake. This is cob country. Over the road, as many a visitor has discovered, there is a shop called Mrs Bunn's Cob Emporium, and very good it is too.

'I'm from Barnsley.'

Like Bird, who is still prodding the pitch.

'Aye, and Boycott. Darren Gough, too. He's a Barnsley lad. And Michael Parkinson, though he wasn't a cricketer. I love Trent Bridge. Of course, it's not far.'

Most people in front of the pavilion, sharing gossip as the players shuffle down the steps, are white and elderly. There is nobody here under 50. They are polite folk, wrapped in fleeces, anoraks and mufflers, waiting for autographs as children used to do. Some look through the papers, hoping to read something about the season that begins in an hour. Others have brought scorebooks, in which they can record every ball and run. They speak in old-fashioned voices that identify them as Nottingham folk. There are no elisions, or rising inflections.

On the field, where Bird continues to wander about, as though looking for a half crown that has rolled away, the players are stretching. None wears a cap, in the way that cricketers of old wore them. The ones that are not bare-headed wear either woolly or baseball-style hats, reversed so that the peaks face backwards. Of all the phenomena to have taken hold of cricket in recent years, this is the most peculiar. Why do cricketers wear hats back to front? Probably because other sportsmen do. It's like getting a tattoo. The impressionable young can feel very lonely if they are not seen to fit in.

The sartorial revolution covers every aspect of headwear, footwear and kit. To a man these players are clad in tight all-black or all-blue outfits, black for Notts, blue for Yorkshire, with training shoes and leggings. Nobody watching them at their exercise would take them for cricketers. They are more like athletes, limbering up before a marathon.

Their form of exercise would also puzzle those who came before. They are playing football, after a fashion, and making plenty of noise, with hugs and handslaps for goals and mock-serious tackles. It is the behaviour of young people, many new to their clubs, who have been encouraged to 'bond' in the interests of team spirit, whether or not this kind of association comes freely to them. There is much enforced laughter. Nothing in all this running and shouting looks natural. It is not true comradeship; rather, an impersonation of it.

Once more the old-school cricket watcher senses a loss of identity. Half a century ago, when most of the spectators here today were introduced to cricket, the players knocked up unathletically in cable sweaters that bore the colours of their club, cream flannels and heavy boots. Each one was distinct. There was no mistaking Doug Padgett from Phil Sharpe in the Yorkshire ranks. The players were easily identifiable in the field, whether they were crouching at short leg or dawdling by the third man boundary. Now the players are fitter – though, paradoxically, they miss more matches through injury – but they are much of a muchness in their fleeces and hats.

There is a touch of comic relief when the announcer on the public address system bids us all welcome. Here, too, there is a touch of affectation. It is time, he tells us, in the sort of well-modulated voice that should always be used to greet people in public places, 'to renew old acquaintances, and familiarise yourself with Trent Bridge'.

At the various stalls around the ground, he tells us, 'there are refreshments you may savour', and scorecards 'you may peruse'. Everybody at Trent Bridge 'extends a cordial welcome' to the visitors from Yorkshire. 'All is set fair,' he concludes. 'Let's hope for an enthralling encounter.' Not a word is spoken ironically. He really does wish everybody well. It's rather touching.

As he reads out the teams there is a good deal of checking names in the new edition of the *Playfair Cricket Annual*, acquired that morning for a tenner, which supplies thumbnail sketches of all players assigned to the 18 first-class counties. There is no Harry Gurney in the Notts team. He has followed Alex Hales, the opening batsman, in agreeing terms only for white-ball (one-day) cricket, and there is a bit of muttering about this decision. There is no Jonny Bairstow in the Yorkshire XI. He is playing in the Indian Premier League, which has become an unignorable feature of the English spring. But Joe Root, the England captain, is playing, and so is Stuart Broad, one of England's best-ever fast-medium bowlers. Enthralling or not, it will be a proper contest.

When Yorkshire invite Notts to bat, those bemuffled members have a chance to see two of their recently acquired players in harness. Ben Duckett, signed from Northamptonshire, and Ben Slater, prised away from Derbyshire, provide the opening partnership, with Joe Clarke, formerly of Worcestershire, and Chris Nash, who joined last year from Sussex, to follow. Zak Chappell, once of Leicestershire, is injured.

The openers are tested by another new boy, Duanne Olivier, who has renounced his South African identity in order to accept a three-year contract with Yorkshire worth £150,000 a summer. Last winter Olivier was bowling South Africa to victory against Pakistan, taking 24 wickets in a three-Test series. Now he is a 'Kolpak' player, currently stateless, though he will be available for England in three years. Boldly, not necessarily wisely, he has indicated that regaining Test status, in England's colours, is his aim. Such is the nature of modern international sport, where identity comes second to ambition.

Until 1992, when they signed Sachin Tendulkar, Yorkshire could select only those men born within the county. There were a few notable exceptions. Lord Hawke, the great stickler, was born in Lincolnshire. But the born-and-bred policy was otherwise written in stone. To some it was pig-headed. To others it was an admirable declaration of identity, even if it left them at a disadvantage in a world of global movement. That tradition is now as distant as the Tudors. Olivier's arrival at Headingley turned no heads. Yorkshire are now like any other club.

At the other end is Ben Coad, a 25-year-old from Harrogate who made his debut three years ago, and has made a good impression. But it is Steve Patterson, Yorkshire's new captain, who takes the first wicket when Duckett pulls him to deep square leg. It is their only success before lunch, when Slater has made 42 of the 112 runs Notts have put on the board. Root, an occasional bowler, has already been called upon to roll a few off-breaks.

After lunch the bowlers continue to toil. Slater reaches a half century, and is 24 runs short of a century when Olivier takes the edge of his bat, and Jonathan Tattersall completes the dismissal behind the stumps. Harry Brook, fielding at backward point, takes a more difficult catch to dismiss Samit Patel as Notts shed three more wickets. Clarke, driving powerfully, will not budge. He completes a fine century just before the close, and is 109 not out when Notts end the day on 324 for five.

Much is expected of Clarke, who doesn't turn 23 until next month. The Shropshire lad played for England at under-19 level, and caught the eye. As a member of the Lions, an assembly of Test players of the future, he stands on the threshold of a significant career. This was a purposeful way to begin the next stage of his life.

When Worcestershire were relegated from the First Division last autumn he traded the Severn for the Trent, and a county ground for a Test stage. It has been the best possible opening day for him, and a good day for the rest of us. We may read about it tomorrow in the national papers, all two that bothered to send reporters to cover a fixture between two of England's grandest clubs. County cricket butters few parsnips on sports desks in London.

And so another season begins, almost apologetically. The opening day is a *bonne bouche*, a taster for 'the summer of our lives'.

It often seems the people who run the game are most apologetic of all for inflicting county cricket upon the public. Although the championship has been a properly constituted competition since 1890, and is still held to be the most important of the three domestic trophies because it prepares players for Test cricket, the game's governors have found so many ways of undermining it that the first-class game seems invisible to the wider public.

Even the most loyal followers of county cricket no longer know what is going on. This season championship matches begin on every day of the week except Wednesday, and there are vast gaps in the calendar. For nine weeks of the summer there is no first-class cricket at all. Those months are given over to the 50-over competition and to T20, a form of the game that resembles 'proper' cricket in the way a giraffe resembles an elephant.

Many factors have merged to rob the county game of its local character, and to deprive the teams of an easily recognisable identity. To begin at the beginning, there are fewer matches. When Yorkshire won the title in 1968 the championship comprised 28 three-day games. Since then the programme has been reduced to 14, through the dominance of limited-overs cricket, and by the schism in 2000 that led to the creation of two divisions.

Test cricket has always been the most visible symbol of the summer. Now it rules like an absolute monarch. The introduction of central contracts in 2000, designed to improve the fortunes of the national team by giving the leading players more time to practise, also granted the England coach the authority to rest players, which has robbed county cricket of its salt.

The best players rarely represent their counties once they have established themselves in Test cricket. They are considered too precious, particularly the bowlers, who must be protected in case they go in the fetlock. Whereas Alec Bedser got himself fit in the post-war years by bowling hundreds of overs, the modern England bowler is considered to be a weakling, in need of constant instruction and medication.

In the past cricketers had local loyalties. Generally they played for the counties of their birth, or where they had been brought up. This was not an ideal world. They were poorly paid in the summer, and left to their own devices in the winter, when many struggled to earn a living, or scraped one by doing low-paid and demeaning work.

The fortunate ones went on the road as brewery reps. The less fortunate worked as undertakers, or signed on at the dole. In retirement many failed to adjust to the exigencies of normal life, and took to the bottle. The incidence of self-harm and suicide among professional cricketers has been well-documented. Many could not contemplate life away from the dressing room, the only place they truly felt alive.

There was little money to be made from playing cricket, even if you played for England as often as Fred Trueman or Brian Statham, giants of the game, so it didn't really matter where you played from a financial point of view. Nor did the clubs care much, so long as you brought your boots back on 1 April each year for another summer of hard toil. Loyalty, in the much-used phrase, was what they stuffed you with.

The lucky players who had served a club for a decade were usually granted a benefit year, if they kept their noses clean.

That meant, quite literally, going round with a bucket so that spectators could reward the faithful servant with a few coins. It was no way to run a professional sport and yet for decades that is how things were done. It was a world, strictly imposed, of masters and serfs.

Trueman and Statham, though national heroes, were local cricketers in the traditions of the county game. Those traditions were established by the likes of Philip Mead, the Hampshire batsman, who made more runs for his county, 48,892, than any batsman has made for any club in the history of cricket.

Every county had them: Don Kenyon at Worcestershire, Dennis Brookes at Northamptonshire, Les Berry at Leicestershire. All turned up year after year, to resume the old ceremony. Winters were spent away from the game, not turning out for clubs in Adelaide or Cape Town. Asked one spring how long it had been since he picked up a bat, Mead replied: 'Last Scarborough festival.'

Their modern successors were batsmen such as Dennis Amiss, loyal to Warwickshire for 28 years, and Graham Gooch, an Essex man in every fibre of his being. They imbibed the lore of cricket, and passed it on to those who followed them. In recent years Paul Collingwood has been a true stalwart of the county game, making his Durham debut in 1996, when they were the championship new boys, and staying there to win three titles. In its understated way Collingwood's career, which ended last summer, is one of the most remarkable.

Certain players flew the coop. Jim Laker, a Yorkshireman, played for Surrey, and Derek Shackleton, from Todmorden, the border town that separates white rose from red, spent

20 seasons at Hampshire. Quite a few Yorkies had to leave home to find a regular berth because the first-choice XI was so strong for so long. Jack Birkenshaw and Chris Balderstone moved to Leicestershire, and went on to play for England. Barry Wood, who joined Lancashire, also became a Test player. But most stayed local. Wages were similar, wherever you played, and local connections helped in finding work during the winter.

Now that there is much more money in the game, with modern players engaged on year-round contracts, and many spending the winter months abroad, county cricket has become significantly more fluid. Players may have attachments to the clubs that raised them but they are no longer defined by an accident of birth. There is some loyalty. There is also a degree of movement between clubs that was unimaginable even 20 years ago.

No fewer than seven members of the Notts team selected to play Yorkshire began their careers at another club. Besides Duckett, Slater, Clarke and Nash, Steven Mullaney was signed from Lancashire and Paul Coughlin came from Durham. Broad had a Nottingham connection through his father Chris, who opened the batting for the championship winners of 1987, and excelled briefly for England. But he began at Leicestershire, having been schooled at Oakham. Leicestershire have provided their neighbours with quite a few players in recent years. James Taylor, forced to retire at the age of 28 with a heart condition, also came to Trent Bridge from Grace Road. Chappell, the latest recruit, is following a well-trodden path.

In all, the Notts staff includes ten men who have been taken from other counties, though one of them, Mark Footitt, began at

Trent Bridge before moving on to Derbyshire and then Surrey. That was a rare case of the grass not being greener. Footitt prospered at Derby but faltered at The Oval and has come back to Nottingham as a squad bowler, not a first-choice pick.

Yorkshire have two recruits in their team. Tom Kohler-Cadmore left Worcestershire two years ago, in search of a higher profile at a Test match ground. Olivier, the South African Test bowler, reveals the other kind of modern recruitment, the Kolpak, named after the Slovakian handball player whose victory in the European Court of Justice led to freedom of movement for sportsmen throughout the European Union.

What does identity mean, to the player or the county, when it is so easy to become 'English'? Olivier is not alone. Essex won the county championship in 2017 thanks in large part to the wicket-taking skill of their off-spinner, Simon Harmer. At the age of 26, with five Tests behind him, the South African should be playing international cricket for the land of his birth. For professional reasons he has found a home in England. Kyle Abbott, yet another South African, opens the bowling for Hampshire as a Kolpak. South Africa cannot afford too many of these voluntary departures. Nor, if we are honest, can England. These men, however gifted, are not English. They are playing under flags of convenience.

There is nothing new about foreign-born cricketers making their way in county cricket. George Tribe of Northamptonshire, Bruce Dooland of Notts and Bill Alley of Somerset played here, as Australians. Allan Lamb and Robin Smith, among South Africans of the recent past, came here because their own country had been booted out of international cricket in 1970.

The most illustrious import was Basil D'Oliveira, the Cape Coloured, who made a name for himself at Worcestershire before advancing to the Test team. But 'Dolly' was effectively a non-person in South Africa. England was his salvation. Olivier, by contrast, has made a choice for professional reasons; a choice he is entitled to make. Season by season the character of English cricket is changing, and those who watch it regularly feel their loyalty is being stretched.

D'Oliveira's purpose could never be doubted. He revealed it every time he put on his sweater. Nor could anybody accuse those cricketers who were born in the Caribbean, or born there and brought up in England, of lacking spirit.

In a shrinking world, when identity can be stretched to have more than one meaning, there is always the possibility that other cricketers will find Englishness convenient. Keaton Jennings was born and raised in South Africa, where his father, Ray, played Test cricket. Jennings junior represented his country up to the age of 19, which should be interpreted as a declaration of identity. He then came to England, where he has played for Durham and Lancashire, and represented England in 17 Tests. He is admired as a cricketer, and liked as a man, but that is by the by. He is not, by any reasonable standards, English.

Another South African made a bigger splash. Kevin Pietersen was also born and raised in the republic, opting to become 'English' in his twentieth year. No sooner had he qualified in 2005 than he had a 'three lions' tattoo embossed on his forearm to prove his loyalty. Later in life, when he had established himself as a star, he told an opponent he was not really English, that he just played here. It was passed off as a joke. Nobody laughed.

Pietersen was a remarkable batsman, who played a handful of great innings for England, and he moved few hearts. Team-mates, like spectators, recoiled from his vanity. One of them thought his inability to understand English humour was the key to the chasm. Irony and sarcasm, the stock-in-trade of English professionals, fell on stony ground when Pietersen shared a dressing room. When he was dropped temporarily from the England team in 2012, and then booted out for good three years later, there was no real regret. For all his gifts he had never chosen to be 'one of us'. Identity, however we define it, matters. Otherwise who are the players playing for?

Root is in the field on this first day at Trent Bridge, so spectators have not been reacquainted with the strokeplay that has made him England's most elegant batsman since his fellow Sheffielder, Michael Vaughan. Observers with longer memories might go back further, to Gower or possibly to Graveney.

He is certainly an exquisite player, and, like Vaughan, productive. They both played for the Sheffield Collegiate club in Dore, that village-like suburb on the south-western fringe of the city, where it meets Derbyshire. Indeed, Derbyshire once played county cricket at Abbeydale Park, where the young Root took his first steps.

Any team would be glad to see Root strapping on his pads. Since he came into the Yorkshire team as a teenager he has brought delight to the crease as well as a touch of vulnerability, like Gorky's 'baby deer'. That's not quite appropriate, because Root has never been the innocent he appears. He grew up quickly. He had to, because he was pitched into Test cricket at 21, in India, which is no place for sophomores.

He plays for the proudest cricketing county, as a record 32 championships confirms. Does he, however, identify as a Yorkshire cricketer? When he was appointed England captain in 2017 he chose to address the press at Headingley, but is he really a Yorkshireman of the old school? He doesn't talk like a Yorkie. Players to him are 'the guys', a word that Hutton never used in all his born years. He smiles easily. He enjoys life, and relishes his cricket. At times he relishes it too much. A batsman of his quality gets out too often when there is a century to be had. That is the way with pleasure-givers. They leave their admirers wanting more.

What really sets him apart from his predecessors is the balance of loyalties. Root has played most of his cricket for England. Born in 1990, he has enjoyed the bounty the modern game has bestowed upon him, as a centrally contracted player. It is hard to imagine him saying the proudest moment of his career was leading Yorkshire to victory over the Australian tourists, as Trueman declared at Bramall Lane in 1968.

He joined the Yorkshire team as a full member in 2011, when he appeared in 15 championship matches. The following year he played 14 matches. Since then he has played 13 matches in six seasons, and didn't play at all in 2015. In 80 Tests he has made 16 centuries. For Yorkshire he has made six, and only one in the last five years. We have come a long way from the days of Wilfred Rhodes and George Hirst.

Eoin Morgan, the Irish-born captain of England's one-day team, has a similar relationship with Middlesex. In 2016 and again the following summer he didn't play a single championship match. His one-day record shows that he has transferred his talents to Bangalore, Sydney, Peshawar and Barbados, among other well-paid assignments.

The most well-travelled modern England cricketer must be Jos Buttler, who left Somerset for Lancashire in 2014. That year he played ten championship matches, making a single century. Since then he has appeared only six times in red-ball cricket for Lancashire, though he has turned out in various bashes for Mumbai Indians, Rajasthan Royals, Melbourne Renegades and Sydney Thunder. In ten years of professional cricket this talented batsman has made only five first-class centuries.

We shouldn't be hard on Root, a young man born into a game that has seen more changes in his lifetime than any period in the game's history. Just as J. B. Priestley and David Hockney, born in the same city, were Yorkshiremen of opposing stripes, Root has little in common with the generation that produced Trueman and Boycott.

There may even be some Yorkies who are happy to close the door on the bolshiness that has scarred the county's cricket. It began when Bobby Peel, the left-arm spinner, was ordered from the field by Lord Hawke for being inebriated. More recently the Boycott wars of the 1970s and 1980s, when members took sides armed with pickstaffs, resembled the Florence of Savonarola. Nobody wants to revisit those wretched days.

Yorkshire cricket was never exclusively about abrasion. There is another side to the club's history, familiar to Rhodes and Hirst. Hutton and Hedley Verity knew it, too, and now the baton passes to Root, a puckish figure who appeals to everybody, wherever they were born.

The season that starts today may not turn out to be the summer of our lives. For the captain of England, entrusted with the task of beating Australia and regaining the Ashes, it will certainly be the summer of his. Root is a superb cricketer who deserves to end as a great one. By September we shall be wiser.

At the end of this pleasant opening day, as the members pack their bags and exchange their see-you-tomorrows, you can't blame J. E. Root of England and occasionally of Yorkshire if his thoughts lie elsewhere.

III

Reference Back

Repton

'The smug and silver Trent,' Hotspur called it in the first part of *Henry IV*, as he grumbled to Bolingbroke about his inadequate portion of the kingdom. It is a river of the Midlands, rising in Staffordshire, and winding through Stoke, Burton and Nottingham towards Lincolnshire, where it meets the Ouse and flows into the Humber. It falls a long way short of majesty, and looks very modest as it slides through the fields of south Derbyshire, a mile from Repton.

You approach Repton from the bridge at Willington, on the Derby road. There is a canal and a railway line, too, giving this village the unusual privilege of having four modes of transport. There is also a popular marina near the power station, which blights the easterly view. When a film production company came visiting in the 1960s, to cast an eye on possible locations for a remake of *Goodbye, Mr Chips*, the scouts took one look at the cooling towers and went back to London.

Repton School, founded in 1557 by Sir John Port, provided the setting for the original film, made in 1939, which brought a Best Actor Oscar the following year for Robert Donat. The Academy Awards prize-giving of 1940 is known to be Hollywood's greatest night. Apart from *Goodbye, Mr Chips* the nominated films were *Stagecoach*, *Mr Smith Goes to Washington*, *Wuthering Heights*, *The Wizard of Oz* and the winner, *Gone with the Wind*. Donat won his gong, and so did Repton, which will always be associated with this tender, some might say sentimental, re-creation of life in an English public school.

The village has many layers. King Penda introduced Christianity to Mercia in 653, and Repton was anointed capital of that Anglo-Saxon kingdom. Work on an abbey began seven years later, and its crypt, which received the Mercian kings, survives in the parish church of St Wystan, after whom the famous poet was named. Auden's father, George, had attended the school.

In 873 the Great Heathen Army of Vikings arrived, and the kingdom of Mercia was no more. The Repton story carried on. An Augustinian priory was established in 1172, and it was on the ruins of that priory that the school took root when Sir John Port left his bequest. By the standards of Winchester (1382) and Eton (1440), Repton is a cheeky new bug among the great schools of England, comparable with Shrewsbury (1552). Its history is no less fascinating. In 1974, when archaeologists came from all over the world to begin a dig that lasted for 14 summers, they unearthed a Viking burial ground containing 200 warriors.

Repton was famous in the last century for producing, either as scholars or masters, three leaders of the Anglican Communion. William Temple, headmaster between 1910 and 1914, was named Archbishop of Canterbury in 1942. Temple was not a great cricket lover, calling it 'organised loafing'. His successor, three years later, was Geoffrey Fisher, who had also succeeded him as headmaster of Repton on the outbreak of the First World War. Fisher was then succeeded by Michael Ramsey, who had been educated at Repton when Fisher was the headmaster.

Not all boys shared the Church's high view of Fisher. Recalling his own days at Repton, when Fisher was the head, Roald Dahl wrote of his miserable time at school, when 'we were groping through an almost limitless black tunnel at the end of which there glimmered a small bright light'. In his 1984 autobiography *Boy*, Dahl recalled, or thought he did, being beaten by Fisher for one of those minor infractions that brought instant punishment. He did not recall well enough. Fisher had left Repton by the time Dahl received that beating, which was administered by Fisher's successor, John Christie.

In those days, between the wars, there is no doubt that school life at Repton, as at all public schools, could be primitive. Personal fagging was considered normal, and prefects were entitled to beat junior boys. Christopher Isherwood, who achieved fame with *Goodbye to Berlin*, which fathered the musical *Cabaret*, published a memoir of his early days, *Lions and Shadows*, that painted the school in only slightly more flattering colours than Dahl was to do four decades later.

Denton Welch, a novelist who died young, was another Reptonian who did not fit easily into the atmosphere of muscular Christianity. In *Maiden Voyage*, yet another memoir, he described being beaten by the Head of House Games for going to Chatsworth, the country home of the Cavendish family near Bakewell, instead of playing football for the Third XI.

Even when John Thorn arrived as headmaster in 1962, Repton was full of dim hearties. In his own story, *Road to Winchester* (the great college he joined as head after leaving Repton), Thorn was dismayed by the philistinism in the school, and sometimes within the common room, where at first he found few allies.

Dahl was a malcontent, who would have been unhappy at any school. When he returned to Repton in 1975, to give a talk, the years had not softened his condition. But the testimony of Isherwood and Welch gives a pretty good impression of the kind of institution so many public schools were, and, in the imagination of those who loathe private education, remain. They have given England some of its finest men over the past 500 years. They have also sent many thousands of dullards into the world, and not always well-educated dullards. The philistinism Thorn sought to address was not restricted to Repton.

A sound mind in a healthy body was the oft-quoted ambition. Occasionally that mark was reached. Harold Abrahams, clever enough to reach Cambridge, and swift enough to win gold in the 100 metres at the Paris Olympics of 1924, achieved a national fame that was carried throughout the world by *Chariots of Fire*, which won the Oscar for best film in 1982.

Two Academy Awards for Repton!

The greatest athlete of all had joined the school a generation before. Nobody defined *mens sana in corpore mano* more completely than Charles Burgess Fry, who went to Repton in 1888. C. B. Fry is, by any estimation, the finest all-round sportsman this country has produced. After his death in 1956 his ashes were interred in the graveyard behind the church of St Wystan, near those Viking warriors.

John Arlott remembered greeting Fry one day, before the start of play at Lord's, with the comradely 'Morning, Charles', only to receive the rebuke: 'Captain Fry to you, sir!' Arlott didn't hold it against him. Fry was, he thought, 'the most variously gifted Englishman of any age'. Harry 'H. S.' Altham, another Reptonian, who later became president of MCC, said that Fry 'could have stepped out of the frieze of the Parthenon'. When one considers the range of his achievements neither witness was guilty of exaggeration.

A classics scholar, immersed from his earliest days in Greek, Fry topped the lists at Wadham College, Oxford, ahead of F. E. Smith, later Lord Birkenhead, noted barrister and politician. Oddly, Fry left university with a fourth-class degree. Beset by debt in his final year, as well as mental problems that afflicted him throughout his life, he went to pieces before finding respite from his woes on the cricket field.

He won twelve Blues at Oxford for cricket, football and athletics, and equalled the world long-jump record at Iffley Road between, he liked to say, puffs of a cigar. He would have added rugby to the roster had he been fit to play in the Varsity match, and in later life played for Blackheath and the Barbarians. As a footballer he was an England international, and appeared as the only amateur in the Southampton team that reached the FA Cup final in 1903. He could turn his hand to anything, from croquet to shove ha'penny, and in his last years he took up dancing.

It was at cricket that Fry truly excelled. For Hampshire, Surrey, Sussex and England he made 94 centuries, and he headed the national batting averages in six seasons between 1901 and 1912. He won 26 Test caps, and captained England in the triangular series with Australia and South Africa in 1906, when they won four matches and drew the other two. In 1901, in the last breath of Victorian England, he made six successive centuries, an unparalleled feat.

Invited by his friend Ranji, the Indian prince who played Test cricket for England, to attend the first session of the League of Nations in Geneva in 1920, Fry took so comfortably to this new stage that he was offered the throne of Albania. 'If I had accepted,' he said later, 'the Italian invasion might never have happened. It would have been ideal in the spring to play some county cricket, and I'd have had pitches ready. If Mussolini had invaded, the Royal Navy would have been obliged to intervene. You can't invade a country with county cricket going on! So perhaps I should have accepted. But at the time it seemed a damn bore.' The Albanians plumped instead for King Zog, and have lived happily ever after.

Fry was hardly less active when he put away his sporting togs. He wrote regularly for a variety of publications, commentated on cricket for the BBC, and stood unsuccessfully in three elections for the Liberals. But his main occupation was running the Royal Navy training ship HMS *Mercury*, in the

Hamble river, as Captain-Superintendent. Life was not always kind. The mental problems persisted, and this formidable athlete spent much of his life under the thumb of a fearsome wife, Beatrice Sumner, who treated him with disdain and the ratings with cruelty.

In 1933, when the National Socialist storm broke in Germany, Fry met Hitler, and found him to be a fine chap, though his efforts to convince the Führer of cricket's character-building qualities bore no fruit. Flawed as he was, he enjoyed 'a life worth living', as the title of his autobiography suggested. Repton is justly proud of this extraordinary man. His gravestone reads: 'Cricketer, Scholar, Athlete, Author – The Ultimate All-Rounder'.

The school can also take pride in producing 153 other first-class cricketers. None achieved Fry's renown, though J. N. Crawford of Surrey and England won acclaim for his batting before he took off for Australia in 1910. Crawford was one of English cricket's mavericks. Had he stayed in England this schoolboy phenomenon would have added significantly to his twelve Test caps, and might have written his name in the record books alongside Fry. Donald Carr of Oxford University and Derbyshire, and Richard Hutton of Cambridge University and Yorkshire, also played Test cricket. More recently they were joined by Chris Adams of Derbyshire and Sussex, who joined the school in the sixth form.

Carr toured India with England in 1951/2, playing two Tests, the second as captain. He went on to serve MCC as assistant secretary, and was then secretary of the newly formed Test and County Cricket Board before it became the ECB, and expanded to incorporate hundreds of staff who did the job

Carr performed, as an old Lord's hand said, 'with two secretaries'. One brother, David, was headmaster of Yarlet prep school, near Stone in Staffordshire, which sent plenty of good young cricketers to Shrewsbury, Malvern and Repton. The other brother, Major Douglas Carr, became secretary of Derbyshire after Donald left the club for Lord's.

Repton's links with Derbyshire were maintained in the 1950s by the cricketing schoolmasters. Guy Willatt captained the county for five years, and John Eggar turned out in the summer holidays. A third master, Dick Sale, played for Warwickshire before he joined Derbyshire. All three men were promoted to headships at other schools when their cricketing days were over. As Malvern College is to Worcestershire, and Tonbridge to Kent, so is Repton to Derbyshire. In recent summers Paul Borrington, Chris Paget, Tom Poynton and Ross Whiteley have played for the county. It is a noble tradition.

The school is very different to the one in Dahl's limitless black tunnel. There are now more than 600 pupils, and half are girls. The facilities for scholarship, once spartan, are magnificent. The 400 Hall, built in 1957 to commemorate four centuries of school life, has been transformed into a theatre of professional standards, and the addition of buildings dedicated to science and mathematics offers a visual reminder of how far public schools have come in the past half century, and how necessary that change is if they are to retain the confidence of parents, many of whom live overseas.

Not all parents looking for an English education have to send their children to Derbyshire. Repton has established four schools in the Middle East, and there are plans for a further six to open by 2021, in Singapore, Egypt, China and Bulgaria. Like many public schools Repton has engaged in a 'branding' exercise that will keep the funds flowing.

The village has also changed. The development of the A50, linking the M1 near East Midlands airport with the M6 at Stoke-on-Trent, means the slip road at Willington offers motorists a chance to drive through Repton, which many take, to the detriment of a settlement that is not equipped to cope with heavy traffic.

Repton now feels more like a small town than a village, and newcomers in sufficient numbers will always alter eating and drinking habits. The Red Lion, a cosy pub enshrined in local legend, is now a featureless bar that caters for lager drinkers. When Dora Bird, a formidable landlady, ran it as pubs used to be run there wasn't any lager to be had, no matter how deep your pockets. She served Marston's Pedigree, brewed six miles away at Burton, by the bucket. Lager, she pronounced, often and loudly, was 'mucky stuff'.

The Boot Inn, which used to be a meeting place for old men, is now a trendy tavern within nodding distance of a gastropub. Who'd a thowt it? The grotty old Boot, which ran to stale cheese cobs, now boasts smart accommodation at £120 a night, offers diners 'smashed avocado with tahini and fennel trimmings', and gets written up in the 'lifestyle' sections of the weekend broadsheets! It also brews its own ale, very well.

This is not the Repton of Penda and Wiglaf, or even dear old Chips, who could recall every pupil in his care. The boys and girls now come from all over the world, yet the school remains strong in sport; stronger than ever. The ideal of muscular

Christianity has gone, and there will never be another Fry, but 'organised loafing' continues to play an indispensable part in making schools such as Repton attractive.

Life rolls on, like the smug and silver river that breaks its banks every winter, flooding the meadows that stretch all the way to the headmaster's study above the Old Trent.

May, with its deep greens and clear light, is the most evocative month. In my case it brings a touch of sadness. In 1976, playing on 'the square' against Wolverhampton Cricket Club, I missed a catch at extra cover and, picking up the ball, saw that a bone in my left thumb had pierced the skin. It was a compound fracture, set right at Burton General Hospital by Dr Davies, brother of Rupert, television's famous Maigret. For five long weeks leading up to A levels my arm was encased in plaster, the fractured bone held in place by a metal pin. The summer of 1976, as those who endured it need no reminding, was the hottest in living memory. Carrying an arm in a sling wasn't pleasant.

Today's visitors to the square are Uppingham, one of Repton's great rivals. The schools have been playing against each other for 154 years and until recently it was a two-day fixture. The pressure of examinations in May and June brought an end to that. Even at well-established cricketing schools the expectations of parents have put such fear into teachers, with an eye on league tables, that the classroom trumps cricket. 'For thirty-five grand a year,' says a teacher who has witnessed the shift of emphasis in the course of a generation, 'they're entitled to ask what they're getting for their money.'

Repton's traditional opponents were always Malvern, Shrewsbury, Uppingham and Rugby, with visits from the wandering clubs – MCC, Leicestershire Gentlemen, Staffordshire Gentlemen and the old boys, the Repton Pilgrims, winners of the inaugural Cricketer Cup in 1967 under the captaincy of D. B. Carr. Some fixtures have slipped off the list but there are still 21 matches for the cricketers and the man who has just joined the school as director of cricket, Chris Read.

It is a swift reversal of loyalty for Read. Last year, his first summer after leaving Nottinghamshire, to end a first-class career spanning two full decades, the former Test wicketkeeper was in charge of cricket at Uppingham. His successor, Trevor Ward, once of Kent and Leicestershire, is acting as scorer for this match, perched in the balcony of the thatched pavilion which, along with the ruins at midwicket, and Pears School behind it, helps to make the Repton ground one of the most pleasing in England.

Read is quite a catch. He played 15 times for England, and belonged to the Notts team that won championships in 2005 and 2010. His title, director of cricket, reflects the significance that schools have come to place on the development of young sportsmen and women. 'Coach' no longer covers it. Direction is everything, though the change of title is unquestionably part of the management-speak that afflicts all aspects of school life.

'Sport has been a core part of every Reptonian's school experience,' declares Ian Pollock, the overall director of sport. He supervises the other directors, of football, hockey, netball, tennis and swimming, as well as cricket, and this emphasis on sport has yielded some notable results.

The tennis players have won 15 national schools titles, and the hockey players have been winners 36 times in national championships across all age groups. This week the talk is of a footballer. Will Hughes joined Derby County when he left school, and is now expected to play for Watford in the FA Cup final against Manchester City.

It's not hard to see why these schools continue to produce so many cricketers. Tradition counts for something, and Repton has a good name within the game. The willingness of staff to get involved in the running of teams is a key factor. Often it is why they were recruited. Pity the state-school teacher, however enthusiastic, who loves his cricket. Life can be very lonely for such people.

By contrast Repton have just appointed a headmaster who grew up with the game in his blood. Mark Semmence, the son of a Sussex cricketer, played for Durham University and the England under-19 team, and used to run the cricket at Rugby. Repton does not, however, offer the sports scholarships available at Malvern, where Worcestershire have established their winter quarters. Indeed, there is a touch of resentment about that recruitment policy, and not only at Repton.

Occasionally the resentment boils over. Radley and Marlborough, two of the great schools, broke off relations two decades ago when Marlborough's late declaration took the competitive sting out of the game. James Wesson, the Radley coach that day, played with me at Repton. The players he brought along included Andrew Strauss, James Dalrymple, Robin Martin-Jenkins and Ben Hutton, so he did a pretty good job.

The most important feature for young sportsmen at these schools is the sheer abundance. The facilities here, running to 15 pitches and excellent nets, are superior to anything to be found in the state sector. Even with exams eating into the summer term the school puts out three senior teams, and often three teams at under-14 and under-15 level. In the winter months there are net sessions in an indoor sports hall. The best of these teenagers are professionals-in-waiting, which is why a man such as Read, recently retired, wants to be involved.

Public schools have never been short of expert assistance. George Hirst and Wilfred Rhodes, the great Yorkshire all-rounders, turned up at Eton and Harrow when their playing days were done, helping the young gentlemen to become better cricketers. Not all the coaches, or cricket masters, were cut from such bespoke cloth. The jobs often went to old pros, short of a bob or two, who were willing to lend a hand.

At Repton that old pro was Eric Marsh, a pipe-smoking miner who bowled slow left arm for Derbyshire in the 1940s and 1950s. Eric was no athlete. Playing against Lancashire at Old Trafford, when Cyril Washbrook was in his pomp, he retrieved a ball 'Washy' had clipped towards the midwicket boundary. 'Buck up your ideas,' he was told. 'There were always three runs in that shot,' he replied, thinking he had returned the ball swiftly. 'Three, Marsh, yes. They ran five.'

Roly-poly Eric spent his Mays and Junes bowling at schoolboys in the nets, occasionally fooling them with the chinaman. On match days he acted as umpire, and could display a shocking bias. Jonathan Agnew, the BBC cricket correspondent, and a decidedly brisk opening bowler for

Uppingham in his youth, was not the only opponent to leave Repton with a dim view of the place, so loose was Eric's interpretation of the game's laws. Reptonian jaws also dropped from time to time at other schools. Such were the perks of being a school pro. 'That's out!'

The master in charge of cricket when Eric was diddling opponents was a gaunt Latin master, Peter Mountford, who had played for the XI at Oxford. In the classroom, between bursts of Virgil, he had rough words for those who forgot to smuggle in a radio when there was a Test on. With his togs on he was a lively fast bowler, who worked up a full head of steam one day playing for the staff against the school. In his sights was Charlie Sale, son of Dick, one of those cricketing schoolmasters.

Three times in an over he peppered Sale about the body. Three times Sale told him to fuck off, starting baritone and ending tenor. In his adult life, as chief rotter on the *Daily Mail* sports desk, Charles Sale as he was by then put that language to good use.

Late spring showers mean that the match, scheduled for 50 overs, will now start at 1.15, with the teams losing ten overs each. Repton have just been beaten by Malvern, so there is a need to bounce back. On the square there is a lot of activity.

Both groups of players look busy in the hour before the umpires, absolutely impartial these days, put the bails on the stumps. Where lads used to warm up by hitting a few balls, and holding a few steepling catches, there is now the kind of athleticism that would not be out of place in the professional game. That is what sport at a school such as this has become, a gateway to a career.

There is the training gear, similar to that the Notts and Yorkshire players wore at Trent Bridge last month. There is the mutual hollering and capering that comes from a shared assumption of what is expected of them. They are conforming to type, in what they wear (the hat worn back to front), what they say, and how they say it. The same words, adopted from the vocabulary of professionals, crop up time and again. Finally there is the huddle, without which no sporting event can be considered authentic.

When Repton bat, the Uppingham fielders supply a commentary on every ball that can be heard clearly from the paddock overlooking the square. The innings is a conversation between ten fielders, punctuated by the occasional stroke. In days gone by the umpires would ask the lads to turn it down, or leave it out altogether, but the game has changed.

All cricket matches, from junior to Test level, must be conducted to a soundtrack of relentless shouts and yelps. Every ball brings a peal of encouragement, or a bark of advice from fielders close to the bat or even in the outfield. One of the things you learn swiftly is that bowlers rarely bowl a bad ball. Another is that, however gloomy the skies, at least two members of the team will be wearing sunhats.

The Repton opening batsman departs, caught behind. As he walks up the steps to the thatched pavilion he lets it be known that Uppingham 'are bowling fucking rubbish'. His team-mates make steady progress, led by a 16-year-old called Berlusconi, not a name that has featured hitherto in the Repton story. His strokes do not impress the men from Uppingham. 'We've given him two lives,' bellows an outfielder to the close catchers, like a mating call. 'Let's not give him a third.'

Berlusconi goes for 62, as Repton make 173. Uppingham are then dismissed 48 runs short of their target, and the players warm down on the outfield before going back to their houses, to revise for exams. One parent, who has been keeping a close eye on his son's performance, is wondering aloud where his lad should be once those exam results are declared. 'We might send him to Radley,' he says. This is the world of the modern public school, where whacking fees and the expectations that follow mean that loyalties, once confirmed for life by tie and blazer, are easily transferred.

The cricketers on the square take the world for granted, as teenagers do. In the common rooms teachers are growing ever more concerned. There is a story in the papers today, generated by comments made by Dr Anthony Wallersteiner, headmaster of Stowe, who has entered the debate about private education with some robust remarks.

'The rise of populists and polemicists,' he says, 'has created a micro-industry in bashing private schools.' He finds the bashing similar in tone, if not in seriousness, to the antisemitism that has inflamed the Labour Party. Whether or not Dr Wallersteiner is over-egging the pudding there is no doubt there is a pudding there. Barely a week goes by without a spokesman for a public school or an Oxbridge college being pounced upon to rebut accusations of privilege. This week it was the turn of a spokesman at Oxford to emphasise the commitment to 'building an inclusive, vibrant' university.

At Cambridge, it was revealed earlier this year, colleges were under pressure to present themselves in a more favourable way to pupils from a Caribbean background. Some, it was claimed, found it difficult to identify restaurants that served food they enjoyed at home. Others couldn't find a barber to cut their hair.

These are some of the new problems faced by the most famous seats of learning in the world. However did Wittgenstein get on at Cambridge without his Wiener Schnitzel?

Apparently it is the public school 'ethos' that puts off sixth-formers from urban backgrounds. To counter the alleged bias of our oldest colleges towards the privately schooled, there is now a deliberate shift of policy towards accepting candidates who may have inferior exam grades, in order to redress the balance. It is a form of social engineering: nobody can deny that. But who benefits?

According to figures published in 2017 public schoolboys and girls accounted for 36 per cent of the places taken up at Cambridge, and 41 per cent at Oxford. There is a clear bias here though that bias reflects, among other things, the quality of teaching at public schools and the poor work (and, frequently, the inverted snobbery) of teachers in the state sector. Social attitudes belong to all classes. For every tutor at Oxford and Cambridge eager to build a bridge for promising pupils, to help them reach the other side, there is a teacher telling them they might feel more comfortable (or less uncomfortable) at Birmingham or Leeds.

That is not to say there is no sense of entitlement, based on a shared inheritance. It is usual in such arguments to quote

Evelyn Waugh, from *Decline and Fall*. 'The social system,' says the ghastly Captain Grimes, 'never lets one down.' That's not so true these days, when people such as Grimes would never be admitted to a public school, no matter how desperate, but the principle is familiar. Too many second-raters have prospered for too long because they went to public school.

David Kynaston, the historian, and Francis Green, the social scientist, have entered this debate on the other side to Dr Wallersteiner. The title of their book, *Engines of Privilege*, leaves little room for doubt. Only 7 per cent of children go to independent schools, and Kynaston and Green offer a painstakingly researched investigation of the influence public schools have had on English (as opposed to British) life over the past century.

It's all there: the bullying, the hand-me-down snobbery, the acceptance of social codes that enable the privileged 7 per cent of insiders (rising to 12 per cent in the sixth form) to retain those privileges, irrespective of talent. Without these schools, and the social and educational imbalances they preserve, the country would be better off.

They present the case thoroughly. Look anywhere in English life, from politics to the national cricket team, and one sees the value of a public school education. In recent years the number of actors and even stars of popular entertainment who went to public schools has become noticeable, though talent may have something to do with it. Eddie Redmayne is not a fine actor simply because he went to Eton. He did, though, benefit from the superb facilities at that school in a way that his peers in the state system, perhaps no less gifted, did not.

In the realm of sport, independent schools consistently punch above their weight, and nowhere is the punching done more effectively than on the cricket field. Joe Root, the captain of England, was a sixth-former at Worksop College, another of Repton's opponents. His predecessor, Alastair Cook, went to Bedford. Cook followed Andrew Strauss of Radley, the Oxfordshire school where Dennis Silk, a former president of MCC, was warden (headmaster) for two decades.

Stuart Broad, who has taken more Test wickets than any English bowler other than James Anderson, went to Oakham; Jonny Bairstow to St Peter's York. Jos 'super scooper' Buttler attended King's College, Taunton. Sam Curran is an old boy of Wellington College. There are dozens of others throughout the professional game.

The influence extends beyond the boundary. The national selector is Ed Smith, who was a star schoolboy at Tonbridge. He is assisted by James Taylor, who went to Shrewsbury. The players are assessed professionally by the BBC cricket correspondent, Jonathan Agnew, an Uppingham man, who fills the shoes worn in the past by Brian Johnston (Eton) and Christopher Martin-Jenkins (Marlborough). Henry Blofeld, the gadfly of *Test Match Special*, was another Etonian.

Look through the history of English cricket, and boys in fancy caps have adorned it, and sometimes dominated, from Lord Harris and Lord Hawke onwards. Douglas Jardine, the unwavering captain of the Bodyline tourists of 1932/3, was moulded at Winchester. After the war came a succession of magnificent strokeplayers: Peter May of Charterhouse, Colin Cowdrey of Tonbridge, Ted Dexter of Radley, David Gower of

King's Canterbury. Fast bowlers, by tradition, came from the north, though it is worth noting that John Snow, one of the finest, went to Christ's Hospital, Horsham.

There is no reason to suppose things will change. Only one in five state schools bothers to play cricket. Of children aged five to ten, only 5 per cent have held a bat or bowled a ball. The figures rise to 12 per cent for 11- to 15-year-olds, but the overall picture is grim. Cricket, the game of summer, is now ranked the eighth most popular sport in English secondary schools, behind football, rugby, swimming, athletics and – this takes some believing – basketball, netball and rounders. There are more than 4000 secondary schools in Britain, and only 333 submit results of cricket matches to *Wisden*, the annual almanack. Of those schools, the vast majority, 246, are selective.

The indifference of teachers is one factor, and the lack of proper pitches is another. Between 1979 and 1997, when the Conservatives were in office, more than 10,000 school playing fields were lost. Chance to Shine, an organisation set up to introduce the game to children in primary and secondary schools, does its best but is fighting against a cultural shift of profound significance. For many modern schoolchildren the joys of playing a makeshift game of cricket, with jumpers for stumps, is a thing of the dim and distant past. They would prefer to play games on electronic gadgets.

Cricket costs money, which is easier to find in fee-paying schools. It costs little to play football or rugby. A pair of boots, a shirt, shorts and a ball, and off you go. To be properly equipped a cricketer's parents may have to spend upwards of

£500 to provide the young player with a bat, a pair of pads and gloves, helmet, boots and flannels.

There is another cultural phenomenon: the public school 'ethos', which has at times smothered cricket like an autumnal mist.

Where did it come from, this much-praised and much-reviled spirit? Historians usually point the finger at Thomas Arnold, the pioneering headmaster of Rugby between 1828 and 1841. It was in the classrooms and on the playing fields of Rugby, the school which gave the world the game of rugby union, that 'muscular Christianity' took root.

Like many well-worn tales it's not entirely true. Dr Arnold did seek to inculcate moral and religious principles, but he sought to do so through scholarship rather than 'organised loafing'. These were the lessons absorbed by his son, Matthew Arnold, the poet and author of *Culture and Anarchy*, which urged educators to pass on the best that had been thought and said. The Arnoldian vision was intellectual. Father and son believed in the power of knowledge to transform the lives of everybody, high and low. Theirs was not the world of William Webb Ellis, who picked up the ball instead of kicking it.

Rugby was also the setting for *Tom Brown's School Days*, by Thomas Hughes, which came to represent the horrors of public school life through the monstrous personality of Flashman, the school bully. The public school novel, such a staple of English literature, begins in 1857 with *Tom Brown*. Nor is it popular only in England. As Donat proved in *Goodbye, Mr Chips*, the oddities of public school life in provincial England may find a receptive audience in other cultures. The international success of Harry Potter, in print and on screen, requires no amplification. People may profess to detest public school life but it seems they are determined to know everything that (supposedly) goes on there. What is *Downton Abbey* if not a continuation of life after public school? It may be tosh but it is popular tosh, across the globe.

That stiff upper lip, mocked for its English rigidity, was never in reality exclusively English. If we are to attribute muscular Christianity to anybody it should not be Dr Arnold but one of his admirers, Baron de Coubertin. The French aristocrat liked what he saw at Rugby so much when he visited England in 1883, and again three years later, that he acted upon it.

In the English public school he found qualities, moral and physical, that inspired him to create the modern Olympics. Based on the ancient Greek ideal of *Citius, Altius, Fortius*, the Games were revived in Athens in 1896. The idea of international sporting competition emerged from the fields of Rugby, and also from the Shropshire town of Much Wenlock, which each year staged its own athletic pageant. Coubertin's vision, which owed so much to aspects of the English life he admired, was an early example of European cooperation. And not a wine lake in sight.

Four years before that Olympiad, at the apogee of Empire, an old boy of Clifton College wrote the poem that really defined the public school ethos. '*Vitaï Lampada*', it was called: The Torch of Life. Sir Henry Newbolt's poem is one of the best-known in the English language, and one of the most sententious. The opening lines are not as familiar as they used to be. But they have the merit of suspense:

> There's a breathless hush in the Close to-night –
> Ten to make and the match to win

Newbolt moves from the final stages of a cricket match in Bristol, on 'A bumping pitch and blinding light', to the Sudan desert, with the unnamed Mahdi engulfing the unnamed General Gordon. No names would have been necessary to Newbolt's readers. This was poetry as metaphor, for life and the sense of duty essential for all officers of the Crown; indeed, for all British subjects. The poem ends with the resounding refrain, drummed out with certainty:

> 'Play up! play up! and play the game.'

Newbolt grew to be wary of the fame his poem brought. Not too wary, though. He also wrote 'Drake's Drum', which fulfilled a similar purpose. The sons of Empire had to be reminded of their duty, to keep the flag flying. By the end of the century the stiff upper lip, unknown to Dr Arnold, prevailed.

What is wrong with lip-stiffening? Applied rigidly it can lead to social atrophy. Put on with greater discretion, it requires no special pleading. Sometimes, surely, it is better to put a brave face on things. A refusal to wallow in defeat, or exult in victory, may be manly. It shows respect for one's self, and for others.

We mock the Victorians for their sentiment. But is our sentimentality more attractive? In modern sport the victors and the vanquished too often engage in behaviour that is unmanly. Holding things in can be as useful as letting them out. In the past we tended too much towards the former. In an age of 'emotional literacy', as some theorists of human behaviour like to put it, the balance has shifted. Expressing strong emotions without restraint is not always healthy.

Social demarcations are not in themselves bad. Proust was in thrall to the Parisian aristocracy. Scott Fitzgerald lived among the nouveaux riches of the Jazz Age, a phrase he coined, while Homer wrote about gods. You could argue, as Philip Roth did, that Western literature began with a beauty contest designed for the immortals, with Helen of Troy playing the role of Miss World.

Whether it is money, breeding or tribe, we are all defined by something we can do nothing about. In England the social distinctions are infinitely subtle. Paul Johnson, the journalist, wrote that the true Englishman could say 'really' in a dozen different ways. Another Paul, Theroux, the American novelist, felt excluded from certain parts of English society because, as an American, he did not understand the laws, and the lore, of cricket.

It is certainly true that English English has more layers of meaning than American English. Irony, sarcasm, understatement and wordplay do not belong exclusively to us. It just seems that they do, and a shared schooling has played a major part in the development of our language and attitudes.

The modern English novel belongs largely, though not exclusively, to those who went to public schools. We read Waugh of Lancing, Huxley of Winchester, Orwell of Eton, Maugham of King's Canterbury, Forster of Tonbridge and Wodehouse of Dulwich. So many leading journalists and broadcasters attended public schools that the London media world sometimes appears to be a closed shop.

There is also that English compound of affection and mockery, expressed by Gilbert and Sullivan in the high tide of Victorian world domination. The English are known throughout the globe for humour, and much of the fun comes directly from the public schools, which are natural incubators of mockery.

Working-class viewers did not, on the whole, seem to laugh at *Monty Python's Flying Circus*. When the BBC screened the first series in the summer of 1969 it came at the end of a decade that had seen a shift in comic tastes, away from the music hall towards satire. The educated tomfoolery started with *Beyond the Fringe* in 1960, and moved through *That Was The Week That Was*, Peter Cook's Establishment Club, and the emergence of *Private Eye* until Python crowned the decade.

With the exception of Terry Gilliam, the American animator, the Pythons were educated at selective schools. *Private Eye* was initially a gathering of Shrewsbury old boys, serenaded by Cook of Radley, who had been the breakout star of *Beyond the Fringe*. When Richard Ingrams slipped out of the editor's chair in 1986, Ian Hislop of Ardingly said 'Bags I'. He's still there. Alan Bennett did not go to a public school but the setting of his first stage play, *Forty Years On*, was Albion House with Sir John Gielgud playing the peppery headmaster.

Kynaston and Green have tapped into the resentment many people feel about these schools, and the way the people who attend them are still able to affect our lives. It isn't possible to read about Boris Johnson without being reminded that he, like David Cameron, went to Eton. The school's name is intended to summon feelings of resentment, and often it does.

For all their influence the independent schools feel more threatened than they have done since the 1960s when Anthony Crosland, a minister in Harold Wilson's government, vowed in colourful language to get rid of grammar schools, 'if it's the last thing I do'. There is a genuine fear that a new Labour administration would seek to abolish the charitable exemption that public schools enjoy, which would lead to a rise in fees that would wound, and in some cases prove fatal.

Jeremy Corbyn loathes independent schools, even though he attended a prep school, then a grammar. A favoured colleague, Diane Abbott, sent her son to the fee-paying City of London School. It is a well-known Labour trait, saying one thing about private education at party conference (boo!) and then behaving in a markedly different way (hello, headmaster!) when their children grow up. Abbott defended her decision to send her son to City of London, saying she was only doing what 'any Caribbean mum would do' for her child. Shami Chakrabarti, another prominent Labour proponent of comprehensive education, said as much after sending her son to Dulwich College. Speaking so, without realising what they had said, they represented all parents who take similar decisions. When the fiercest opponents of private education opt to send their children to selective schools it is hard to sustain the argument.

It will carry on until kingdom come. The Labour Party will continue to be led by men such as Clement Attlee, who went to Haileybury, Hugh Gaitskell of Winchester, and Tony Blair, an old boy of Fettes College in Edinburgh. The radical left will be roused to indignation by the successors to Tony Benn, a Westminster man, and Corbyn, who went to a rather less distinguished school in Shropshire, though his aide-de-camp, Seumas Milne, is yet another Wykehamist. Lord Longford, who detested pornography, devoured it to make sure he hated it. That helps to explain the Labour position on private education. They can't live with it, or without it.

There may no longer be the sense of duty that existed in the days of Empire, when public schoolboys were groomed for a life of service. There is still a sense of mission, and parents demand value for money. That is particularly true of parents from overseas, who believe that an 'English education', public school followed by Oxbridge, will bring social respectability. Being good at games is no longer a matter of imparting moral values, though sport can shape character. Providing excellent facilities for young cricketers is a practical imperative. It is one way of keeping Repton, say, ahead of Shrewsbury and Rugby.

Where cricket is concerned the public schools are likely to become even more dominant. For all the talk of greater opportunity in the state sector the game will continue to be played best by those who enjoy the centuries-old benefits of a private education, where cricket is not a dirty word. Schools such as Repton, which have done so much to promote the game, will turn out talented cricketers as long as the staid and smug Trent wanders towards the North Sea.

'Reclothe us in our rightful mind', goes the great hymn, 'Dear Lord and Father of Mankind', composed to the tune of 'Repton'. Our rightful mind, and our lively bodies. And give that money tree a good shake. Now, more than ever, the piper must be paid.

It took a Berlin friend to spell out the value of a public school education, when he praised the more attractive qualities of those fortunate enough to have been granted the privilege; qualities that some who have enjoyed the benefits prefer not to acknowledge. 'We Germans are educated to be obedient,' Andreas told me. 'You English are educated to be independent.'

With a single arrow the Prussian archer spliced the tree.

IV

I Remember, I Remember

Ramsbottom

The view from Holcombe, the hill above Ramsbottom, is nothing like Malvern. On the West Pennine Moors there is a wildness you won't find in Worcestershire. This is no land of orchards, well-bred cattle and revelations by the riverbank. It feels like another country: harsher, darker.

Ramsbottom is one of those old-fashioned English words that make people chuckle. Sooty and Sweep, children's favourites in the glory days of early evening television, had a pal called Ramsbottom, a snake who slithered on to greet them now and again when Harry Corbett, who worked the gloves, got bored. 'Look, it's Ramsbottom!' he would say to his warring puppets, and everybody laughed.

To outsiders Ramsbottom may be a name that suggests a soft-focus image of cobbled streets and chimneys, with a brass band playing in the background. They might get a shock if they came here, for the town has altered significantly in the past decade, as a slog up Holcombe reveals. It is not a wealthy town but life here is certainly more bountiful than in other parts of Lancashire, where signs of decline are stark.

By the Peel Monument, a tribute in stone to a local man who changed this land irrevocably, the climber can take in the desuetude of post-industrial England. Bury, five miles south, is the traditional home of black pudding. It has a fine market, and some good shops. A Debenhams, even. The neighbouring towns are not so well-equipped. Bolton has lost its grandest store, Preston's the jewellers, which proudly claimed to be 'the diamond centre of the north'. Rochdale, a town without a bookshop, looks post-apocalyptic.

To the north lie Blackburn and Burnley, where the Catholic recusants took refuge in the days of the Pendle witches. *Mist Over Pendle*, written by Robert Neill in 1951, was once a popular novel. In 1960 Bryan Forbes shot a delightful film, *Whistle Down the Wind*, in that haunting part of east Lancashire. Even Lancastrians consider Burrrn-leh, where they drink Bénédictine in the pubs, to be a town apart. Some nights, it is whispered, you can still see witches flying about on their broomsticks.

The Peel Monument, or Peel Tower, was erected in 1852 to honour Sir Robert Peel, twice prime minister, who had died two years before. Born in Bury, Peel was no ordinary fellow. Educated at Harrow and Christ Church, Oxford, an unusual path for a Lancashire lad, he was a Tory in a county of free-trade liberalism and religious non-conformism which became receptive to organised labour.

As Home Secretary he established the first police force, known colloquially as 'Peelers' and 'Bobbies'. The second term is still in common usage. The world over, British policemen are known by Peel's affectionate diminutive. Prime Minister Peel repealed the Corn Laws, which split his party, and, after wrestling with his doubts, he sponsored Catholic emancipation. His relationship with Queen Victoria and Prince Albert helped to bolster the monarchy in an age of revolution. Peel was one of the great figures of the nineteenth century, and is held to be the father of the modern Conservative Party.

On one of those clear days beloved by crooners you can look across the plains of west Lancashire where the Manchester Ship Canal, that masterpiece of nineteenth-century engineering, rolls towards Liverpool. Further up the coast is Blackpool, famous for a different kind of tower; more like a giant vinegar pot. It is not a conventional 'view', whichever way you look, yet it has a rugged appeal for the people who live in these valleys, flanked by hills. In Lancashire, often to the surprise of visitors, there are hills everywhere.

Lancashire is not rich. It has no towns like Ilkley and Harrogate, over the Pennines. Away from the Crown Estates, in the Trough of Bowland, where the River Hodder meanders through picturesque villages near the border with Yorkshire, urban Lancashire is grim. The settlements where cotton was king are worse than grim. They are very rundown indeed. The idea of a 'Northern Powerhouse' seems a cruel joke.

This is a familiar tale in the post-industrial parts of the realm, far from the gleaming commercial spires of the metropolis. For Lancashire, read south Wales, the old West

Riding of Yorkshire or the north-east. The wealth that accrued from the Industrial Revolution was never shared by the people whose toil did most to create it. The political and social movements that emerged from this communal working life shaped our national life, and there are occasional echoes. Much has been lost. Many of these towns are sad places, with little hope of renewal.

Sport led the social change. The men who worked together played together, at football, cricket and rugby. The Rugby League was established at the George Hotel in Huddersfield, so that players could benefit financially from playing a game that was nominally amateur. Payment in union was forbidden until 1990, though everybody knew that money could easily be found in the boots of the favoured. Rugby union tolerated unpardonable snobbery in the old days, when scouts would be dispatched to sniff out league triallists playing under the cover of 'A. N. Other' so they could be cashiered like errant soldiers.

Six of the twelve founding members of the Football League played in Lancashire. Our family grew up with Bolton Wanderers, who won the first FA Cup final at Wembley in 1923, the 'White Horse' final, so-called because a mounted police officer was obliged to maintain order among a crowd of 120,000. My mother's father was among the spectators that day.

The Trotters won the Cup again in 1926 and 1929. In 1953 they lost the most famous final of all, the so-called 'Matthews final', in which another Stanley, Mortensen, netted the least talked-about hat-trick in football history. My mother represented the family at Wembley that afternoon. Bolton were back at Wembley again in 1958, when Nat Lofthouse scored the two goals that beat Manchester United. 'The Lion of Vienna' won 33 England caps, and scored 30 goals. He is one of the heroes of English football.

He wasn't the greatest footballer to come from Lancashire. That honour goes to Tom Finney of Preston North End, one of the other founding members. Finney and Lofthouse once went to Grimsby, to play in a benefit match, and received no payment. Except, as Lofthouse noted in many an after-dinner speech, in the local currency.

'I got cod and chips,' he said, 'and Tommy got a haddock, which was only fair. He was the better player!'

Finney, eventually Sir Tom, was not merely the greatest Lancastrian footballer. He is considered by those who played with and against him to be the greatest English player. One day in Edinburgh, on meeting Johnny Haynes, the former England captain, who had joined a group of mutual friends, I bowled a half volley: who was the best player he had played with?

'I'm surprised you have to ask.' And Haynes, the master passer, was not an easy man to please.

When Brian Clough, another of Finney's admirers, called Johan Cruyff 'the Catherine Wheel', he might have been describing 'the Preston Plumber'. He never won a trophy, and earned less in his career than some modern players get in a day, yet he won the love of all who saw him play.

Burnley, Blackburn Rovers and Accrington help to, make up the red rose domination of that pioneering dozen. Only Burnley, the Clarets, can be said to be doing well now. There is no room for sentiment in modern football, which is run for the benefit of foreign billionaires who have no emotional attachment to the clubs they have bought. 'English' football only exists in the lower leagues, below the salt.

As well as playing sport, men and women also came together to sing in choirs, play in orchestras and brass bands, and act in am-dram. These were truly communal activities, based on the mills and factories where they worked, the inns where they took their leisure, and the churches and chapels where they worshipped.

The brass band is a miracle of musicianship. It was, and in some communities still is, stuffed with talented men and women, boys and girls, for whom band life offers a release from drudgery. Anybody who wants to see musicianship in its least affected mode should begin with the brass band. It offers the authentic sound of working life in this country.

Two of the greatest singers of the last century came from this part of Lancashire. When Kathleen Ferrier died at the age of 41 in 1953 the nation mourned, for her story moved all hearts. Within the space of only ten years this telephonist from Blackburn, largely self-taught and entirely natural, conquered the world with her contralto voice and a modesty that underpinned all she did.

Appearing with the Vienna Philharmonic at the Edinburgh Festival of 1947, to sing Mahler's song-symphony, *Das Lied von der Erde*, under the baton of Bruno Walter, she left out the final words, a repeated *'ewig'* (eternally), as she was in tears. 'We should all weep,' Walter told her afterwards, 'if we were all artists such as you.'

When Ferrier died of cancer in the year of the Queen's coronation the conductor paid a greater tribute. He had been

Mahler's protégé as a young man in Vienna, and conducted the first performance of that composer's ninth symphony. Yet he said the two greatest things that had happened to him 'were to know Kathleen Ferrier and Gustav Mahler, in that order'.

To this day Ferrier's recording of the folk song, 'Blow the Wind Southerly', is one of the most-requested records on *Desert Island Discs*. That unique voice (we don't hear contraltos any more) continues to speak to listeners who were not born when the great Kate lost her fight for life. And it had been a fight. Singing in *Orfeo* at Covent Garden in February 1953, despite the ravages of breast cancer, the audience heard her hipbone crack. She couldn't move, yet she carried on, singing as she was born to do, all the way to the grave.

John Tomlinson, 'JohnTom', was born in Oswaldtwistle, the town that gave us 'Ossie' Clark, the dandy who befriended David Hockney in the 1960s. Tomlinson is the great Wagnerian bass of our day. He sang all the great roles during 18 consecutive seasons at Bayreuth, as well as the opera houses of Berlin, Munich, Vienna, New York, Milan and London. Like Ferrier he grew up singing in the house, and in the local choir; part of that great tradition of amateur music-making that has been overwhelmed by the virus of instant entertainment.

I first met John after a performance of Britten's *Billy Budd* in Manchester, conducted by a mutual friend, Elgar Howarth. Cricket helped to open the door. In his youth he used to watch the game at Church, his local club in the Lancashire League.

In September 2002, after a performance of *Die Walküre* at the Bavarian State Opera in Munich, conducted by Zubin Mehta, we popped into an Italian restaurant just off Maximilianstrasse to

I REMEMBER, I REMEMBER

celebrate his birthday. He had just sung Wotan, the chief of the gods, and brought along Wotan's spear as a jest. Taking my leave in the early hours, after swapping tales of Lancashire cricketers, I found myself carrying the spear through the streets of the city, to the puzzlement of folk who, we were astounded to learn, had never heard of Noddy Pullar. Actors tend to disdain the carrying of spears. Non-actors are not so picky.

Lancashire is well-known for its comedians. That has something to do with people living in cramped conditions in mill towns, and the necessity of getting on with the neighbours. But the main factor is the openness of the Lancashire character, and the warmth and timbre of the voice; the old Lancashire voice, not the modern Mancunian whine that has blown through the satellite towns like tumbleweed. It's difficult to be funny when you sound confrontational.

Ken Platt's catchphrase, 'I'm not taking me coat off, I'm not stoppin" wouldn't pass muster in a Birmingham voice: the tone is wrong. Brummies tend to sound puzzled. Nor would Albert Modley's 'In't it grand when you're daft?' work in a London voice. It needs the flat A. In Lancashire it sounds right, and funny. There is an impish quality to the Lancashire character. Unlike Yorkshire there is little bombast. Lancashire folk are direct. They are rarely rude.

Platt and Modley were comics of the old school. 'Not stand-up,' as Ken Dodd told me one night in Eastbourne over fish and chips. 'They were known as front-cloth comics, because they stood in front of the cloth. What's a stand-up? Doesn't everybody stand up?'

It is not a word Platt and Modley would have known, either,

or Frank Randle. The star of *Randle's Scandals* rarely ventured south of Manchester, so he didn't gain the national recognition enjoyed by his successors. He preferred to stay in Blackpool, where he entertained holiday makers with boisterous shows when he could be persuaded to leave licensed premises.

Randle was the sort of performer Trevor Griffiths had in mind when he wrote *Comedians*, produced in 1975 at the Nottingham Playhouse. With Jonathan Pryce in the leading role, and with a meaty part for Jimmy Jewel, a real music-hall comedian, it went to the West End and then Broadway, making a star of Pryce.

Lancashire comedians dominated the old music hall. George Formby of Wigan and Gracie Fields of Rochdale were big stars before the Second World War, and became international figures during the conflict. 'When I'm Cleaning Windows' and 'Sing As We Go' were songs that everybody recognised.

Eric Morecambe, the clown, and Les Dawson, the droll, were two of the most widely-loved comics of the post-war period, Jimmy Clitheroe one of the less appealing, and Bernard Manning one of the most explosive. Manning, to the fury of his detractors, was often brilliantly funny. 'Anybody can tell a dirty joke,' Esther Rantzen told him one night on *Parkinson*, her face a bag of spanners. 'All right,' he replied, 'let's hear you.'

Peter Kay and Victoria Wood, who left us far too early, have kept Gracie's aspidistra flying in the past two decades, and found large audiences beyond their native heath. The impish Lancashire spirit animates their humour. Lancastrians are, as they say up here, gradely folk. There are exceptions to the rule, of course. Little and Large got off lightly when a television reviewer described them as 'that execrable end-of-pier duo'. They were, however, marginally funnier than Cannon and Ball.

Liverpool, which has a strange relationship with its parent county, has a tradition of its own. There are even traditions within the city. There are Liverpudlians, and there are Scousers, and it's not difficult to tell one from t'other. 'Manchester man, Liverpool gentleman,' Doddy liked to say. He belonged to the old school, and when he died, in March 2018, more than a century of an old English tradition went with him.

As Eric Sykes of Oldham said, Dodd should have been available on the NHS. On stage he was the greatest comedian of all. To watch theatregoers wander out of a show nearer 1 a.m. than midnight, almost physically reeling from a four-hour fiesta, was to witness something very rare. Kenneth Arthur Dodd was a jester, a magician, a genius. Every night he went down a waterfall in a barrel, and took everybody with him.

'Building a bridge with the audience' was his summary of the act. Occasionally there were a few faulty steps. At Buxton one night, when he returned for the second part of the show, he wasn't bringing his bat down straight. The lines sounded tired, the laughs weren't coming. Like a batsman approaching a century, who has spent an over or two playing and missing, he took a fresh guard, eyed the bowling with renewed intent, and regained the audience's trust with strokes that restored him to glory. It was a pro's performance.

In the last 15 years of his life I got to know him well. On another night at Buxton he invited me to join him on stage an hour before the show, as he tuned up. After thousands of performances, in almost every theatre in the land, he liked to get the feel of the building before he went on, 'to sniff the audience', as Laurence Olivier said.

There was nothing malicious about his comedy. He liked people too much. He gave everything of himself, yet the self-regard that taints so much contemporary comedy was absent. Right to the end, in his ninety-first year, he retained a child's sense of wonder. 'The laughter of children,' he used to say, 'is the most beautiful laughter of all.'

Where did he spring from? Billy Bennett, 'almost a gentle-man', was a Liverpool comedian of the previous generation who also liked to play with words. It was inspired nonsense, and sometimes hit the spot. But he wasn't a jester like Dodd, who waved his tickling stick at people nightly.

Another Bennett, Alan, recorded in his diaries that Liverpudlians all 'want to do their little verbal dance for you', though he took a less flattering view of the way they did it. Dodd, like Robb Wilton and Tommy Handley, showed there was another side to the reflexive chippiness many people, including Bennett the playwright, associate with Liverpool.

Dodd had no time for the 'Scouse, not English' line peddled by some Mersey separatists. He was proud of his city, and also of his Englishness. After all, which comedian was ever more joyously English? He played with our language like a virtuoso, a fact recognised by John Osborne. In 1965, when Dodd was breaking the house record at the London Palladium, playing two shows nightly for 42 weeks (and three times on Saturday), the dramatist took the entire company from the Royal Court Theatre to see a master at work.

His funeral, at Liverpool's Anglican Cathedral on 28 March 2018, was packed with Liverpudlians paying their respects on behalf of the city, and the nation. There were hundreds outside the cathedral, and thousands lined the streets. No comedian entertained so many people in the variety halls of England. Doddy knew every one, and every person who worked in them.

In May 2009, distraught at losing a booking at the Royal Concert Hall in Nottingham, he rang me up, hoping a favourable story might help to win it back. Local media had reported that audience members had left while Dodd was on stage, passing judgement on the act. As anybody could have told them, they had buses and trains to catch! Doddy went on longer than the Grateful Dead, and you would expect the press to know this. Dodd got his show back, which cheered him up no end, because Nottingham was the city where he had made his professional debut in 1954.

Liverpool did him proud on the day of his funeral. The public buildings were festooned with tickling sticks, and the eulogies gave a thorough account of the man's life and work. At the end of the service, as we processed down the nave, those sticks were there again, waved proudly by fans conferring their own blessing. He was stingy, some said. They can never have seen him on stage, where he gave everything. A performer in a million.

By the end he had been knighted, 30 years late. He should really have been given a tower, like Peel, where he could wave his tickling stick – by Jove! – at passers-by. Doddy was the last of the great Lancashire comedians, by way of Knotty Ash.

* * *

The town that nestles beneath the Peel Monument has grown a new limb in recent years. Since the BBC relocated members of London staff to the corporation's palace of varieties at Salford Quays many of the incomers, awarded bonuses for hazarding the journey north, have ended up in 'Rammy'.

'They came here in coaches,' says a chap forking his steak and kidney pudding in the local chippy. 'It wa' like being in a zoo.'

Not all the locals like the new Ramsbottom. 'We used to have five banks here,' says an elderly lady on Bridge Street. 'Now we've none.' Her point is well made. They're putting up a 'premises to let' sign on one of those banks. Across the road a café has opened, offering avocado on toast. There was a time, not so long ago, when putting avocado on a menu in Lancashire might have led to an appearance before the magistrates first thing next morning.

'We've three supermarkets,' says the lady, warming to her theme, 'but we've no shoe shop. The shops have all gone, and everything seems to be an eating place. We used to know one another in Rammy. Now we don't.' It's a familiar lament, which pits 'citizens of somewhere' against those who belong nowhere in particular. In Ramsbottom that *kulturkampf*, to use a good Lancashire word, stands out like the Peel Tower.

A short walk reveals the scale of this transformation. Cafés serve 'artisanal cakes', 'ethically sourced coffee' and 'luxury ice cream'. There is a cheese shop, the Mouse Trap, a deli that styles itself 'eclectic', and a chocolatier. A tearoom boasts of twelve selections, including 'Russian Caravan', just the thing when you're entertaining friends from Haslingden. They haven't lost their humour. 'Ration books welcome!' says a sign in one window.

Nobody need starve. The restaurants are Indian, Chinese, Italian, Thai and Spanish. If it's Lancashire hotpot you're after, however, you may be disappointed. Nor is the serious toper overlooked. There's a first-class vintner, tucked away in a back street, and enough bars to furnish a much larger town. One has 32 'premium' gins on its list. 'The quickest way out of Manchester,' it used to be said in the days of slums and destitution, 'is gin.' Now the spirit associated with tipsy old ladies is the drink of choice for the fashionable young.

The lamp shop, run by Denise Smith, a lady of local repute, is a bistro. The newsagent's round the corner is a gift shop. Tommy Topping's butcher's, an emblem of the town, has become a ladies' boutique. Some antique shops remain – for the time being.

When Charles Dickens visited the town in the 1840s he met the brothers Grant, William and Daniel, who had given their name to the town's hotel. The novelist, it is believed, used them as models for the optimistic Cheeryble brothers in *Nicholas Nickleby*. Now the Grant Arms is smothered in scaffolding as builders equip it for a new life as an office block.

For two centuries these towns used to make things. Now the chimneys, fragments of the buildings that once stood proudly, proclaiming Ramsbottom to be a town of work, bear witness to a past that seems as distant as Ethelred the Unready. The modern creed is consumption. Even the East Lancs Railway, which chuffs through Ramsbottom on its way up the valley, is an entertainment for day-trippers. It catches the eye, but is strictly ornamental.

Beyond the railway line, something does work: a cricket club. Ramsbottom have been playing at Acre Bottom since 1845, when Peel was the prime minister, and in 1892 they were one of the founding members of the Lancashire League. In 1904 the club constructed a pavilion, coated in cream and green. It's a lovely building, the essence of what a cricket pavilion should be.

Inside are photographs of all the professionals who have spent their summers at Acre Bottom, and it's quite a list. Emmott Robinson, the Yorkshireman of whom Cardus spun so many tales, spent six years here from 1908, but the biggest name is Ian Chappell. The man who went on to captain one of Australia's strongest teams spent the summer of 1963 at Ramsbottom.

He was not the only Australian batsman to make runs here. Keith Stackpole, David Hookes and Michael Clarke turned out for Rammy. Clive Rice, Brian McMillan and Faf du Plessis of South Africa did too. Wasim Raja of Pakistan and Keith Arthurton of the West Indies wore the colours, as did Tony Lock, the slow left-arm spinner who played for Surrey. Nobody did better than Chris Harris, the New Zealand all-rounder, who spent three summers here in the 1990s. In his first year, 1995, he scored 1231 runs at an average of 87, and took 112 wickets at 12 apiece.

On this day, two months after he passed away at the age of 74, members are thinking of Seymour Nurse. The Barbados opening batsman spent three years in Ramsbottom in the early 1960s, as he was becoming a star of West Indies cricket. The club has placed an obituary from the *Daily Telegraph* on display, so that younger members can discover what a fine cricketer he was, and how fortunate they were to have him as their 'pro'.

There is also newspaper coverage of another paid man, whose life took a different course. When Rambottom signed Ary Molenaar in 1948, it was a bit of a coup. The fast bowler was the first Dutchman to play in the Lancashire League, or would have been if he had pulled on his boots. No sooner had he given his word than Molenaar was arrested, with two other men, and charged with the murder of a Dutch shopkeeper in 1945.

Today, as India are playing Pakistan in the World Cup, 15 miles away at Old Trafford, before a television audience of hundreds of millions, Ramsbottom are playing Clitheroe, newcomers to the Lancashire League. Clitheroe used to play in the Ribblesdale League, transferring their allegiance when the Lancashire League extended its membership to 24 clubs, and two divisions, three seasons ago.

For one couple, who have driven down from 'witch country', Ramsbottom is a fresh adventure. 'Our scoreboard at Clitheroe isn't really up to it,' says the husband.

'The other week,' says his wife, 'a batsman was applauded for making fifty, and when he was out he found out he was three runs short.'

'It was a bit embarrassing, to be honest,' says the husband.

They're sitting in front of the clubhouse, next to the pavilion, with blankets keeping them warm, for the weather is uncertain.

In the tearoom adjoining the clubhouse, some folk are playing the game of 'Whatever happened to him?'

'He went to Australia, I believe.'

'Wrexham.'

A local clergyman arrives. The talk moves on to what will happen at Old Trafford, not that they've seen much of the World Cup on the telly, with it being on so late at night. Holidays, too.

'Last year we went to Cornwall. Had a beefer.'

Beefer! That great Lancashire word. The years roll away.

The tearoom, like the pavilion, is everything such a place should be. For £3.50 you can get a pie with mushy peas and gravy. For afters there is custard tart, Manchester tart, vanilla slice, Eccles cake, Chorley cake, lemon cake, trifle, blueberry pie and scones, and nothing costs more than a fiver. You don't get this at Lord's.

As we wait for the rain to subside it's time for a stroll around the ground. From the far side there is a fine view of the Monument. This really is the most handsome of club grounds. Not pretty. Lancashire has no use for prettiness. It's not that sort of county. Handsome will do. It's a more admirable quality, in nature and humankind.

The advertisements by the whitewashed perimeter wall tell the story of old Ramsbottom, before the New Salfordians arrived. Local travel companies, stonemasons, paint and body shops and building contractors jostle for business. Nino the barber offers 'special OAP rates'.

When the rain abates Ramsbottom are invited to bat. All clubs rely on certain families to replenish the team, and the current Rammy XI can call upon three Fieldings: Jonathan, who played a few games for Lancashire in his youth, and his sons Brad and 16-year-old J. J., who belongs to the county's academy. In the long ago there was another Fielding, Brian,

Jonathan's father. It's not quite the Kennedys of Cape Cod, but it's a fair effort.

In the pavilion the chairman, Rod Hamer, is reflecting on a month spent on the road. He has been to Newport, on the Isle of Wight, to watch Hampshire play Nottinghamshire, and popped into Guildford, for Surrey's match with Yorkshire. This week it was Swansea, another ground to tick off the list. There aren't many left now, he says, though he would like to have got to the recent Notts match at Welbeck Colliery.

On the field the noise from the fielders assaults the ears. Compared with this lot the schoolboys of Uppingham were library quiet. As they say in courts of law, everybody has equal rights of audience. One by one the men from Clitheroe, donning the kind of grey-green hats worn by soldiers on manoeuvres, take up a verbal baton, just as they handle the ball on its way back to the bowler.

'Bowled!'

'That's the one!'

'Keep going, lads!'

Yes, the lads must keep going. They've been out there for all of two overs. They need constant encouragement if their spirits are not to wilt.

At square leg one fielder bellows 'Come on, boys' eight times in an over, adding 'Come on, pro' four times more. He claps 27 times within the space of six balls.

Maurice Haslam, a club stalwart, is talking about the club's big function next week, when 200 guests will attend a Gold Cup day, which includes a four-course dinner. That's Lancashire dinner; the meal you eat at midday. This promises to be an

'Ascot gavotte' with a northern twist. They don't expect to see the back of those guests before nightfall. By the end of the day they will be significantly richer, and every penny helps.

Overall, Haslam reckons, there are 500 members at Acre Bottom, of whom 'around ninety' are players. Ramsbottom put out two senior teams besides the first XI, and field age-group teams from nine to fifteen. 'Though it seems the same people do the work from one year to the next he doesn't sound angry'. He knows this is the way of the world, and clubs such as his are run by men and women with big hearts for the benefit of others who are usually grateful for their efforts.

Not all clubs prosper. Milnrow, a well-regarded club on the other side of Rochdale which belonged to the neighbouring Central Lancashire League, joined the Lancashire League when it was reconstituted. Now they have asked to leave because they failed to field a team for a second XI fixture last month. There is sympathy for their embarrassment, and an unspoken fear that other clubs may suffer it.

Occasionally one of the Ramsbottom lads breaks through. Alan Ormrod, a graceful batsman for Worcestershire, and John Savage, who bowled off-spinners for Leicestershire and Lancashire, played county cricket for many years. John Simpson, the current Middlesex wicketkeeper, grew up at Ramsbottom, where his father Jack was a notable wicketkeeper-batsman. The quality of cricket, though, is not what it was. Everybody agrees on that. They will also tell you, quite rightly, that this league produced James Anderson, a Burnley player not so long ago, who has taken more wickets in Test cricket than any other Englishman.

It is heavy going in the middle. George Linde, the South African pro, is run out by Sam Halstead, a Rammy old boy. The immutable law of the ex, as Italians say of footballers who score against their former clubs. There is some chortling in the clubhouse. Pros are not supposed to be run out.

Jonathan and Brad Fielding, father and elder son, then come together in a stand that pushes Ramsbottom towards an all-out score of 174. If the weather holds they should win.

The weather doesn't hold, but it doesn't matter. When the rain drives the players from the field for the last time Ramsbottom have completed 25 overs, more than enough to count as a game, and Clitheroe are languishing on 47 for five. Fielding senior has taken three cheap wickets, and Linde's eight overs bring him two for six. According to the rules for shortened matches devised by Duckworth and Lewis, Ramsbottom are the winners by 97 runs. In the clubhouse pints are ordered for the players. No jugs. There were no outstanding performances to merit a communal swill.

If there is such a thing as a hub of the community in a town that has changed as much as Ramsbottom then it may be found in this clubhouse. There is no ethically sourced coffee at Acre Bottom, and the place is no worse for its absence. There are decent folk, who were born in the town, and will die here. The club is part of their lives, a part they are pleased to hand on to those who follow.

Next month there is a festival of real ale, that staple of English life. There is a jigsaw tournament in the autumn, which is a novelty, and September brings the annual black-pudding lobbing 'world championships', though 'world' really means Bury and district.

You can paste as much avocado as you like on your toast, and swill premium gin by the quart. Ultimately what matters is the people who will remain in these out-of-the-way places when the caravan moves on. At the Theatre Royal, round the corner from a tapas bar, the Summerseat Players are putting on a series of northern dramas. At Acre Bottom they are still playing cricket, in the old Lancashire manner.

Here, in this crucible of social transformation, one of the great cricket clubs of England is doing its bit to keep local traditions alive. Good for them. Three cheers for Rammy.

Seymour Nurse was not the only great West Indian cricketer to play in the Lancashire League. You can drive from Ramsbottom to Nelson, 20 miles to the north-east, and find evidence in almost every club you pass of a profound Caribbean influence. In the days before widespread overseas employment in county cricket this is where the great and the good came to play as the club pro, and their involvement was felt beyond the clubhouse. Without ascending the pulpit, or playing to the gallery, these men helped to change attitudes.

Haslingden, the club nearest to Ramsbottom, was a summer home to George Headley, the Jamaican batsman, in the 1930s, and three decades later to Clive Lloyd from Guyana. Headley, sometimes called 'the black Bradman', was the first great West Indian batsman. His son Ron, who opened the batting for Worcestershire, also played Test cricket. Ron's son, Dean, was a third generation international cricketer, though he represented England as a fast-medium bowler. A very good one. In 1998 his wickets helped to win a Test match in Melbourne.

Lloyd occupies an exceptional place in the history of cricket. As captain of the all-conquering West Indian team of the late 1970s and early 1980s, he is credited with bringing together the different factions of the English-speaking Caribbean, and their unprecedented run of success tends to support that argument. It is sometimes overlooked that before he became captain he was the most thrilling of batsmen, and a cover fielder without equal. When he threw at the stumps he generally hit, as a host of defeated batsmen found out the hard way. If Garfield Sobers and Vivian Richards were the monarchs of West Indian batsmanship then Lloyd served as a splendid regent between their reigns.

Haslingden greeted him in April 1968. The night before his first match, billeted with a local family, he was granted the luxury of sleeping in the marital bed. 'Well, he's the club's new pro,' as the selfless husband explained later. The following summer Lloyd was a Lancashire player, and his feats at Old Trafford are the stuff of legend. In 1986, as he wound down his career, Lloyd became a British subject out of respect for the way he had been accepted in his adopted country.

Everton Weekes played at Bacup, and Clyde Walcott at Enfield. In the twilight of his days. Richards, 'King Viv', spent a year at Rishton, a club that also engaged Michael Holding, one of the greatest fast bowlers. Holding was following a path trodden by Wes Hall (Accrington), Charlie Griffith (Burnley) and Roy Gilchrist (Bacup). The neighbouring Central Lancashire League was served at various times by Sobers, Frank Worrell, Andy Roberts and Joel Garner. No league anywhere in the world has known such a concentration of high talent.

Lloyd is not the only West Indian to form a permanent attachment. Sonny Ramadhin, the mystery spinner from Trinidad who bamboozled England in 1950, when West Indies won here for the first time, played a year of county cricket for Lancashire in 1964 and still lives locally. His grandson, Kyle Hogg, wore the red rose in the first decade of the millennium. For years Ramadhin ran the White Lion at Delph, one of the villages beginning with D (Denshaw, Diggle, Dobcross) that crouch beneath Saddleworth Moor, and are often impassable in winter.

Cec Wright, the Jamaican fast bowler, has played in the local leagues since 1959. This summer, at the age of 85, he is finally bringing down the curtain on one of the game's most extraordinary careers at Uppermill, another Saddleworth club, where he turns out for the second team. He doesn't tear in these days. But the fact that he plays at all, for the sheer love of life, is remarkable.

To find the pioneer you must go to Nelson. When Learie Constantine, the Trinidad all-rounder, accepted an offer to be the club's paid man in 1929 it was the start of an astonishing story that really did change cricket. Other players may have achieved more remarkable things on the field but no West Indian cricketer, living or dead, achieved so much in his life as the man Neville Cardus said he would include in an all-time XI for his fielding alone.

There were few black faces when Constantine left Trinidad for a new life in north-east Lancashire. It was a world of terraced houses and cotton mills, and the Depression touched everybody. Yet the townsfolk accepted him as one of their own. In his decade at Nelson they were champions seven times, and he established a reputation as a cricketer and man that subsequent years have embellished.

Cricket turned out to be a prelude to a life decorated with honours. He was an Honorary Bencher of the Middle Temple, served as Trinidad's High Commissioner in London and was a knight of the realm. In 1969, when he became the first black member of the House of Lords, he was gazetted as Baron Constantine of Maraval in Trinidad and Nelson in the County Palatine of Lancaster. He did so, he said, to dignify his place of birth and those who had made him so welcome when he came to England.

When he died in 1971, at the age of 69, 'Learie' was granted the signal honour of a memorial service at Westminster Abbey. By then the Race Relations Act was enshrined in law, partly as a consequence of Constantine's suit against the Imperial Hotel, London, which had refused to accommodate him in 1943. In small-town Lancashire he encountered occasional puzzlement (as white people can do today in the Indian sub-continent) but no hostility.

Interviewed by Mike Brearley in 1987 for Channel 4, C. L. R. James said neither he nor Constantine were victims of racial prejudice in Nelson. Constantine had invited James, his fellow Trinidadian, to join him in Lancashire. Once there, James found journalistic work at the *Manchester Guardian*, thanks to Cardus. In his view the cricket played in the Lancashire League was harder than Constantine would have encountered in the county championship.

In the course of a life in education and culture James

became one of the foremost historians of the Caribbean, teaching at Harvard before ending his days in Brixton. He is perhaps best-known as the author of *Beyond a Boundary*, a book about cricket which, as the title implies, extends to other subjects. Any true love of cricket, it may be argued, includes life beyond a boundary. James's main interest, unusually for a Caribbean Marxist, was English Romantic poetry.

Constantine's was not the first sporting memorial at Westminster Abbey. That honour went to Sir Frank Worrell, whose death in March 1967, at the age of 42, was mourned far beyond Barbados, where he was born, and Jamaica, where he served as a senator. As the first black man to captain the West Indies, Worrell was another pioneer.

He also had a Lancashire connection, as pro for Radcliffe in the Central Lancashire League when he was a student at Manchester University. Radcliffe, between Bury and Manchester, was the club where Sobers played as well. It was in these small towns that the great West Indian lineage was forged, from Constantine to Richards, by way of Headley, Worrell, Sobers and Lloyd. The six cricketers who did most to make Caribbean cricket great, and make the game a source of pride for their people, all had a connection with the County Palatine.

There was a form of symbiosis, or at least mutual recognition. By degrees, over the course of seven decades, each side contributed to an understanding of the other, and a relaxing of social codes. There is no absolute in racial tolerance. Fear of the other exists in all societies, at all times. But cricket in Lancashire, through the appearance of so many outstanding players from the Caribbean, carried a torch for civilised values. Their legacy is more profound than is sometimes acknowledged, because it owed nothing to political movements. It was all to do with people rubbing along together.

Another foreign-born cricketer came to England in 1960. Basil D'Oliveira, the Cape Coloured, was barred from selection for the South African Test team. John Arlott, who took up his case after the player wrote to the commentator to find him a suitable instrument for his talent, helped to get him a place at Middleton in the Central Lancashire League. 'Come now,' he told D'Oliveira, 'it's the best chance you'll ever get.'

It did not go well at first. Unfamiliar with slow pitches, 'Dolly' struggled against the kind of medium-pace bowlers who could nip the ball around at will. But he persevered, and the runs came. From Middleton he went to Worcestershire in 1964, where he became a county champion two years running, and from New Road he was promoted to the England team in 1966, where he stayed for six years.

Brought up as a second-class citizen in Cape Town, D'Oliveira was astonished by the openness of English life, where he was accepted as a human being of equal standing. His tale has been told often, and remains vivid. His non-selection for the MCC tour of South Africa in the winter of 1968/9 had political consequences that helped to dismantle apartheid. Like Constantine, he responded to provocation with a modesty that unmanned the peddlers of intolerance. 'He was challenged many times,' said Arlott. 'But he never rose to it. I never admired a man more.'

Lancashire cricket owes a debt to D'Oliveira. Having settled down in Middleton, he sent word back to Cape Town, to his friend Cec Abrahams, who followed him to England within a year. Cec's eldest son, John, played his early cricket at Milnrow, where his father was pro, and later became the captain of Lancashire. In retirement he has coached young cricketers, and managed the England under-19 team. Just as important, he has retained his reputation as one of the most decent human beings in a game that boasts quite a few.

Throughout the 1980s and 1990s cricketers born in the West Indies, and the sons and grandsons of Caribbean immigrants, played for England regularly. Roland Butcher of Middlesex was the first to win selection in 1981, after which the doors opened for his county team-mates Wilf Slack, Norman Cowans and Neil Williams. There followed a mighty rush as Gladstone Small, Phillip DeFreitas, Devon Malcolm, David Lawrence and Chris Lewis emerged as fine bowlers.

There are cultural reasons for the failure to find their successors from within the West Indian population. Young people in the inner cities, black and white, are attracted more to football, which enjoys a higher public profile and offers the gifted players untold riches. The game that meant so much to previous generations means less to young men who were born here, whose connection with the Caribbean becomes slighter with each decade that passes.

Cricket cannot fail to reflect the changes in habit and custom. The immigrants, or sons of immigrants, who have played for England in recent years have come from the Indian sub-continent. Nasser Hussain led the way, and ended up as captain, one of England's finest. Monty Panesar, Ravi Bopara,

Moeen Ali and Adil Rashid have known successful days, and a few disappointing ones.

In the Lancashire towns where the West Indian cricketers were received with such warmth life is very different. Over the past half century, as the nature of work has shifted, and immigration from the Punjab has altered the character of places such as Burnley and Blackburn, there has been a social revolution. In such towns the ideal of 'multi-culturalism', as defined by people who live in more prosperous parts of the country, often appears to be an abstraction.

The towns known for cotton mills and comedians are better known now for sex scandals. Rochdale, over the hill from Ramsbottom, was represented at Westminster for two decades by Cyril Smith, a Liberal MP whose monstrous behaviour, frequently alluded to while he was alive, has become a matter of record since his death in 2010.

In the past decade Rochdale has become associated in the public imagination with the sexual grooming of teenage girls by gangs of Pakistanis, many working out of taxi firms. Rochdale does not stand alone in its infamy. The Casey Report, published in 2015, the year that 12 men from the Keighley area were jailed for sexual grooming, revealed that as many as 1400 white girls in Rotherham had been sexually abused.

When Ann Cryer, the Labour MP for Keighley, voiced her concerns about sexual exploitation of white girls by Pakistani gangs in 2002, she was ignored. Police officers, social workers and members of the Pakistani community in Keighley preferred not to listen. She was even denounced by members of the Labour Party for her 'racist' conduct in raising the matter. Jack Straw, the Labour MP for Blackburn, and Home Secretary, was also criticised for asking constituents to take off the burka when they visited him at his office.

After Andrew Norfolk prepared an outstanding series of reports in *The Times* in 2012, detailing the extent of the scandal in Rotherham, there was nowhere for the rebukers to hide. Not everybody felt a sense of shame. Denis MacShane, the former Labour MP for Rotherham, admitted to Martha Kearney on the BBC's *World at One* programme that he had heard rumours of criminal activity but, 'as a *Guardian*-reading liberal', he didn't want to rock the boat.

Despite the evidence, which led to convictions in courts across the land, the word 'Islamophobia' was tossed about with the gladdest of hands. It was sometimes lost in the course of this shameful parade that the man presenting the case on behalf of the Crown Prosecution Service, Nazir Afzal, is a Muslim. After the trial in 2012 that saw nine men from Rochdale sent down for sexual trafficking and rape he made the salient point that most crimes of a sexual nature were committed by white men. In cases of grooming the perpetrators were overwhelmingly Muslims. It was a message many people within that cloistered world did not want to hear.

Social cohesion in the towns of Lancashire and Yorkshire has not broken down irreparably, though there have been incidents of unrest. But it cannot be denied that there have been fractures. Whereas the West Indians who came to Britain were rooted in the values of the Judaeo-Christian world, the Muslim dimension to the recent wave of immigration has introduced a cultural difference that bland platitudes about 'multi-culturalism' cannot disguise.

Most Muslims live decent lives in harmony with their neighbours. A significant minority, it cannot be denied, have made little effort to integrate within British society, and closed societies encourage hostility towards outsiders. Those differences are seen most clearly in places such as north-east Lancashire, where Learie Constantine was made so welcome.

The walls that exclude may be found in cricket, which has done so much to bring people together. Fewer players from a Pakistani background engage with league clubs, to the detriment of both parties. The drinking culture that has always been part of British sport does not appeal to Muslims, for whom a night in the pub, and the japes that accompany it, is a manifestation of Western life many of them cannot understand.

There is a well of talent in danger of running dry. Lancashire have found some players, most recently Haseeb Hameed and Saqib Mahmood, but more young men from their background should be coming through. And Hameed owes his promotion to the bespoke facilities of Bolton School, thanks to a sports scholarship Lancashire arranged to prevent him leaving as a 13-year-old for Malvern.

'Only connect,' wrote E. M. Forster, referring to the competing faculties of reason and feeling. It is a sound precept to live by, in real life and in the puppet world of sport. Constantine and those who celebrated him in Nelson provided lessons of tolerance that make us all richer. It's time to hear that song again. Sing out, Learie.

V

Long Lion Days

Scarborough, Chesterfield, Cheltenham

'Welcome to Yorkshire,' proclaims the advertisement at North Marine Road. 'England's biggest and most glorious county.' That's how they like their brew up here, hot and strong.

The English Bavarians are gathering once more in Scarborough. Like Freistaat Bayern, a territory in its own right, Yorkshire affects to be a country within a nation, and the natives do not always hide their sense of otherness. Like Bavarians, Yorkshire folk sometimes bridle when people do not take them at their own estimation. All that's missing this morning is a blue and white flag above the pavilion, and *Mädchen* in dirndls.

A signpost by the main entrance indicates that we are 190 miles from Lord's. The inference to be drawn is that Lord's is 190 miles from Scarborough. On this Sunday morning, when

Yorkshire, the most famous cricketing county, are playing Surrey, the current champions, the town's north bay is a bracing place to be. It is July, the height of the year, and we do like to be beside the seaside.

Many of the traditional grounds, festive or occasional, are no more; at least not used any longer for county cricket. Somerset do not go to Bath or Weston-super-Mare. Hampshire have put all their eggs in a single basket, at Eastleigh, which means fare thee well to Bournemouth and Basingstoke, where the young John Arlott grew up. You won't find Buxton or Dover on a map of the modern championship, although first-class cricket did return earlier this summer to York. The World Cup scheduling led to that happy accident.

In an ideal world, most championship matches would be played on these grounds, where the dimensions are modest, and the mood jolly. The players appear to be better disposed, too, even if they mutter about the quality of some pitches. Taken away from the main grounds, and shunted off to the seaside, they too feel liberated. When the sun is out, as it is today, there are few happier places to watch cricket than Scarborough.

The town is unbalanced. Although the coastal fringes are still loved by elderly holiday makers, keen to relive old glories, the centre has become shoddy. It is a world away from the glory days of the 1930s when its reputation gained it a famous admirer; from the land of dirndls, as it happens. With Europe his to command, Herr Hitler dreamed of dancing with Eva Braun in the Grand Hotel. The ballroom of romance indeed.

This is no longer the resort of the Führer's fevered

imagination. Like so many seaside towns Scarborough is a sorry-looking place, stuffed with tattoo parlours, pawn shops, grotty pubs and hotels barely fit for purpose. The decline, a puddle at first, has turned into a torrent in the last two decades. Despite its superb location, situated between two bays, Scarborough has surrendered its dignity.

It should have a strong hand to play. There are some handsome buildings, and a history that, though not gilded, beckons the curious traveller. For decades this was a respectable place, which welcomed families from all over the north for a fortnight of fun by the shore. Generations of cricket lovers frolicked on the beach for hours on end, improvising games with their neighbours. Now you may spend all day on those sands, and not see a single child or adult pick up a bat.

Scarborough's most celebrated resident is Alan Ayckbourn, the writer-director, who worked here as an actor in the 1950s, and stayed. His plays, beginning with *Relatively Speaking* in 1967, have conquered the West End, and made him a rich man. 'With all that money,' a local stalwart once said, 'you'd have thought he would live in Bridlington.'

It's a line that could have come from one of his plays. No dramatist has examined the foibles of middle-class life so precisely, so humorously or, as his work darkened, so tragically. Watching the procession of men and women wandering through his adopted town by day and night, it's not unfair to think he is painting from memory.

There is social tragedy here, but not the kind that animates *Absurd Person Singular*. It is the stench of physical decay. This is not confined to Scarborough but it is more apparent here than other places because this town, a long-established resort with decades of capital in the bank of public goodwill, should present a more cheerful face to the world.

Ayckbourn is not necessarily the first writer who springs to mind when people think of Scarborough. Anne Brontë is buried in the churchyard at St Mary's, up the hill from North Marine Road, where many of those holidaymakers are heading this morning to fulfil their annual ritual. The youngest of the Brontë sisters, whose novels did so much to reveal Yorkshire to the world, died here in 1849, at the age of 29.

The town also has a significant theatrical connection. Charles Laughton, who won an Oscar for his kingly performance in *The Private Life of Henry VIII*, and went on to direct that disturbing masterpiece, *The Night of the Hunter*, with Robert Mitchum in the leading role, was brought up here, the son of a hotelier. He worked with Billy Wilder, too, on *Witness for the Prosecution*, so he was acquainted with true greatness.

What a rebuke the ground offers to the town! The spectator may go back in time, to the palmy days of county cricket, like those non-cricketing couples staying round the corner in guesthouses called Seacliffe and Bay View. Morning is the best time to catch both sets of holidaymakers, as they parade on the promenade overlooking the North Sea, wondering whether the weather will last beyond lunchtime, and where all their yesterdays went.

Scarborough is where people come to forget, and to remember. My response on entering the ground is to stand at midwicket and imagine through half-closed eyes Fred Trueman's surge to the crease on that September day in 1965, when he parted five Derbyshire batsmen from the crease. Bowling at the other end was Richard Hutton, son of Leonard, who had the rare gift of halting 'F. S.' in his verbal tracks when the fast bowler's tales entered the realm of fantasy.

One evening, as Trueman polished his halo ('another five wickets for me') before an audience which was not encouraged to interrupt, Hutton asked: 'Fred, would you describe yourself as a modest man?'

A younger generation think of Trueman, if they think of him at all, as a sour old-timer forever banging on about the glory days, failing to understand what was 'going off' in the middle. Some may remember him as the presenter of *Indoor League*, a Yorkshire Television programme from the mid-1970s, when he would bid farewell to viewers by pointing his pipe towards the camera, and saying: 'Ah'll si'thee!' By then the mask had worn into the face. He didn't talk like that in real life.

There are a few folk on this ground today who could put the scoffers right. Although he retired from first-class cricket in 1968, reappearing briefly in Sunday League matches for Derbyshire four years later, Trueman still inspires more tales than any other cricketer except Ian Botham. He was a great bowler, perhaps England's greatest. He was also an important figure in our country's post-war social history, a fact not sufficiently recognised when he died in 2006.

He didn't always play the role of the cheerful Tyke. A friend, Peter Myers, who later ran a well-known English grocer's in Manhattan, recalled going to the Scarborough Festival as a ten-year-old to watch the Gentlemen take on the Players. 'My uncle Mark told me to get his autograph but when I approached him he told me to fuck off or he would wrap his bat around my head.' The Bedser twins, Alec and Eric, obliged the young chap, so the day wasn't entirely wasted.

He was a rough diamond, F. S. Born in 1931 near Maltby, when south Yorkshire had a coalfield, the young Trueman was an authentic working-class hero in those post-war years, just before the novels of Alan Sillitoe and David Storey helped to make that type of man fashionable. Distinctions of social class were policed more rigidly in those days, and the young Trueman was undoubtedly a victim of prejudice.

When listeners south of Northampton heard him speak on radio and television, after he had become England's cavalier in 1952, many were shocked to discover that people talked like that. In the Yorkshire dressing room, too, there were dissenters who thought of him as a common man from mining country. Trueman did not sound like J. B. Priestley or Wilfred Pickles, whose warmer, slightly diluted tones were reassuring. He sounded unvarnished, a short step from savagery.

After 1956, the year of Suez and *Look Back in Anger*, attitudes changed, and doors hitherto closed to young men in northern towns banged wide open. Actors from working-class backgrounds, or, like Albert Finney, thought to be from working-class backgrounds, stormed the stage and screen. The pop explosion in the early 1960s, led by four lads from Liverpool, gave another shove, though it would be misleading to suggest that pop music was rooted in the proletarian experience.

John Lennon, the most comfortable of those 'rebels', played at being a horny-handed son of toil. When the Beatles broke up he wrote 'Working Class Hero', which referred directly to another 1950s literary landmark, John Braine's *Room at the Top*, as if he had some kinship with those who had known genuine hardship. It was a mawkish song, which recalled James Joyce's definition of sentimentality, 'unearned emotion'.

In his younger life this gifted self-romanticiser, on whom *Private Eye* based Spiggy Topes, the pop singer forever searching for a cause, grew up on Menlove Avenue, which for generations has defined respectability in suburban Liverpool. A decade later Simon Rattle was raised on the same road. To the barricades, comrades!

Trueman never gave peace a chance, or demanded power for 'the people'. His pleasures came in a pint glass and a pipe full of old shag. In his later years, when he had settled snugly into the role of a grand old man, he antagonised many who had grown up lauding him, who thought he had gone over to the other side. Temperamentally he came to stand beside the most unlikely of comrades, T. S. Eliot, who declared himself to be Anglo-Catholic in religion, classicist in literature, and Royalist in politics.

Conservative or bolshy, proletarian or classless, there can be no argument about his status. Trueman takes his place alongside Botham and Denis Compton in English cricket's post-war trinity. They were not 'characters', as the modern idiom has it. They were stars, as in twinkle, twinkle.

The people who flocked each summer to Scarborough understood Trueman. Most lived in towns such as Rotherham and Barnsley, the heartland of Yorkshire cricket. For them Scarborough was a place where they could set their cares aside, and watch a game they played in the local leagues. Fred was their representative, the man who fleshed out their hopes with a hatful of wickets, and won matches for Yorkshire and England. They didn't resent his urge to hog the follow-spot. That's what stars do.

North Marine Road was the place not only for championship jousts but also for end-of-season revels. Cricketers from all over the land set off merrily each September for contests between Yorkshire and the Yorkshiremen, and turn out for T. N. Pearce's XI. Scarborough was known for cakes and ale, first out in the middle and then in the town's inns when stumps were drawn. All parties would convene in the bar of the Royal Hotel towards midnight, to tell tales of their adventures. Trueman's were not always the tallest.

There are 4000 spectators present this morning, most of them seated beneath the Tea Room at the Trafalgar Road end, and behind the arm at the sea end. These are the most patient attenders of cricket in England, and they are seated a good hour before the start of play, armed with newspapers and thermos flasks, preparing to watch Yorkshire make plenty of runs.

A few hundred have no direct allegiance to either county. They have come from other parts of England, to absorb the Scarborough experience. A man in the popular enclosure, where the rows of unsupported wooden benches haven't seen a minute's maintenance since the old king died, is happy to tell people this is his first cricket match. 'I'm a Tottenham fan, you see.' He seems surprised by the blank looks.

Many Yorkshire members, who plan their weeks here with the rigour of generals in the field, are happy to get away from Headingley, the prosaic ground in Leeds that is the county's headquarters. In days gone by Yorkshire played at Bradford, Harrogate, Middlesbrough and Hull as well as Leeds and Scarborough. They also played, until 1973, at Bramall Lane, where Sheffield United play football. For many Yorkies of the old school Bramall Lane distilled the essence of Yorkshire cricket.

In the clubhouse, above the dressing rooms, it is possible to feel the weight of history. W. G. Grace played on this ground, and Donald Bradman made his last appearance in this country at Scarborough in September 1948, making a century. It's not quite like Olivier and Gielgud at the Old Vic, perhaps, but those are grand names to bag.

The boards record the men who have served as presidents of Scarborough Cricket Club. The Duke of Edinburgh, the Duke of Norfolk and the Earl of Harewood have all lent their names to this club, situated on the north bay of a seaside resort. Leonard Hutton (twice) and Herbert Sutcliffe represent the aristocracy of Yorkshire cricketers. Somewhere in between are Michael Parkinson and Tim Rice, knights of the realm who love their cricket. Another knight, Paul Getty, was cricket's greatest modern benefactor, who held court in his box at Lord's every summer as though each Test was a garden party.

Philip Hodson, the current prez, could have walked out of a novel by Storey. Not *This Sporting Life*, which Lindsay Anderson turned into a fine film starring Richard Harris as the turbulent star of rugby league. Storey, good enough to play league for Leeds, wrote an even better novel, *Saville*, which won the Booker Prize in 1976, apparently on the toss of a coin. Two other superb novels were shortlisted that year, William Trevor's

The Children of Dynmouth and Brian Moore's *The Doctor's Wife*. In those days, before it became a media event, the Booker was a prize worth winning.

Like many novels, *Saville* is a disguised autobiography. Colin Saville, born in a pit village, and educated at the local grammar school, leaves his home for London, as did Storey, who attended Queen Elizabeth Grammar School before winning a place at the Slade School of Art. Though it is largely forgotten now, like the man who wrote it, *Saville* is one of the most convincing post-war English novels, all the better for being unfashionable. But then, as Tom Courtenay, star of *Billy Liar* and *The Loneliness of the Long Distance Runner*, has said: 'When you see who's considered to be in fashion, it's a relief to be out of it.'

Hodson went to Queen Elizabeth Grammar School, and still lives nearby, though he is a rich man – he earned his pile in insurance – with homes in France and South Africa. A fine amateur cricketer, who won a Blue at Cambridge, he is a former president of MCC, and married Sally Anne, Tony Greig's sister. He is also one of the game's strongest evangelists.

In Scarborough, he admits, it's a labour of love. There is little money in the town. The club budgets for a loss of £50,000 each year, relying on sponsorship and bequests to keep county cricket here, in a place where it shines most brightly. Next summer there is talk of inviting Durham to play a championship match, to extend the festival.

Adam Lyth and Will Fraine, left and right, open the batting for Yorkshire. They also diverge in experience.

Lyth is almost at home, as he grew up in Whitby, a few miles up the coast, beyond Robin Hood's Bay. Four years ago he was called up by England, and played seven Test matches, making a century against New Zealand at Headingley. He didn't fail, therefore, but neither did he make an unanswerable case to be Alastair Cook's regular partner, and, approaching his thirty-second birthday, the years are against him.

Fraine, 23, is from Huddersfield. He returned to his native county after spending his formative professional years at Worcestershire and Nottinghamshire. This is an important year for him. The Yorkshire batting has wobbled in the last couple of seasons, without the permanent presence of Root and Bairstow. There are places to be won, and reputations to make.

Bairstow is opening the batting for England today, in a World Cup match against India, and the spectators are keeping a close watch on events at Edgbaston. There are cheers when 'Bluey's lad' reaches his century, and a few smiles from the Surrey fielders, who seem to be enjoying their northern tour. On their balcony Alec Stewart, their director of cricket, is recalling his first experience of Scarborough, half a lifetime ago, when Geoffrey Boycott's word was still writ. 'When he was out, half the crowd went home!'

Lyth pats a long hop to extra cover, after helping to make 116 for the opening stand. Fraine carries on regardless. Last month at York he passed up the chance of making a significant score, the kind he needs to retain his place, when he clipped a catch to midwicket. He is more resolute today, and completes his maiden championship century in the middle of the afternoon, before he is the fourth man out, caught behind off the South African fast bowler, Morne

Morkel. Jordan Clark, Surrey's medium pacer, a native of Cumbria, then takes five wickets as Yorkshire surrender the ground they had gained in the first two sessions, and Surrey, through Mark Stoneman and Dean Elgar, launch their reply with confident strokes.

The spectators return through the back streets to their guesthouses. At St Mary's it is time for evensong, and 'the day thou gavest, Lord, is ended'. Not a big and glorious day this time but a very good one, with the promise of three more to follow. And a happy day for young Fraine, who may tell his children's children of the fine Sunday afternoon he walloped Surrey, champions of England, around the meadow for 106 well-crafted runs.

'Greetings to you all,' says the man on the public address, as spectators assemble in the tree-lined ground at Queen's Park, Chesterfield, for the second day's play between Derbyshire and Northamptonshire. 'And remember, England are the world champions.'

This is true, though the people spreading rugs in the warm sunshine are not inclined to crow. The previous day, after a 'super over' made necessary by the teams making identical scores, England were deemed to have beaten New Zealand in the World Cup final because they struck more boundaries during their innings. Queen's Park is not basking in the afterglow, as some places might. There is gentle applause and a handful of cheers, more ironic than exultant.

Triumphalism does not sit well here. Most visitors to

Chesterfield are from solid Derbyshire stock, which means as solid as England gets. The old-fashioned virtues have never become outmoded in this part of the kingdom, where mining country meets the Peak. You are close to the pits, or where the pits used to be, and just as close to Chatsworth, seat of the Cavendish family, one of those stately homes Noël Coward used to sing about. 'We know how Caesar conquered Gaul, and how to whack a cricket ball . . .'

It is the kind of morning that makes anybody want to whack a ball; a day when poets sharpen their pencils, and painters prepare their brushes. The chestnuts stand proud on either side on the sightscreen, near the solitary tulip tree, and an avenue of silver limes offers shade on the mound beneath the bandstand to spectators who have camped near the van that sells the superb ice creams supplied by Frederick's. Signor Frederick has his own gelateria on the other side of the park railings which offers, as many happy cricket lovers have discovered, a Bakewell tart-flavoured ice cream. Just the thing for the hour before tea.

Derbyshire have not had much luck at Chesterfield in recent years. In 2016, and, barely believably, again in 2017, they lost all four days of championship matches to rain. There is talk of playing all first-class cricket at Derby, the county's much-improved headquarters. Even Chesterfield loyalists know that Queen's Park, with its basic facilities for the players, struggles to maintain the standards required by a professional game.

Yet here, below the greenhouse, where pupils gather to dodge 'the toad work', there is a ground of becoming rightness. Its good nature quiets the restless soul. Even the agitated young man walking along the path behind the members' enclosure, muttering oaths, ready to take offence at anything said or left unsaid, makes peace with himself.

John Cater, Chesterfield born and bred, has been watching the cricketers since childhood. 'I sometimes say that, if it hadn't been for cricket, I would never have gone to Derby!' His first summer was 1956, when he sang as a nine-year-old in the choir at the parish church, the one with the twisted spire. 'I was a junior subscriber, and it cost ten and six. In those days there were six matches at Derby, and six at Chesterfield, with other games at Buxton, Ilkeston and Burton-on-Trent.'

Those were the years of Donald Carr, Les Jackson and George Pope. Bill Grundy, the journalist and broadcaster, once interviewed Pelé, who told him he had met the Pope. 'I take it,' Grundy, by no means sober, told the great footballer, 'that you are referring to Mr George Pope, the famous Derbyshire all-rounder.'

If any man represents the spirit of Derbyshire cricket it is Jackson, the county's most successful bowler with 1670 wickets. Born in Whitwell, near the Nottinghamshire border, Jackson went down the pit at 16, a traditional background for fast bowlers from this part of the world. They were strong men, who knew about hard work. To play cricket for a living, however modest, was a boon. Others were less fortunate. Jackson's brother died in the Creswell colliery disaster in September 1950, which claimed the lives of 80 miners.

He enjoys a stellar status in these parts, admired for his supreme skill and pitied for the misfortune of playing no more than two Tests, 12 years apart. The other fast bowlers of the day, Fred Trueman to the fore, thought the world of Jackson, regarding him as a superior craftsman.

In 1949 he played against New Zealand. In 1961 he was recalled in his forty-first year to bowl against Australia. It was a desperate throw of the dice, and established the longest separation between Test appearances in the game's history. Jackson's forthright views in an age of deference were considered to have been held against him. The amateur ethos of 'good chaps', not all of whom were good, prevailed.

There was also the matter of geography and history. Winners of the championship only once, in 1936, Derbyshire have never been a fashionable club. Even when Bob Taylor, Mike Hendrick and Geoff Miller played for England in the 1970s, followed by Kim Barnett, Dominic Cork and Devon Malcolm, it was possible to hear the gritting of selectorial teeth.

In or out of fashion, Chesterfield has seen some remarkable scenes. In 1969 Peter Eyre, the man whose hairpiece fell off when I saw him at Old Trafford two summers before, took six for 18 against Sussex in a Gillette Cup semi-final. Eleven years later, when the West Indies unleashed Andy Roberts, Malcolm Marshall and Joel Garner on a fast pitch, John Wright, the New Zealand batsman, made 94 going in first. It is an innings lovingly remembered in the Peak, where Wright is honoured for his chivalry as much as his talent.

In 1973 there was a peculiar day when Brian Bolus, the Derbyshire captain, instructed Alan Ward, his fast bowler, to leave the field. Ward had been badly treated in his opening spell by John Hampshire, the Yorkshire batsman who later joined Derbyshire, and didn't feel up to the task. In that case, his captain told him, you're no use to me. He found support from Brian Clough, the highly quotable manager of Derby County, who used his newspaper column to remind readers that, as a cricket lover, he thought Bolus had acted as any captain should. By Guy Fawkes Night Cloughie had left the Baseball Ground, a victim of his own quest for sainthood. But he bounced back in Nottingham, as all the books confirm.

Mohammad Azharuddin was responsible for one of Chesterfield's happiest tales. The opening championship fixture of the 1994 season brought John Morris back to his former club. Morris, a strokeplayer of considerable gifts, had left Derby the previous year for Durham, newly admitted to the roster of first-class counties, and he made 90 as they won, handsomely. But it is the Indian captain's double century in a losing cause that people remember.

Six times he drove David Graveney, Durham's left-arm spinner, over the sightscreen between the chestnuts. Every stroke, it seemed, was a masterpiece of timing and balance. He teased the fielders, placing the ball past the left hand of cover point, for instance, and then, once the fielder had shifted his position a yard or two to anticipate the next stroke, and deny the batsman runs, he placed it past his right.

It must have been like this in the Golden Age, one imagined, when Ranji was at the crease. On a dank April day, real two-sweater weather, Azharuddin played like a sorcerer, making captives of us all. 'Master class' sounds too formal. It was as if he had intended to compress the history of sub-continental batsmanship into four hours, for his own pleasure. The 2000 souls present will never forget some of his strokes that day. High talent requires no quorum.

Derbyshire, resuming on 34 for one, could do with an hour's batting as golden as the sun. Alas, they soon lose Wayne Madsen, their main source of runs. Madsen has given them 11 summers, the best years of his life, and there will be a mighty hole to fill when he puts away his bat. Though associated with Derbyshire, and long resident in the county, Madsen was born in South Africa. More than most clubs the Peakites must cast their net widely.

The days of Jackson and his new-ball partner, Cliff Gladwin, also from mining country, are long gone. Only one member of this team, Harvey Hosein, the wicketkeeper, born in Chesterfield, is a native of the county. The others come from Trinidad, Afghanistan, London, Sussex and Lancashire as well as South Africa. Billy Godleman, the captain, is on his third club, after Essex and Middlesex. Tom Lace, a batsman, is on loan from Middlesex for the summer. Fynn Hudson-Prentice, an all-rounder, has been picked up from Sussex on the basis of 'let's have a look'. This is the way of the world for the less prosperous counties.

In the press tent, to the right of the clubhouse, there is mock dismay as the wickets tumble, for the scribes are well-versed in disappointment. The ball is moving around, and by lunch Derbyshire are 121 for eight, as Ben Sanderson and Brett Hutton take full advantage of a pitch that we learn is considered 'below par'. This will not do Chesterfield's reputation much good. A surface that was once considered lively and true is, on this evidence, one that bowlers would happily roll up and carry around with them.

Journalists have had a lot of fun in that tent. One of the joys of covering county cricket, in a way it is no longer covered, was the spirit that existed among those who wrote about the game. It wasn't so long ago when the broadsheets sent reporters to a handful of championship matches every week, and the ranks were swelled by locals and agency men.

It was a collegiate world of friendly rivalry punctuated by pranks, and laughter was never far away. A drama critic who popped into the old press box at Lord's for an afternoon was astonished by the ease with which journalists swapped tales. 'If any theatre critic has an opinion,' he said, 'or what he thinks is an original insight, he keeps it strictly to himself.'

The Derby box could be an unsettling, occasionally forbidding place for newcomers. The old guard, led by Michael Carey, a fine writer for many newspapers, and eventually the *Telegraph*'s cricket correspondent, gulled the unwary so frequently it became a badge of honour to pass the entrance exam. One writer for a national title failed to pick the verbal googlies, took fright, and never returned for a second innings.

Others did come back but were not always equal to the challenge. Carey's allies included Neil Hallam, a noted wit, whose mastery of many subjects would impress the High Table of any college of knowledge, and Gerald Mortimer of the *Derby Evening Telegraph*, whose well-rehearsed impression of a curmudgeon couldn't conceal the fact that he enjoyed the company of his peers, at least some of the time.

Henry Blofeld swallowed the well-baited hook that Major Douglas Carr, Derbyshire's patrician secretary, and Donald's brother, was absent one Saturday morning because he ran a disco called 'Doug's Place' in Swadlincote on Friday nights, and occasionally spun the discs. 'Oh, Douglas, you racy old thing!' Blowers told a befuddled Carr.

John Thicknesse, the long-standing correspondent of the *Evening Standard*, was sold a pup of Cruft's pedigree: Fred Swarbrook, Derbyshire's slow left-arm bowler of the early 1970s, was the only Hungarian to have played first-class cricket. His real name was Ferenc Schwarzenbec, and he had come to Derby with his family as a young boy after the Budapest Uprising of 1956. 'My word,' said Thickers, 'that's a new one.'

A hapless reporter from Nottingham informed his readers that Dallas Moir, a slow left-arm bowler who stood six feet and eight inches, played basketball for Japan in the winter, 'qualifying through his wife'. Another scribbler was persuaded that John Morris, the stylish batsman, should really be called the Revd John Morris because he was a Methodist lay preacher. Bernie Maher, a wicketkeeper, became a novitiate in the Church of Latter Day Saints, where he hoped to bag a Mormon wife or two.

One by one they were reeled in by the Derby glee club, who generally threw them back in the water once they'd had their fun. Thicknesse couldn't win either way. Hearing one afternoon that Jack Warner, a medium-pace bowler of Caribbean parentage, spent his winters in New York City, riding shotgun for his brother's security firm in the Bronx, he spluttered, 'You buggers won't catch me this time!' The tale was true!

The national papers now find little value in covering county cricket, even though readers of the broadsheets, having grown up with the game, would surely welcome a broader approach.

Press boxes have become silent places, where young bloggers outnumber reporters from the traditional organisations. The sharing of information, for instruction or amusement, is considered desperately old hat.

In the past the lore of the box meant that customs were handed down, as in any other trade. Young journalists learned how to write, and think, about cricket by listening to those who had been doing it for decades. In an age dominated by the soundbite, and the need for instant opinions, refreshed hourly, youth does not always defer to age. Readers are not necessarily better off.

A new kind of sportswriter has emerged, whose style owes more to the world of fanzines. The Careys, who favoured wit, will not come again. One windswept evening, covering a football match in the far north-west, Carey dictated to the *Guardian* copy-taker: 'Barrow comma in fairness comma'. Today's bloggers, expert in every kind of technology, less assured in the social graces, might not get the joke. They certainly wouldn't understand the idea of dictating words written by hand to a lady in London wearing an earpiece.

The Derbyshire innings, meanwhile, limps along to a total of 146. Hudson-Prentice makes 56 of them, unbeaten, to supply a coat of respectability. He is then among the wickets as the Cobblers of Northampton are dismissed either side of tea for 122, leaving Derbyshire a target of 319. When play ends at 6.44, they have knocked off the first 155 for the loss of five wickets. Lace represents their best chance of victory. He has batted sensibly in the last hour, and resumes tomorrow with 34 runs on the board.

There are not many optimists to be found. On this day of midsummer madness 24 wickets have fallen, and most spectators expect the Tudor Rose county to push over the five remaining wickets in the morning. But there are no grumbles. Memories of those two washouts in successive years mean that every day at Chesterfield must be savoured, rather like the scooped delights at Frederick's. Wallace Stevens was on to something when he wrote there is no emperor like the emperor of ice cream.

There are many pleasant ways to approach the college ground at Cheltenham. You can drive in from Evesham, past the racecourse, which stages the famous National Hunt festival every March. You may roll in on an easterly breeze from Burford, the town with the filmset of a main street that makes Americans coo with delight.

Or you can drop down, as I do this morning, from Winchcombe, and enjoy the view from Cleeve Hill beyond Tewkesbury. The landscape opens up, and there to the north-west are the Malvern Hills, where the spirits of Elgar and Housman may be gazing back at you.

Cheltenham is a famous Regency town. It is also the festival town in excelsis. Hardly a month goes by without thousands of people arriving to bet on horses, talk about books, listen to music of all kinds, and watch cricket. In July the festivals of classical music and cricket overlap, making a visit to Gustav Holst's birthplace particularly attractive. Gloucestershire, as usual, are playing two championship matches on the college ground. Last week they won the first, when Leicestershire collapsed in their second innings. Today the visitors are Worcestershire, neighbours from across the Avon.

Relations with the pear county have not always been cordial. In 1960, when Tom Graveney told Gloucestershire he wanted to leave, having been relieved of the captaincy in favour of Tom Pugh, an amateur of no great ability, the club played rough. They made him spend a summer kicking his heels before he could join Worcestershire where, in 1964, his batting helped his new county win their first championship, a title they retained the following year.

It was a shoddy way to treat any cricketer, never mind one of Graveney's stature. Yet that was the way of the world, when counties secured their professionals with a ball and chain. By a quirk of fate Graveney ended his days streets away from the college ground he graced so often, first caring for his wife, who suffered from dementia, and then slipping away himself in 2015.

The Glorious Glosters are one of three counties never to have won the championship, along with Northamptonshire and Somerset. With the great batsmen they have produced, you wonder why. Grace, the man who invented the modern game, was a Gloucestershire man, and usually got his own way. Wally Hammond may have been the greatest English batsman of all. Before Graveney, that handsome strokemaker, there was Charlie Barnett, who lived up the road at Sudeley.

That lineage is something to be proud of, and Gloucestershire folk are. There is still something reassuringly rustic about the way they come here every year from Slad and Painswick, like their fathers and grandfathers before them, to watch cricket on the college ground. They come from further afield, too. The Cheltenham experience, like Scarborough, is something that attracts locals and dippers-in alike.

The ground, framed at the town end by the college chapel and at the other by a row of tents, is almost a postcard representation of festival cricket. The austere college buildings at midwicket, adjoining the dressing rooms, do not detract from the conviction, created by word of mouth over many decades, that this is festival cricket's ground of grounds. Scarborough is king of the seaside venues. Cheltenham in midsummer speaks resonantly of the shires.

In 1968, when radicals believed they could change the world, Lindsay Anderson used the college chapel for the closing scenes of *If*, a film that raised a few eyebrows upon its release. Malcolm McDowell, armed with a sub-machine gun, takes aim from the college roof on Speech Day at parents of the pupils; the kind of people that Anderson thought needed shaking up. It was a fantasy come to life, and it wears its years poorly. Anderson was a flaneur.

Those radicals left little impression on Cheltenham. There is not just money here; there is real wealth. There are well-known public schools for boys and girls. There are good hotels and well-regarded restaurants, excellent shops and thriving wine bars. That is why people bring their custom here all year round. The book festival in October regularly attracts 40,000 visitors. This is not, begging their pardon, Scarborough or Chesterfield.

You can see the social disparity in the ground. The stalls offer a wider range of food. In the tents the lunches, impressive in quality and value, are wolfed down by happy regulars, though there is no longer a tent run by the Montpelier wine bar, one of the town's best-known establishments. There is also a well-stocked bookstall by the electronic scoreboard.

John Light, who has been watching the cricket for 70 years, is typical of many men of his age and background. Raised in Burford, the son of a forester, he recalls 'coming on a bus with my dad to watch Surrey in 1949. The first ball I saw was bowled by Jim Laker to Jack Crapp, who jumped out to hit it and was bowled. Years later my father's last lucid sentence to me was that he wasn't bowled. Arthur McIntyre stumped him. I looked it up, and he was right.'

In 1950, when the West Indian tourists came, 'it rained, and Sonny Ramadhin took eight for 15. Tom Graveney didn't play that match but John Mortimore did, and took two wickets with successive balls. Clyde Walcott got a hundred.' Young eyes don't miss much.

'The shame of living in Burford, in a minor county, was soon overcome. One day my father asked me, "How would you like to go to the same school as Wally Hammond?" So I went to Cirencester Grammar, which was socially splendid and academically variable.' He played cricket, 'made lots of runs', and was made head boy, the first step on the road to university and a career in the classroom, which ended with a headship in London at Hackney Free and Parochial School.

Barnett he remembers clearly. 'C. J. Barnett. He sold fish and game. You usually saw him cutting the head off something or other. Hunted with the Beaufort, too.' Sam Cook, the left-arm spinner who is inked into the fabric of Gloucestershire cricket like a dye, was another he observed at close quarters. 'I was his postman.'

Playing for Rodmarton in the league, and alongside public schoolboys in country house cricket, Light acquired a social confidence he might otherwise have struggled to find. 'When I went to university in Reading I had never been to London, never been in a lift or on an escalator, and seen the sea at Weston once.' This is the world described by Laurie Lee, who was cousin to Light's father, in *Cider with Rosie*. Jack Lee, the writer's brother would later live in Australia, 'but whenever he came home to Sheepscombe he would talk about cricket with my father'.

Today, as a member of the club committee, Light is watching play from a tent opposite the college chapel. There is talk, as always, of Barnett, Cook and Graveney. Other heroes of Cheltenham, 'Bomber' Wells and David Allen, the clever off spinners, feature in any conversation. Both men came to the festival every year with a fund of memories, and goodwill for all. Right to the end, in 2008, Wells would sit in his wheelchair and spin tales as he did the ball.

Get in at Cheltenham, the old pros would say, and you may enjoy a feast of runs. The ball will go through for the quicker bowlers but if the batsmen get through the first hour without a clatter of wickets they should prosper. No professional ever feared the quality of pitches here, where crowds have seen some cracking matches down the years.

A couple of early wickets go down when Gloucestershire bat. Chris Dent, the captain, and Gareth Roderick repair the damage before they get out when they should be settling in. It's a hodge-podge of an innings. Then Tom Smith and Ryan Higgins put bat to ball. Smith makes 83 and Higgins, who was among the wickets during the Leicestershire match, adds 76 spanking runs. Watching him get after the bowling you wonder why Middlesex let him go. He looks a fair cricketer.

Brett D'Oliveira, son of Damian and grandson of the great 'Dolly', is given the chance to bowl his leg spinners, and is denied two wickets when fielders drop chances that should be grasped with both hands. He's 27 now, hardly a lad, but it has never been easy to be a wrist spinner. Joe Leach, the opening bowler, enjoys more fortune. One of county cricket's great triers, he reaps six wickets for 79 as the Gloucestershire innings ends on 354. A decent total, not a formidable one.

The tents are full of cider and ale, supplied by the excellent Wye Valley brewery over the county's other border, in Herefordshire. When Light was a lad these tents would be chockful of farmers and men who worked the fields, who would dampen their beards one last time before driving home on tractors. Now the car park is full of posh cars, and the villages and valleys are full of the new rich.

'Cheltenham' will continue, though the social transformation of the past two decades means it will not be quite the event it was. The south of the county, around Cirencester, has seen an invasion by the London set, which affects everything: the price of property, the character of the pubs, the tone of the villages. The newcomers have bought land, but they are not of the land. There is bound to be a dislocation.

'When I grew up,' says Light, 'many more people worked in agriculture. Farm workers came to Cheltenham by the wagon load, and I used to see many people I played cricket against. Lots of vicars, too. Now it's the incomers who play, the public schoolboys who have a few bob and buy houses here. Village cricket continues but the agricultural workforce has gone.'

Light does his bit. With his wife, Penny, he sponsors the T20 competition in the Cotswold League. He's putting something back, in the proper tradition of cricket folk, so that younger people may in time enjoy the kind of memories he has of Barnett and Graveney. 'And don't forget M. J. Procter. He could play a bit.' He certainly could. Mike Procter, denied a meaningful Test career by South Africa's banishment from international cricket in 1970, gave his all to Gloucestershire. Nobody will ever forget 'Procky'. He had plenty of offers to take his talents elsewhere, and he stayed with the club that gave him his chance.

There is a happy personal memory of Cheltenham. It was here in June 1974 that I made the only century of my life, playing for Repton under 16s against the college lads; not on the main ground, but over the road. That evening a group of us were chased out of a takeaway by an angry Chinese man, wielding the kind of knife that cuts ribs to slivers of meat. We were watching Holland in the World Cup on the television above the counter, bewitched by Johan Cruyff's sorcery when we should have been ordering grub.

Arranging Scarborough, Chesterfield and Cheltenham in order of precedence would trouble the most orderly mind. Look what happened to King Lear.

Yorkshire beat Surrey by 123 runs, taking eight wickets cheaply on the final afternoon. Derbyshire fell 73 runs short at

Chesterfield. The Cheltonians saw the Glosters win by 13 runs. At each ground the commonwealth of cricket lovers, gathering by bookstalls and ice-cream vans, remembered they were not alone. Away from the world 'of telegrams and anger' there are still unnumbered thousands who love cricket in the way people always did.

This year the palm goes to Chesterfield. On that sun-kissed Monday, when 24 wickets fell, Queen's Park felt like 'a summer with a thousand Julys'. At close of play I drove through my favourite county towards the sun limning the hills, listening to the great Ellington band of 1940. That was the Duke's 'team of all the talents', with Johnny Hodges, Ben Webster, Harry Carney, Cootie Williams, Rex Stewart, Lawrence Brown and Jimmy Blanton sharing the honours.

After a day of deep pleasure I sat on the balcony of the Old Poets pub at Ashover and watched the sun sink, knowing that when it rose in the morning life would not be the same. Not quite.

VI

Summer Nocturne

Leicester, The Oval

It is a sweltering day at Grace Road, the hottest of the year, and the forecasts indicate that winds from north Africa are pushing more heat our way before the week is out. In old money it's touching 90 °F, and it feels uncomfortably humid as Leicestershire and Yorkshire knock up on a summer-brown outfield before this Vitality Blast match, which starts at 6.30.

The knockers-up are the T20 cricketers, not all of whom feature in the championship. The Vitality Blast requires a different kind of player, some brought in specifically for this competition, which will occupy them for the next five weeks. It's really a season within a season, with the four semi-finalists playing off at Edgbaston on 21 September.

Nicholas Pooran, the West Indies left-hander known for his mighty hitting, has boosted the Yorkshire ranks, and Dom Bess, the off-spinner, has been signed on loan from Somerset.

Not that they are called Yorkshire in this giddy romp. Their designated name is Yorkshire Vikings, which is less absurd than Lancashire Lightning, if only by the width of a stump. The home side, naturally, answer to the Foxes.

Officially this is now the Fischer County Ground. Few people beyond the club offices, situated next to the dressing rooms, know it by that name. To the world at large it remains Grace Road, twinned with Desolation Row. Hemmed in by streets of mainly terraced houses, a mile south of the city centre, this is the most functional ground in England. It may be only 30 miles from Trent Bridge but in this celebratory week, when the world is marking the fiftieth anniversary of the first moon landing, the distance seems lunar.

Even on pleasant days this can seem the most forlorn of homes, and over the years it has attracted some odd folk. The baronet who used to take pot shots at balloons that floated over his estate, pretending they were zeppelins. The bedraggled member who wore his lunch on his shirt, and lurched through the gate by the Cricketers Arms with the cry, 'I'm on me way!'

In the 1970s, when Raymond Illingworth brought himself on for an exploratory over of off-spin ahead of Jack Birkenshaw, to see if the pitch was turning, this man would shout: 'Get Birky on!' If championships were awarded for contributions to care in the community, Leicestershire might have won as many titles as Yorkshire.

The people who have given their lives to this club deserve the highest praise. Charles Palmer leads the list. He served Leicestershire as captain and then, in retirement, as secretary, chairman and president. He also served as president of MCC.

Without men such as Palmer and Mike Turner, who did a long term as secretary, in the days before chief executives, clubs such as Leicestershire would not exist.

One can only commend the men and women who gather here in the summer months, striving to keep cricket alive for a constituency so small it may be measured in hundreds. The membership is just over a thousand. In this century the club has appointed no fewer than seven chief executives, the latest being Karen Rothery, who took over the reins from Wasim Khan when he was lured away by the Pakistan Cricket Board.

Khan's was a bold appointment. This is a city with a south Asian population that accounts for four out of ten people who live here. The problems, though, are immense. The county of Leicester is loyal to rugby, and the Tigers, one of England's best-supported clubs. The city inclines towards football. The other Foxes, Leicester City, won the Premier League title in 2016, that year of wonder when Claudio Ranieri, the Italian manager, waved a wand and dreams came true in blue and white. Then the wand snapped. Within nine months he was gone.

Trapped between these rival attractions, the cricketers have always struggled to make themselves heard. There is no great love for the summer game, which means that Leicestershire face a constant struggle for survival, living off scraps, picking up players stamped 'NGE' by other clubs. The riches offered by the Hundred cannot come a day too soon. An annual subsidy of £1.3 million is a boon they crave, like serfs clutching the sleeve of a prince.

Leicestershire have had their moments. When Illingworth, fed up at Yorkshire, was persuaded to come here in 1969 he transformed Grace Road. County champions in 1975, they won four one-day trophies in six seasons, including two Lord's finals. Towards the end of that run the teenaged David Gower announced himself as the batsman who finally put some grace into Grace Road.

They were champions again in 1996 and 1998, though Gower had left by then, for Hampshire. James Whitaker, a Yorkshire lad who had attended Uppingham, was the captain of a team that included scrappers such as Paul Nixon, the combative wicketkeeper, who is now the club coach, doing his best to make their cricket competitive. There has been an improvement since his arrival, though these things are relative. Memories are still sharp of the three seasons they went without a championship victory. This year, with a single victory from ten championship matches, they are bottom of the second division.

In the Meet, a large hut at midwicket that serves as bar and eating place, the Friends of Grace Road have gathered to carry round buckets. There are 3000 spectators at the ground tonight, so they are hoping to collect a few bob, and persuade people that cricket is a game worth following.

'Friends of Grace Road': are there four sadder words in cricket? This ground wears its melancholy like an overcoat. Tonight, to cater for the T20 crowd, there is some sense of purpose. The noodle bars are busy, as well as the burger vans. There is an Indian food outlet, next to the Red Monkey playpen and, more improbably, there is a stall by the big scoreboard that offers 'street food' from Barbados (Birstall, more like). The mood is one of prescribed jollity, not a quality that comes naturally in this parish.

The indoor school carries endorsements that accompany large photographs of two men who have worn the county colours. They must be taken with a cellar-full of salt.

'Walking out to represent Leicestershire and England,' says James Taylor, 'were the two proudest moments of my life.' Zak Chappell is no less clear: 'Grace Road is an inspirational place to play.' But not to stay. Chappell has gone to Nottinghamshire, like Taylor before him. They followed the road to Trent Bridge that Stuart Broad had previously measured, step by step. Grace Road, which once claimed Gower's loyalty for a decade, is now little more than a nursery for its northern neighbour.

In the shortest form of the game there is hope. Nixon and his Foxes will have noted that Derbyshire beat Yorkshire comfortably in the first T20 fixture three days ago. Now is the time to show the first-time visitors to the ground what they can do.

Leicestershire's captain Colin Ackermann decides to have a bowl when he wins the toss. The fielders, clad in black pyjamas, wander on to the field through an arrangement of children bearing, rather than waving, flags. More enforced jollity. There is a blast from the hunting horn, the traditional greeting in this land of red coats, to signify 'tally ho, off we go'.

To the second ball, bowled by Dieter Klein, Adam Lyth withdraws a yard to the onside and cuts a short, straight ball deliberately high towards the boundary at third man. Callum Parkinson gets his mitts on the ball as it dips but cannot catch or stop it. Six runs. A burst of pop music. Cheers from the Yorkshire followers, many of whom are on their second pint.

The second over, bowled by Chris Wright, brings 17 runs, 16 of them to Lyth from four strokes. More pop music. Ben Mike is given the third over, and Ackermann entrusts himself with the fourth. Tom Kohler-Cadmore, Yorkshire's captain tonight, heaves the second ball over long-on for another six. There are 20 runs off the over.

After the fifth over Yorkshire have made 69, and Lyth has gone to his half century from 21 balls, with six fours and three sixes. There are beery cheers from spectators who do not appear to be following the cricket closely.

Parkinson, who bowls slow left arm, is given his chance. Kohler-Cadmore clatters him into the bleachers at midwicket. Six. Then it is the turn of Arron Lilley, who rolls off spinners. Kohler-Cadmore thrashes him straight, on to the television gantry. Six more.

On 116, Lyth slogs one up to deep square leg, where Klein is the catcher, and the fielders engulf Parkinson, the successful bowler, though that adjective flatters him a bit. There's a grand celebration, to maintain morale. Lyth made 69 from 39 balls, and hit four sixes.

Pooran the biffer comes in now, and at once makes the boundaries, 20 yards short of the advertising boards, look even smaller. When Parkinson lets slip a beamer he swats it for six. There are 27 runs from the over, as Pooran reaches his half century from 22 balls, with five sixes.

Kohler-Cadmore is not exactly becalmed. He drives Wright over the sightscreen, and pulls Mike high over the rope at midwicket. Then he bashes him down the ground, his third straight six. Pooran slices Klein to third man and departs for 67, which required only 28 balls. Six he hit for four; six for six.

When the innings is complete Yorkshire have made 255 for two, five runs short of the competition record they established two years ago against Northamptonshire. Kohler-Cadmore is 96 not out, with eight of the 19 sixes the batsmen have plundered. One six more, and they would have equalled another record, set three days before by Essex, when Cameron Delport made 129 off just 49 balls against Surrey.

Delport, a South African, played for the Foxes last summer, but Leicestershire can hardly claim him as one of theirs. In the past decade he has been a hired hand in T20, picking up his bat for Kwa-Zulu Natal, Sydney Thunder, Trinidad and Tobago, the Dhaka Dynamites and the Kolkata Knight Riders. He has even played in Afghanistan. A modern cricketer, you might say, who goes like those Texas riders of old to those who have coins in their purse.

As Kohler-Cadmore and Harry Brook run from the field there is no trace of dignity. They are cricketers doing a job. There is no joy to be had in it, only a sense of professional obligation. Rimbaud comes to mind: 'I alone hold the key to this savage parade.'

The floodlights go on between innings. So does the quaffing and troughing. This is a big night out for the locals. The cricket, for many, is incidental. Those who are keeping an eye on the match know the Foxes will not catch the men from the Ridings but nothing is going to sully this midsummer frolic.

At 8.30, almost by decree, there is the first chorus of 'Sweet Caroline'. Neil Diamond's hit, beloved of pub drinkers at chucking-out time and revellers on skiing holidays, has become the theme song of the Vitality Blast. It is to these crowds what 'Land of Hope and Glory' is to Prommers at the Last Night, or the *Radetzky March* to the well-heeled Viennese at the New Year's Day concert in the Musikverein. It gets a muted performance here, as if the singers are doing what is expected of them. There is some ironic laughter, and the song doesn't come back.

The cricket by now is played by rote, though Lilley and Lewis Hill ensure their team is not humiliated. Lilley, defiant to the last, smashes Bess for three sixes in an over. When the match is done Leicestershire have added a dozen sixes of their own to Yorkshire's 19, and few of the spectators will, if they are honest, recall a stroke of genuine pedigree when they wake up on the morrow. Off they shuffle, in good heart.

'Doubt, or age, simply?'

Age. The younger spectators have few doubts. They have been entertained, to the tune of 456 runs in two and a half hours. They have cheered 31 strokes that cleared the ropes, and in this cricket the basher of sixes wears a crown. But there has been no genuine excitement. In cricket, as in any sporting event, there must be a context for the action to have a proper meaning. There was no sense tonight of a tale unfolding: no shape, or variety, or change of pace. It was a beer match, performed for the benefit of incurious drinkers.

It wasn't rowdy. There was no unpleasantness in the crowd, which looked about 20 per cent Asian. It was a good-tempered assembly, and clearly some of the spectators enjoyed what they saw. But no lover of cricket will have taken home anything to

171

recall with fascination or pride. No player could have taken pleasure from his part in the jamboree.

There is no story to tell in this cricket. The bowlers are fodder for cannons, the batsmen pirates without eyepatches. There may be occasional moments of brilliance – Kohler-Cadmore played a couple of strokes that would have graced a proper game – but the overall effect was benumbing. The aim was to raise spirits, with mascots, flag-bearing children and loud pop music. Instead the indifferent quality of the cricket lowered them. One almost wished that bewildered soul of yesteryear had stumbled into the ground, late as usual, and bellowed: 'Get Birky on!'

My word, this was boring. And there are five weeks to go.

'You must never forget, love, some people can see farther than others.'

Robert Tear liked to say that, whenever the conversation about modern manners turned gloomy. Born modestly in Barry, Bob was a choral scholar at King's, Cambridge, where years later he was awarded a fellowship; partly for his life in music, partly for intellectual qualities that raised him into that rarest of categories, the polymathic. He wore his learning lightly, found common ground with all kinds of people, and was lively company.

Bob could see farther than most. He was a writer and painter, as well as a singer good enough to take major roles in the world's great opera houses. For years he was Benjamin Britten's tenor of choice at the Aldeburgh Festival before he fell foul of the composer. The Suffolk coast is full of 'Ben's corpses', and Bob was miles away temperamentally from the tetchy Britten, a great composer and a cold, thin-skinned man.

'I came out of the dressing room one day, after a rehearsal of *Death in Venice*, wearing *Easy Rider* glasses and singing to myself "with you and me, dear, arm in arm, Rome can sleep secure". I bumped into Ben, who had a face like thunder. "Do you really think this is the way to treat my grand opera?" So I wasn't expecting to return the following year, and I didn't.'

In pubs near his home in Ravenscourt Park he would gossip about the gifted people he had met. 'Leonard Bernstein actually put his tongue down my throat on stage. Not during the performance, of course.' Of E. M. Forster, whom he had known at King's, where the novelist was quartered in his final years, he was fond but not indulgent. 'He liked Schubert, Morgan, and would invite some of us to come to his rooms so we could listen to recordings of lieder. Lovely man, though to be honest he knew next to nothing about it.'

After a few pints he would quote from Eliot ('we shall not cease from exploration') and Thomas Traherne. He liked to remind you that 'we have no choice in what we do, no choice at all'. This was the Buddhist in him speaking, not the rhetorical Welshman. He genuinely believed that, this side of paradise, all was folly. 'There is nothing we can do about it. Nothing.' Are we not blessed with free will? 'No, nothing.'

He was amused, rather than appalled, by what he called 'the pliable, mediocre taste of the multitude'. He knew, being well-read, and professionally acquainted with great music, that art had a life of its own, which owed nothing to popular acclaim. He was upset by philistinism, but not surprised. Some people choose not to see.

Playing in a game at Ealing to celebrate the fiftieth birthday of our mutual friend, Martin Campbell-White, Bob and myself shared a brief stand. Watching from the pavilion was Ted Dexter, who used to live around the corner. Sadly, Lord Ted's presence did not spur us into audacious strokeplay. The partnership was not fruitful. Our friendship was. On that day of days in September 2011, when Lancashire won the county championship outright for the first time since 1934, I took myself instead to St Martin-in-the-Fields for Bob's memorial service. I owed him that much.

What fun he would have had this summer, when the pliable taste of the multitude can be seen in freshly painted coats of bogus populism. The Hundred, designed to attract a new, younger audience that is not apparent to others, does not exist in solitude. It has been swept in by the most powerful tide of modern life, 'accessibility'.

True accessibility is a good thing. The best educators, such as Bernstein, are generous hosts. They invite others to see the world from an exalted plane. 'Lenny' was a pianist of recital standards, a conductor of genius in his inspired moments, and the composer of *West Side Story* and *Candide*. Wearing his telly hat he introduced millions of American schoolchildren to music they might not otherwise have heard through his Young People's Concerts in the 1960s, broadcast by CBS.

André Previn, another American pianist-conductor-composer, became a star of BBC Television in the 1970s, demystifying orchestral music without betraying his calling. Those men had confidence in their ability to act as mediators between the composers they loved and the audience. They also had confidence in that audience to follow them. They never talked down because they knew that great music, given the chance, will speak for itself.

If accessibility has any meaning, Bernstein and Previn revealed it. So did Kenneth Clark, whose *Civilisation*, screened in 13 parts in 1969, opened up the world of Western art for millions of viewers who may never have visited a gallery. Television will be judged in future, said Huw Wheldon, the man who commissioned the series, by its willingness to produce such programmes.

Clark was followed by Jacob Bronowski, another genuine intellectual, who explained difficult things about the world of science in *The Ascent of Man*. Robert Hughes, a different kind of critic, presented *The Shock of the New*, a series about twentieth-century painters that really did break new ground. Hughes was that rare being, the expert who spoke in the crisp and clear tones of the common vernacular without surrendering his scholar's robes.

Nobody makes programmes of such ambition these days, partly because critics of wide learning are harder to find; more specifically because the people who do the commissioning have lost their nerve. When the BBC screened *Civilisations* in 2018 they entrusted the authorship to three historians, so there was no unifying voice. If the series was planned as a partial rebuke to the unashamedly patrician Clark (and the plural title indicated it was), it failed. He aimed high, and was rewarded with a vast worldwide audience. The three popularisers sought to be accessible, and missed the target altogether.

Clark's success was rooted in a single, unarguable fact: civilisation is created by human beings of exceptional gifts, not -ologies or -isms. As he told viewers in his introductory programme, if he were forced to believe either the speeches made by a Minister of Housing or the buildings erected on the Minister's watch, he would believe the latter. Human sympathy, from Giotto to Henry Moore, meant more than ideology.

Post-Clark, the relativists have become bolder, and accessibility has acquired a different meaning. Instead of inviting viewers and readers to see the world through their eyes, scholars have been encouraged to believe the subjects Bernstein and Bronowski spoke about so naturally must be presented in a demotic manner. Things must never be 'difficult' because the audience can't take it.

This argument, ostensibly an exercise in democracy, has led to a loss of confidence in those things that bring joy and meaning to our lives. All voices, however untutored, are deemed to be 'relevant'. The virus of phone-ins, Twitter feeds and talent shows for exhibitionists is uncontainable. It is unfashionable, almost unconscionable, in the worlds of media and academia to suggest that some things may actually have greater merit than others. It puts a person above the common herd.

Anthony Burgess, who had the sharply focused lens of an outsider, was appalled by this inversion. 'Only in England,' he said, on one of his last visits to the land of his birth, 'is the perversion of language regarded as a victory for democracy.' It is a useful way of describing the avalanche that has covered more than language. When words such as 'irreverence' and 'subversion' are used as forms of approval, it is clear our culture has twisted in the wind.

It is a brave person who swims against the tide of relativism. That kind of independence can destroy careers. The pliable taste of the multitude is now the engine of social advancement. Drip by drip, the urge to 'reach out' in the interests of 'accessibility' and 'diversity' has turned generations of human behaviour upside down. The benefits of this cultural rupture are not always clear.

In the Church of England what began with the amending of the old liturgy, to make some of the most beautiful words in our language less opaque, has led to a self-abasement so profound that even non-believers feel sorrow. The King James Bible and *The Book of Common Prayer* do not belong only to worshippers. They are part of the intellectual property we all share.

Mystery is part of language. Otherwise why do poets order words as they do? It is part of faith. To make supposedly difficult words accessible destroys that sense of the numinous, and alters meaning.

'In the beginning was the Word, and the Word was with God; and the word was God.'

Why would anybody want to amend the opening line of St John's Gospel, to make it 'clearer'? It is one of the most glorious sentences in our language. But nothing is sacred any longer. The modernisers have even altered the Lord's Prayer.

It has been a dismal summer for the established church. Norwich Cathedral introduced a helter-skelter standing

55 feet tall so that revellers could slide down it for £2 a scoot, contemplating the paradox of the Holy Trinity. 'For such a place,' said the Rt Revd Dr Gavin Ashenden, 'steeped in mystery and marvel, to buy into sensory pleasure and distraction, is to poison the very medicine it offers the human soul.'

At Rochester Cathedral the gimmick was crazy golf. The central aisle was given over to models of bridges, through which golfers could strike balls. Revd Rachel Phillips, the cathedral's canon for mission and growth, thought that visitors 'will reflect on the bridges that need to be built in their own lives and in the world today'. Golfers normally reflect on getting the ball in the hole, and they do it in the open air, not a cathedral.

Never two without three, they say. At Southwark Cathedral there was a frock show, as part of London Fashion Week. The Rt Revd Ashenden had something to say about that, too. It promoted 'a narcissistic, self-referential display for the very rich'.

It is difficult for the Church of England to engage with the modern world. Priests take the long view of human folly, because their teachings promise eternal life and the possibility of redemption. They try to speak, wherever possible, in a language that brings people towards the church, to listen to their message of hope. With the best will in the world, it is hard to see how crazy golf and helter-skelter rides will bring younger people closer to the Kingdom of God.

This populism is no less rampant in the secular world. The National Trust, obsessed with quotas, has come to see its principal duty as a social service, with spokespersons bleating that not enough black people visit its properties. The Arts Council's funding is determined by how enthusiastically its clients demonstrate their 'relevance' to all members of the 'community', words that take their place alongside accessibility and diversity in the vocabulary of modern thought. The quality of work, which used to be the most important consideration, is incidental.

It is happening in that English institution, the pub. In June, just as the World Cup was getting under way, the London brewers, Fuller, Smith & Turner, decided to put the company's own manager into the Coach and Horses in Soho, one of London's best-known boozers. A spokesman said Fuller's were determined to uphold the pub's traditions. 'The only tradition here,' said Alistair Choat, the outgoing tenant, 'was Norman Balon (the previous guvnor) telling people to fuck off.' That lofty phrase, 'upholding traditions', usually gives the game away.

More excuses that make them all needs.

The most defiant example of the new populism came in 2016, when Emma Rice was appointed artistic director of the Globe Theatre, on London's South Bank. Created by Sam Wanamaker as a modern home for Shakespeare, the Globe had been well-served by the previous directors, Mark Rylance and Dominic Dromgoole. One was a fine actor, the other an interpreter immersed in Shakespeare's world. Rice, by contrast, was a babe in the wood. She had directed only one of the 37 plays, *Cymbeline*, and immediately upset the applecart by saying she found Shakespeare difficult. In that case, why appoint her?

Being a woman didn't hurt. The theatre world is sensitive to accusations of bias on grounds of sex. There was also an urge, which should have been suppressed, to be irreverent. The Globe, as most observers sensed at the time of her appointment, had backed the wrong horse.

Her first production, *A Midsummer Night's Dream*, jollied along by strobe lighting and loud pop music, earned few admirers. One of the more sympathetic reviewers, straining every sinew to be charitable, called it 'charmless'. Two years into the job, her greenness exposed, she departed, leaving the Globe management to reflect that a bit more reverence might have served them better.

Rice came to the Globe from the Cornish theatre group, Kneehigh. A small touring company was surely the best place for her, or possibly a role in theatre education where her zeal for sonic and visual effects might impress young minds. What she had no aptitude for was a feeling for language, a drawback no amount of 'inspiration' can redeem. Without a respect for words there can be no true direction.

The race towards the bottom carries on, in the search for younger audiences. At English National Opera, a company of world class shattered into shards by maladroit stewardship, the new chief executive hatched a daring plan. Stuart Murphy proudly stated that regular critics from the traditional outlets would no longer be offered a 'plus one' ticket to opening nights of ENO productions. Those seats would go instead to 'opera fans', to 'broaden' the range of opinion.

As night follows day ENO invited La Rice to direct a new production of Offenbach's *Orpheus in the Underworld*. A bottle-aged critic, not one of the happy clappers, considered it to be 'half as witty and twice as earnest as it should be'.

A member of the ENO high command, speaking informally, let it be known 'she won't be coming back'. What was she doing there in the first place? Her record was there for all to see.

Critics who can't tell Mozart from a corncrake commenting on the performances of professional musicians. Directors for whom opera is an exotic plaything given the chance to be irreverent. It is the musical world's version of crazy golf in the aisles of our most sacred places, inflicted on believers in the name of accessibility.

The arrogance is twofold. Directors, often unversed, have the gall to imagine they know more about the work than the writer or composer. Humility, in the face of greatness, is essential. One of the reasons Peter Hall was such a fine director of actors and singers is that he started from the premise that Shakespeare and Verdi knew best.

Then there is the belief that audiences, living in a different age, are unable to understand what the great writers were doing unless their work is cut up in easily digested chunks, like slabs of meat, and told 'this won't hurt'. If viewers and listeners were trusted to respond naturally, the modernisers might be pleasantly surprised to discover that great work, presented in good faith, generally finds favour.

This crisis of confidence has corrupted the BBC, where the light of knowledge Lord Reith urged the corporation to shine in the name of public service broadcasting grows dimmer by the year. This is where diversity, defined by race, sex and youth, is considered the *sine qua non*. Every week the BBC puts out programmes on radio and television that appear to be directed overwhelmingly at slow-witted children.

The opening night of the Proms, just after England had won the World Cup, gave viewers of long standing the chance to make comparisons with the corporation's traditional coverage, in the days when Richard Baker and James Naughtie were the hosts. They were not flattering.

Katie Derham, the presenter, and the three supposedly expert voices assembled to assist her, could hardly utter a sentence without bursting into giggles. Every performance was deemed to be 'incredible', 'amazing' or 'awesome'. The lady expert, billed as 'a tech CEO', opted for 'electric' by way of variety. It was clear she had an interest in orchestral music. It was equally clear she would not be allowed to express it in case she put people off.

Sir Henry Wood, the founder of the Proms, was patted on the head for 'championing women'. The concerts they had lined up for us lucky viewers in the forthcoming weeks would be all about 'diversity and inclusion'. There was silly talk of 'international superstars'. The tone was breathless, uncritical, trivial. They could have been talking about a baking contest, or a football match. It was as if they felt embarrassed by their love of classical music.

Radio 3, the home of classical music, suffers from the same lack of confidence. The recruitment of presenters who speak in a less 'stuffy' manner is another manifestation of this virus. So it's goodbye to Geoffrey Smith, the expert American presenter of a superb jazz programme that has been binned to make way for a show called *Freeness*, and hello to a tribe of breezy word-manglers.

It is not only the highbrow programmes where the grades are down. Radio 2, a station of middlebrow tastes, has become a province of excitable young voices. An old-fashioned broadcaster like Russell Davies, who proved every Sunday evening how to write and read a script of elegance and wit, is required no longer. In this brazen new world, where he – or, increasingly, she – who shouts loudest is rewarded most handsomely, the qualities demonstrated by Terry Wogan, David Jacobs and Brian Matthew are not needed. The implicit is now explicit, the understated overstated, the subtle obvious.

'Modern demotic' may also describe the self-willed decline of *Test Match Special*. The programme shaped carefully by John Arlott and others as a cricket commentary, leavened by a touch of humour, has been invaded by noisy show-offs. The distinction between commentary and summary is breached almost every over as new members of the team, unaware of the show's patiently nurtured traditions, take turns to spin supposedly comic tales.

A programme that traditionally spoke to a Radio 4 audience has been turned round to satisfy the more demotic demands of Five Live. Moz Dee, a former managing editor of Five Live, let the cat out of the bag when he said that 'every ball must be an event'. In Test cricket, played over three sessions of play, that is not possible.

There must always be room for humour, and in the old days the *TMS* commentators were happy to provide it, when the laughter flowed naturally from events they were describing. Arlott brought a poet's sensibility. Brian Johnston supplied whimsy. Christopher Martin-Jenkins lent a good-natured dignity. Jonathan Agnew, who succeeded C. M.-J. as cricket correspondent, does his best to live up to the example they set but his is only one voice.

Now the lines are written in capital letters: WE MUST NEVER BE BORED. Many old-fashioned listeners are, bored witless by the relentless adolescent ragging.

This is how the Hundred comes in, on a wave of self-abasement. Colin Graves, the chairman of the ECB, didn't use the words Emma Rice did on joining the Globe, nor speak the language of the churchmen at Norwich and Rochester. But he thinks every ball must be an event, and that 100 balls, from soup to port, is quite enough.

Young people, he said in 2018, when the Hundred was in the early stages of development, were no longer interested in cricket. The T20 experience, of full grounds across the land, would suggest that many young people were. No, said Graves. They think it's boring, and the only way to convince them otherwise is to pretend we're not playing cricket at all. The counties fell into line, attracted by the largesse of television, and in 2020 cricket will get its shortest tournament yet.

When the game's governors turned towards Gillette for sponsorship of the first limited-overs trophy in 1963, there was a genuine necessity. Interest in championship cricket had waned after the big crowds of the post-war years. The Gillette Cup, initially played over 65 overs an innings, proved an immediate success.

How distant the recent past can appear to contemporary eyes. Brian Close said any team that scored 190 in 65 overs to beat Yorkshire would be worthy winners. Donald Carr, in his final season as a player, featured in one Gillette match for

Derbyshire. 'I didn't bat or bowl,' he said years later, 'and I touched the ball only a few times in the field. But at the end of the day I was dog tired.'

That was how the Gillette Cup, the T20 of its day, struck the old pros. Whatever would they make of an innings lasting 100 balls?

In 1964 the competition was reduced to 60 overs a side, which was how the competition remained through its years of sponsorship by Gillette and, after 1981, by NatWest. It was cricket's attempt to get with it in those years of social change when, as Roger Miller sang, 'England swings like a pendulum do'. The 60-over game fused the elements of instant and 'proper' cricket to make a potent brew. The Gillette final, played at Lord's on the first Saturday of September, was a big event, carried live on the BBC.

The summer of 1969 brought another innovation, the Sunday League, sponsored by John Player, and games played over 40 overs. Spectators attended in large numbers, though they were less eager to turn out for the Benson and Hedges Cup, which began, for no compelling reason, in 1972. That was how it stayed for three decades before T20 arrived like a typhoon in 2003.

By today's standards the Gillette scores were low. Sussex beat Worcestershire in the first final by 14 runs after making a far from formidable 168. Apart from a rare feast in 1965, when Geoffrey Boycott's 146 against Surrey propelled Yorkshire to the improbable heights of 317 for four, totals were modest. No team exceeded 300 again until 1993, when Warwickshire overhauled Sussex's 321 for six in the most memorable final of all.

The final of 1971, which to my 12-year-old eyes seemed so marvellous, looks ordinary from this distance. Yet the red rose loyalists who were there that day reckoned Lancashire's 224 for seven would take some getting. They were right. Kent, for all the brilliance of Asif Iqbal, were bowled out for 200. It wasn't an ordinary game at all. Everybody thought they had witnessed a classic contest between two very good teams.

At Grace Road Yorkshire made 31 runs more than Lancashire did on that great day, in 40 fewer overs. Is this not progress? As Bernard Shaw wrote, and Chuck Berry sang, it goes to show you never can tell.

One ground has come to define the Vitality Blast. A week after Grace Road was lit by a burning sun it is raining c's and d's in south London, as Wodehouse of Dulwich College might have written. The downpour hasn't stopped 20,000 people from turning up at The Oval for Surrey's game with Kent Spitfires. Had the weather been kinder they would have put up the 'house full' notices. Gates of 25,000 are common. The Kennington Oval, to put the handle of history on its jug, is the fortress of T20.

Viewed from the tower-like pavilion, which seems to grow taller by the year, Leicester is a different country. Surrey are the richest county club by far, the only one that could hold their own without subsidy from the ECB. They have been steadfast in their opposition to the Hundred, and on evenings such as this it is not hard to understand their lack of consent. The T20 matches staged here represent, by cricket's standards, a goldmine. Full houses and full bellies every time. Surrey expect to shift £250,000 worth of business at each match. What need have they for another competition?

The Oval is richer in history than any ground except Lord's, owned by Marylebone Cricket Club, the grandest name in world cricket. This is where Jack Hobbs, the maker of 197 centuries, batted in the early years of the last century. 'The Master', they called him; Sir John Berry Hobbs, the first cricketer to be knighted, who wore his honour, John Arlott said, 'with the dignity of a prince'.

Surrey were already smothered with honours by the time Hobbs joined them in 1905. Champions six times in the early years of the county championship, they were fired to victory by the fast bowling of Tom Richardson, and the runs of Bobby Abel and Tom Hayward. Hobbs found a productive partner in Andrew Sandham, and these names can be found within a pavilion that greets the visitor walking up from the tube station with four Doric columns decorated with the Prince of Wales feather, for this is Duchy land.

'Ich dien': I serve. There has always been a touch of nobility about this club, tempered with south London realism. Many Surrey members belong to that black-and-white world described faithfully by V. S. Pritchett and, going back a bit further, H. G. Wells. They are the last remnants of the traditional skilled working class; mild and bitter men if you like, who live in places such as Bromley and watch Charlton Athletic in the winter. They may still be found here during championship matches, recalling Stuart Surridge and the county's seven successive titles in the 1950s.

The spectators here tonight are worth a serious look. As The Oval is half a mile from the Thames, on the unfashionable side of the river, the social and racial blend of the crowds who flock to T20 matches is revealing. To use the word in its proper sense this is the most diverse cricket ground in England. There are stockbrokers and trans-pontine artisans. There are also plenty of Asian and black faces.

This social mix may be seen in the naming of stands in this much-changed ground. The most resonant names in Surrey cricket since Hobbs have been Alec Bedser, who was also knighted for services to cricket, and Peter May, known to the world by his initials, P. B. H.

Bedser, a working man from Woking, was the leading English bowler in the period straddling the Second World War. He was a belt-and-braces cricketer, who never missed a day's work through injury, and could be heard in retirement lamenting that fings ain't wot they used to be. 'I read these days about an effort ball,' he used to say. 'I bowled one of 'em every time I ran up.' Eric, his twin, was usually by his side, nodding assent like Churchill the insurance dog.

May was one of cricket's aristocrats, who refined his batting on the pitches at Charterhouse and Cambridge. He is considered to be the greatest post-war English batsman, his on drive a fluttering of peacock feathers. He retired at 31, and went into the City, when the square mile was a more gentlemanly place. Like Bedser, who was better suited to the job, he served as a chairman of the Test selectors.

Other stands honour players who also left a mark on Surrey and England. Jim Laker, the Yorkshireman who took 19 wickets in the Old Trafford Test of 1956, the most remarkable individual performance in the game's history, shares a stand with Tony Lock, the aggressive left-arm spinner who took the other wicket in that match. Laker and Lock go together like Morecambe and Wise, or Pinky and Perky. They bowled thousands of overs as Surrey won those seven successive championships from 1952.

That team was bolstered by the runs of Ken Barrington, the soldier's son from Reading, and the most indomitable of batsmen. 'He who endures, conquers,' his wife told him when his fortunes ebbed. Barrington conquered to the tune of 57 runs every Test innings, earning a place at the high table of English batsmanship. When he passed away in the spring of 1981, acting as manager of the touring England team in the West Indies, the mourning was shared by all cricket lovers, who recognised in Barrington something essential in the game's spirit. It went beyond money, or fame, or personal glory, to the core of his being.

Micky Stewart was one of Barrington's comrades for club and country, and the pavilion bears his name. As player, captain, coach and president, still looking full of beans at 86, Stewart is the living embodiment of Surrey. Alec, his son, played 137 times for England. The gates at the Vauxhall end are his. Father and son memorialised on the same ground: now that is something.

It would be wrong to say Stewart junior has merely followed in the tracks his father left. He was always his own man, who plotted his course without special favours. Like Micky, Alec is now the panjandrum at The Oval, as director of cricket, rather than coach. He can be seen on the outfield this evening as the Surrey lads prepare for the match. Surrey have won one of their four T20 matches so far. Kent have won three out of three.

We're supposed to have a match of 13 overs a side. But the rain, which has never gone away, returns after a single ball, delaying the resumption until 8.50 p.m., when the umpires decide we can get in a game of seven overs each. The ground staff have been sweeping away water for three hours but Sky's cameras are here, and the show must go on.

Ben Foakes, who is not alone in thinking he should be playing in the first Test against Australia at Edgbaston later this week, is in a Surrey team happy to receive Ollie Pope, fit again after dislocating his shoulder in April. These are two fine players, who have tasted Test cricket, and are eager to sup from that spoon again, and soon. The Kent team is more of a mix. The names take us around the world, like Phileas Fogg: Kuhn, Nabi, Viljoen, Qayyum and Klaassen.

The rain drives some spectators away but there are still 12,000 people in the ground when Will Jacks gets the Surrey innings under way by cutting Viljoen to the boundary. The 'dragons' at the Vauxhall end immediately roar bursts of flame into the night sky, and everybody cheers. Then the batsman biffs the bowler to extra cover, where Zak Crawley accepts the catch, and Sky's cameras search the stands for people happy to do some jolly gurning. They do not have to look far.

Pope played for England last summer, at the age of 20, and has some catching-up to do after his injury. He gets off the mark with a reverse sweep, which the modern batsman can play in his sleep. Then he slogs Mohammed Nabi, the Afghan all-rounder, to deep midwicket. The dragons roar, the gurners gurn, the Sky director earns a silver star.

In the last over Aaron Finch plays another of those strokes that would have made a man like Bedser wonder whether he had wasted his life. The ball from Adam Milne is on a good length just outside off stump, where bowlers have been hoping to land it since those evenings on the Downs. Anticipating its length and direction, Finch stoops to his knees and, with perfect calibration of his wrists and lower arm, lifts the ball behind him, over the wicketkeeper's head, and over the ropes at third man for six.

Heavens above!

It was not a stroke Hobbs could have contemplated. But games evolve, and the best players find ways of adapting to different conditions. Just as Ranji patented the leg glance, which was acclaimed by Edwardians as a stroke of daring, so batsmen such as Finch have adjusted to T20 with shots of their own. In the manner of its execution this was extraordinary.

Finch's unbeaten 36 accounts for more than half of Surrey's 54 for four. Kent looked snappy in the field. If they bat so directly they will record a fifth successive victory.

Daniel Bell-Drummond, playing against his old club, goes in the first over, lbw to Tahir, who runs halfway towards the Vauxhall end in celebration. Nabi comes to the crease, and within three overs he carries Kent home.

First he pull-drives Rikki Clarke for a mighty six into the seats in front of the old Cricketers pub. Adjusting his sights a few degrees, he pulls the next ball into the spectators by the scoreboard. The last ball of Clarke's over is pitched up, and Nabi drives him on to the second tier of the pavilion.

Tahir is not accorded more respect. Rocking back into the crease, Nabi belts the leg spinner high over his head for six more jaw-dropping runs. Another straight six follows, this time off the front foot, and Kent have won by nine wickets. Nabi's share is 43 from 12 balls, with five sixes. Each could have counted 12, so big were they.

Nobody can pretend this was great cricket. You can't have a proper contest that lasts only 11 overs. Yet the ferocity of Nabi's striking was remarkable. If there was an element of slogging about the pulled sixes there was nothing counterfeit about the three drives down the ground. Those shots took some believing but there were 12,000 witnesses who can confirm that he played them even if the majority, being Surrey supporters, would rather he hadn't.

Although the match was reduced to seven overs each, The Oval on this rain-sodden evening offered a more authentic cricketing experience than Leicester did on a day of blazing sun. Any game is shaped by the setting, and the occasion. The Vitality Blast is a big event at The Oval, which stages these matches with conviction, and Surrey are rewarded in turn by the loyalty of supporters who trust them to do it right.

This cricket will never make converts of those who prefer the longer game. But it is permissible for sceptics to dabble now and then. There are evenings when the basic appeal of T20 can pierce the armour of the most unyielding unbelievers, though Brian Close and Donald Carr may have taken some persuading.

Tonight, between the showers, one could see how T20 can work when everything comes together. At The Oval, although Surrey have not enjoyed as much success in this competition as they would expect, it usually does. An unpromising evening turned out rather well. Despite the rain, and a result that went against them, there was laughter in the air. Happiness, almost.

VII

Many Famous Feet Have Trod

Lord's

One sodden night in October 1988 I took refuge in P. J. Clarke's, a well-known bar on Third Avenue where it crosses 53rd Street. It enjoyed a reputation as 'a mid-town saloon for the tasselled loafer set', and offered the toper a vision of plenty: an oak counter, a cosy backroom with gingham tablecloths, and a jukebox that played to the strengths of the Great American Songbook.

Billy Wilder mocked up Clarke's in *The Lost Weekend*, which starred Ray Milland as the sottish writer. Johnny Mercer, the 'sentimental gentleman' from Savannah, Georgia, who contributed so much to that songbook, was a real-life regular, as I found out when I commended Jerry, the guvnor, on his interesting selection of discs.

'Thank you, sir. I chose every record myself.'

'I'm glad you've got this.' It was Sinatra singing 'One for My

Baby', Harold Arlen's bar-room classic that should only be attempted by scholarship candidates.

'Mercer wrote the words right here.'

'Did he now?'

'Ask that man,' he said, directing me towards a tall, white-haired barman, Tommy Joyce.

'Mercer was standing where you are. I poured him a cocktail, then one more. He asked me what I was called, and I said "Tom." He said, "Doesn't work, you'll have to be Joe."' That, as everybody knows, is how the song goes: 'So set 'em up, Joe . . .'

No cocktail for me. A pint of 'Bass ale' instead. In those days you could find the Burton brew all over Manhattan. As I took a preliminary swig one of the tasselled loafers pulled me up short. 'Is this the MCC, or what?' Even in midtown Manhattan a well-modulated English voice may summon images of the club that is held to represent an ideal of effortless superiority.

George Miller, it took all of five minutes to learn, was friendly, and well-connected. A permanent fixture at the business end of Clarke's, where he made urgent-sounding calls at the payphone, he was a good man for a newcomer to know. What he did for a living wasn't exactly clear, though it was obvious he was a busy chap. Once, he told me, he helped a British pop star move into an apartment in Greenwich Village, and received payment in class A narcotics.

Miller was a Cornell man, and an Anglophile who had married into a blue-blooded English family. His son had served with the British Army in Northern Ireland, which was not something he talked about openly in an Irish-American saloon where one of the barmen, who Tommy Joyce refused to acknowledge, was an IRA fundraiser.

He was a generous host, who opened a few doors on that first trip to Manhattan. And what a cheerful greeting! For him, as for many people around the world, the famous club that owns Lord's represented something significant in English society. It belonged to that many-headed monster, 'the establishment'. A monster that is there for all to see, or so it seems. Like Macavity the mystery cat, it's never quite where you think it is, or what.

How do you define Lord's? In the view of Michael Billington, the *Guardian*'s long-standing theatre critic, 'it's a reason for living in London. Growing up in Leamington Spa I dreamed of spending my afternoons there.'

According to Philippe Auclair, a French journalist, broadcaster and author, who never misses a Lord's Test, it is 'a pendant to the Royal Parks of London'. Whether you take to it or not, and some are happy to let you know they don't, Lord's is a unique temple of sport.

The cathedral of cricket. HQ. Cricket's House of Lords. Marylebone Cricket Club, and the ground it owns, have answered to many descriptions. Len Hutton thought the spectators who watched from the pavilion were the best-informed on any ground. Ian Botham thought the place was full of 'gin-swilling dodderers'.

Some members let the side down. Auclair, with an outsider's eye, indicts 'the blazered buffoons' who wear the club's egg-and-bacon colours at all times, even in bed. 'They think, or so I imagine, they are trying to re-create the Golden Age. What they don't seem to understand is that men like Ranji and Grace were pioneers. They weren't trying to turn the clock back. They were pushing the game forward, full steam ahead. Buffoons. I don't like the people in red trousers either.'

Lord's has become a form of shorthand for the old ways, and the old days. England may no longer go on tour draped in MCC colours but the club remains the custodian of the game's laws, and is very keen on what it calls 'the spirit of cricket'. Each summer a distinguished former player is invited to give an address on that thorny subject.

There is an establishment in England, as in all countries, and it isn't always easy to define. As societies change, so does the nature of the people who occupy positions of influence. It is patronage, rather than power, that defines the establishment, at least in liberal democracies. In France a place at the *École Nationale d'Administration* is the first step towards a life in government. Americans who want to get on tend to pass through Harvard Law School.

The phrase, 'the establishment', has been attributed erroneously to the journalist Henry Fairlie, a High Tory wastrel who ended up in Washington, a lover of most things American. A column he wrote in 1958 for the *Spectator* identified a group of opinion-formers where the link was social, rather than professional. Fairlie, educated at Highgate and Oxford, could be said to belong to it.

He didn't identify the other members of this set but it is not hard to make certain assumptions. His establishment had in common schooling, professional attachment and tribe.

Therefore we can start with Eton, Winchester, Oxford and Cambridge, and move from there to the Inns of Court, the Foreign and Commonwealth Office, the Brigade of Guards, White's Club, the upper reaches of the Church of England and the BBC general staff. Add, for good measure, the MCC committee.

It is a view of English life that has been parodied very well, and very badly. The satire boom of the early 1960s, starting with *Beyond the Fringe*, supported by *Private Eye*, took a wrecking ball to the establishment. Peter Cook, the queen bee of that world, mockingly called his club in Greek Street The Establishment. Now the *Eye* itself may be said to be part of the new establishment, based on the London media world.

The case for MCC's membership is not difficult to prosecute. You have only to look at the board listing the club's presidents. There is a prime minister, Sir Alec Douglas Home, who holds rank above a field marshal, an admiral of the fleet, a marshal of the RAF, and enough baronets, earls and viscounts to keep Vienna in operettas until the restoration of the Habsburgs. But even he must bend the knee to the Duke of Edinburgh, who served two terms.

When you walk through the Long Room, as the players do at least six times a day, the sense of the past is palpable. The great and good stare from the walls, reminding those who still have breath that much is expected of them. Players from overseas may be inspired more by this atmosphere than the natives. England have beaten Australia at Lord's only once in the twentieth century, in 1934, when Hedley Verity, Yorkshire's left-arm spinner, took 14 wickets.

Tradition can claim the loyalty of some unlikely people. Harold Pinter did not fit easily into any definition of the establishment but he loved cricket, and Lord's. In his eyes the Long Room was 'the greatest in the world'. When the BBC hosted a tribute to Pinter at Lord's in 2003 some bright spark thought it was a good idea to entertain the guests with amplified music. The playwright exploded. 'We can't have that in the Long Room!' For Pinter, the lover of Lord's, it was an outrage.

The men who held sway here for so long were cut from similar cloth, and may be found on the walls of MCC's inner sanctum. Lord Hawke, the first great tartar of English cricket, ran Yorkshire cricket with a rod of iron, even though he was born in Lincolnshire. He was one of many Etonians who advanced through the game to claim its highest honours. The presidency of MCC was no less than his due.

Lord Harris, another Etonian, ran Kent as a personal fiefdom. He was a treasurer and trustee of MCC, as well as president. 'Gubby' Allen, born George, had to make do with a knighthood. Yet another Etonian, he played for Cambridge and Middlesex, and captained England. In retirement he was chairman of the Test selectors. These men, bred to inherit the family silver, would have felt quite at home in Dorset Square, MCC's former home, quaffing bumpers of claret with Mulberry Hawk.

MCC, until fairly recently, meant England. The national team played abroad under the club's cloak until 1976/7, and players wore MCC colours on tour for a further 20 years. When Michael Colin Cowdrey, as he was, published his autobiography in 1976, the book's cover photograph made his identity clear, as if the initials did not. He was wearing an MCC sweater.

These portraits – and MCC have more than 3000 pictures in their collection – do not speak exclusively of the cricketing elect. There is a nod towards the great players from overseas. Don Bradman and Keith Miller take their places with Grace and Hutton in this hall of fame. The modern players are represented by Shane Warne, Brian Lara and Kapil Dev.

The most striking image is Vivian Richards, 'King Viv', painted in 2006 by Brendan Kelly. This year it has been hung at the top of the stairs that lead from the main entrance towards the bowlers' bar, and that is where it should remain. It's a magnificent portrait, which catches the great Antiguan batsman's physical power, and also his grandeur, which is not the same thing. The artist has applied the paint boldly, to match the audacity that typified the subject's batting.

This is not a mask of Ozymandias: 'look on my works, ye mighty, and despair'. The glint in his eye certainly reveals the certainty of a great cricketer, who has the measure of all things, but the portrait falls short of arrogance. It hints at glory, not boastfulness. Great players do not always see their greatness reflected truthfully on canvas. Anybody looking at this painting, whether or not they had the slightest interest in cricket, could see that Richards stood apart.

Richards has been joined on the wall leading to the visitors' dressing room by the Sri Lankan batsmen, Mahela Jayawardene and Kumar Sangakkara. In 2017, when the paintings were hung there, Sangakkara walked past his own portrait as he went out to bat for Surrey against Middlesex. It was the first time a cricketer could make that claim. To prove they had chosen the right man, he made centuries in both innings.

Other paintings work less well. The portraits of Graham Gooch and Michael Vaughan are poor, and Ian Botham's reveals little about the man. The ones that stand out are the group shots of famous players from the 1950s and 1960s, which compel the viewer to take a long look. Here are two-dozen great cricketers, caught in characteristic poses, engaged on equal terms in a conversation that will last for ever.

Allen and Pelham 'Plum' Warner (Rugby and Oxford) lend their names to the stands on either side of the pavilion. The stands that acknowledge other ranks are found at the nursery end, where Denis Compton and Bill Edrich are given their due. Nobody gave more pleasure to more people on this ground than the Middlesex twins did in 1947, when their run-making helped Londoners banish the memories of war and deprivation. Compton made 3816 runs that summer, with 18 centuries, records that will stand for ever. No knighthood, though. He wasn't officer class.

Establishments evolve. The Conservative Party used to elect its leaders when chaps of Fairlie's kidney nodded through one of their own. The men in suits, they were called. Then, in 1975, Margaret Thatcher unseated Edward Heath. She was provincial, from a lower middle-class background, and a scientist. Not one of the chaps at all. Some never forgave her.

There has been no revolution at Lord's, though the ground has shifted. In the last three decades the change has been visible, starting with the redevelopment of the Mound Stand in 1987 when Michael Hopkins, the architect, stripped off the old roof and created a 'tented village' above. With that stroke Lord's looked more relaxed, and in the intervening years no part of the ground has remained untouched.

A conservative club, stewed in decades of tradition, MCC have shown great enterprise in their plans for the new Lord's, which will bring the long overdue improvement of the Compton and Edrich stands. Members have repeatedly drawn the line, however, at selling land at the nursery end for residential development, despite a £150-million offer from the Rifkind Foundation.

One part of the ground has not improved. The Tavern concourse, where so many spectators gathered to meet old friends, make new ones, and drink indifferent beer, was covered by seating in 1986. The demand for Test-match tickets from the club's 18,000 membership persuaded MCC to make use of land that had been communal. It's a loss. That place gave Lord's something that cannot be replaced.

The original Tavern was a pub, with an entrance outside the Grace Gates. 'For the price of a pint,' wrote Ian Nairn, the architectural historian, 'you could enjoy a view of the most famous meadow in the kingdom.' A modern Tavern now squats on the other side of the Grace Gates. It is not so much a pub as a simulacrum of a pub, which puts diners before quaffers, who are not encouraged to stand at the bar. During Test matches they honour reservations only. It is not the most attractive part of the 'Lord's experience'.

MCC could also give some thought to the banners and billboards that tell everybody what a great place the ground is. Lord's doesn't have to tout for business, like a hawker in the Strand. The world knows what it is. The home of cricket. A pendant for the Royal Parks. A reason for living in London.

* * *

The dramatist who loved Lord's so much entered my life in the Michaelmas term of my second year at school, when an English teacher, a gifted director of plays, invited us to read *The Birthday Party*. That was Pinter's first full-length play for the stage, which baffled so many people at the Lyric Theatre, Hammersmith, in 1958 that it was taken off after a week. Only Harold Hobson of the *Sunday Times* heard a new voice, and his notice appeared the day after the show closed.

Those early critics missed Pinter's tone, which seems so natural to modern audiences. They missed the humour, too, pitched between absurdism and the music hall. They were not the only ones to misunderstand Goldberg and McCann, the ominous boarding-house gate-crashers, who interrogate Stanley the lodger. The line, 'who watered the wicket at Melbourne?', was once translated in a German production as 'who pissed against the city gate?'

My first Pinter on stage, *No Man's Land*, came at Wyndham's Theatre, in Leicester Square, on 4 August 1975. The day is etched in memory because it was a Monday, the fourth day of the Lord's Test against Australia. It was Tony Greig's first match as captain, and he marked it by making 96 superb runs on the first day.

David Steele, plucked from county cricket to play his first Test at the ripe age of 33, made a valiant half century, and received hearty cheers for standing up to Dennis Lillee and Jeff Thomson, who had battered England into submission the previous winter. How dare they bowl short at an old man? Steele, unbowed, pulled them repeatedly to the pickets. By December the white-haired veteran, known to his team-mates at Northampton as Crime for his supposed reluctance to pay, was the BBC Sports Personality of the Year.

Lillee's ferocious bowling from the nursery end on the first morning, when he took four wickets, remains the clearest image of that match. Ross Edwards made 99, denied a century by Bob Woolmer's full toss that hit him on the toe in front of middle stump. John Edrich piled up 175 runs second time round like a miser counting his coins. John Snow was received by the Warner Stand like a hero back from the Napoleonic Wars. There were plenty of good things. But Lillee stood out, for that opening spell. He wielded his bat well, too, belting three sixes into the Grandstand on the second afternoon.

No Man's Land was one of those 'threshold' moments, when a curtain parts, and you are bidden to enter a new world. It has puzzled a few people, even those who admire the writer. Ken Tynan, for instance, found it very strange. It resonated with my teenage mind at once, and remains my favourite Pinter. A play of memory, which nods towards the Eliot of *Four Quartets*, it is a poetic meditation on the passing of time, touching and funny. It also begins, on the page, with a stage instruction that evokes a mood before a word has been spoken. It says, simply: Summer. Night.

Pinter was well served by his collaborators. Peter Hall directed that first production, initially at the Old Vic, before it moved into the West End. The leading roles of Hirst and Spooner were taken by those great knights, Ralph Richardson and John Gielgud, 'baritone' and 'tenor'. Subsequent London productions have brought together other well-matched double acts: Pinter and Paul Eddington at the Almeida; Corin Redgrave and John Wood at the National Theatre; Michael

Gambon and David Bradley at the Duke of York's; Patrick Stewart and Ian McKellen at Wyndham's, again.

Every show worked, although nothing could efface memories of that opening production. Pinter, Hall, Richardson, Gielgud made a convincing top four. I paid 70 pence to sit on the floor that Monday night, at the back of the stalls. In 2016 I paid £99.50 for a seat in the fourth row, and that was not the most expensive ticket. They were selling 'premium seats' in the last two weeks of the run, a producer told me, for £250. As Dickens wrote in *Nicholas Nickleby*, the best way of filling a theatre is to tell people they have no chance of getting in.

There are four characters in *No Man's Land*, and each bears the name of a famous cricketer from the Golden Age. George Hirst, the Yorkshire all-rounder, and R. H. 'Reggie' Spooner, the Lancashire batsman, were opponents from Roses matches. R. E. 'Tip' Foster, one of seven brothers who played for Malvern College and Worcestershire, made 287 on his Test debut at Sydney in 1903, the best score on that ground until Michael Clarke made a triple century against India 109 years later. Johnny Briggs, a left-arm spinner, took more wickets for Lancashire than anybody except Brian Statham.

Foster and Spooner, who had been schooled at Marlborough, were 'gentlemen', amateurs who batted. Briggs and Hirst were 'players', professionals who bowled (though Hirst did make 36,356 first-class runs). Foster, uniquely, captained England at cricket and football. Spooner played one match for England at rugby. Even by the standards of the age, set by C. B. Fry, these were remarkable sportsmen.

Briggs was a tragic case. Born in Sutton-in-Ashfield, in the Nottinghamshire coalfield, he was brought up in Widnes, and was a talented hockey and rugby player as well as a good enough bowler to go on six tours of Australia. But he had mental problems, and was confined to an asylum where he died in 1902 at the age of 39.

As a cricket lover, Pinter was aware of the contrasting skills of these players. Batsman and bowler, amateur and professional, left and right, Lancashire and Yorkshire. It is not the most important feature of his play, though it lends some flavour, as does the reference to a googly in one of the exchanges between the two main characters, as they jostle in that Pinteresque manner for supremacy through language.

Like all his plays it is, in part, a struggle for territory between those who dominate and those who are dominated. Spooner begins as a supplicant, a second-rate poet craving Hirst's approval when he finds himself in the latter's Hampstead mansion. In the closing scene, the transformation complete, he is granted the lines of benediction, to which Hirst can only reply: 'I'll drink to that.'

There is a direct cricketing reference at the beginning of the second act. Hirst, presented in the first act as an old soak, oblivious to the conversation taking place in his living room, bursts into that room the following morning, refreshed, as though nothing had occurred. 'Our last encounter,' he tells Spooner, 'I remember it well. Pavilion at Lord's in '39, against the West Indies, Hutton and Compton batting superbly, Constantine bowling, war looming.'

That is *echt* Pinter, the dramatist and cricket lover speaking with one voice. Hutton was the hero of his youth, and retained that status for the rest of his life. He may have been born in Hackney, but Pinter followed Yorkshire, and one Yorkshireman in particular. He was eight when Hutton made 364 against Australia at The Oval in 1938, and he never got over his reverence for the batsman he put above all others.

His English teacher at Hackney Downs School, Joseph Brearley, was a Yorkshireman who passed on his love of cricket and literature. As master and pupil walked around east London they would talk about the great writers, notably John Webster, the Elizabethan tragedian. In 1947 Brearley took a school party to see *The White Devil*, with Robert Helpmann and Margaret Rawlings, which knocked the future playwright for six. 'Life to the power of ten,' as one of Pinter's school pals recalled it.

In 1969 Pinter contributed an essay to the *Sunday Telegraph* magazine, called 'Hutton and the Past'. His hero's bat, he wrote, was 'part of his nervous system'. Every stroke Hutton played surprised him. In later years he said that whenever the cares of the world became overwhelming he would take down a copy of the 1954 *Wisden* and read how Hutton made 36 at Sydney, going in at number seven.

Did he ever meet Hutton? I once asked. 'I saw him at The Oval, at the end of a day's play. He stood about six yards from me. But I couldn't bring myself to say hello.'

Hutton helped to form a bridge between us. I first met Pinter in July 1992, outside the Bell and Crown pub, near Kew Bridge. I had been at Lord's that day, and was talking to Sebastian Faulks, who was working at the time on *Birdsong*, his magnificent novel of the Great War. He had been playing cricket at

Gunnersbury Park against the Gaieties, the team Pinter turned out for, and wondered if I would like to meet him.

'I gather you were umpiring today, Harold.'

'Umpiring? I was fucking playing!'

Middle stump flattened. M. R. P. Henderson bowled Pinter 0.

He had indeed been playing, unlike the day at Gunnersbury that Tynan described in his *New Yorker* profile of Tom Stoppard. On that occasion he burst into the pub when the match had been completed, to offer praise and criticism of performances he had not witnessed. It was, Tynan wrote, 'like listening to Wellington if an attack of gout had kept him away from Waterloo'.

Pinter was a batsman who valued his wicket, and was never so pleased as when Arthur Wellard, the former Somerset and England all-rounder who became the Gaieties coach, commended one of his innings. He wrote a fine tribute to Wellard, who bequeathed him his England sweater, in a book of essays called *Summer Days*.

When I mentioned I had been at Lord's while they were playing at Gunnersbury, and used to ghost Hutton's column for the *Observer*, there was a sharp change of tone. He presented what Michael Billington called his 'dentist's grin'. 'Lord's?' And off we went, talking about cricket and cricketers, and *No Man's Land*, in which he was about to appear at the Almeida.

Lunches followed. The most memorable, certainly the most expensive, was at Sally Clarke's restaurant in Kensington Church Street in June 2000. We cast from strength that day. Michael Parkinson and Tim Rice opened the batting, with middle order support from Stephen Fry and Robert Tear. Bob Willis and Mark Nicholas represented the real cricketers.

Pinter and myself sat on our bats, gazing at the scoreboard as the runs ticked over.

Like an eager child, which he resembled when cricketers were present, Pinter couldn't help himself. 'Have you heard the story about Larwood when he was bowling fast as you like?' We had, but allowed him to tell it. 'Don't invite Harold again,' Willis joked later. 'He'll tell us all about Larwood and Voce.' Bob had a point. You wouldn't dream of telling tales about Olivier and Redgrave to a table of actors.

On his own turf, as one might imagine, he played strokes of absolute command. He could even tell stories against himself.

'I flew into JFK one day. I'd just been to Nicaragua, and had my passport stamped. I was waiting in the queue at customs, with my passport open, and held it out to the officer, thinking "take a look at that". He asked me, "Are you Harold Pinter?" "Yes." "Harold Pinter, the writer." "Yes." "Welcome to the United States of America, sir." It rather took the wind out of my sails.'

He didn't suffer fools. 'After Auden died [in September 1973], they put on a reading in London, and people were invited to talk about his poetry. That chap Clive James spoke, but it was all about him. I shouted, "We've come here to learn about Auden, not you." He got to the point, eventually; he didn't know it was me.'

Cricket featured in *Accident* and *The Go-Between*, two of the three screenplays he wrote for Joseph Losey. In the latter, which won the Palme d'Or at Cannes in 1971, ahead of Visconti's *Death in Venice*, the game serves as a valuable metaphor. Young Leo, the twelve-year-old messenger, staying with the Maudsley family in the summer holiday, catches Ted Burgess, the tenant farmer played by Alan Bates, in the annual match between the hall and the village.

'You caught me out,' Ted tells Leo, played with nervous intoxication by Dominic Guard. He did, and what a price he paid.

The Go-Between is that rare example of a famous novel adapted by a film-maker with no loss of emotional power. It's a great book, and it's a great film. Michel Legrand's Bach-inflected score, introduced by five doom-laden notes on the piano during the opening credits, is an augury of the loss of innocence about to unfold. The cinematography, which catches the Victorian summer's parting sigh, casts a shimmering spell. The performances, of which Margaret Leighton's Mrs Maudsley is the standout, are pitch-perfect.

Pinter's script, meshing past and present, is a Huttonesque innings of skill and judgement. It has, as the young Maudsley says of a batsman's stroke in the village match, 'such elegance and command!' By introducing Michael Redgrave as Leo in adult life, returning to Norfolk to make amends for a past blighted by hypocrisy, he supplies a layer of knowledge, not in the novel. All the elements of film-making come together in *The Go-Between*. It is a masterpiece, and the cricket match is at its heart. How he must have enjoyed writing it!

During the Lord's Test against West Indies in 2007, I popped into Pinter's box in the Tavern Stand. Four of his pals were present: Ronnie Harwood and Simon Gray, whose plays he had directed; Tom Stoppard and David Hare. Pinter had gathered them together, like a captain who thinks it's time for a spot of hey-lads-hey, and invited them to guess his favourite line in the whole of drama. It turned out to be Sir Andrew Aguecheek in *Twelfth Night*: 'I was adored once too.'

That afternoon I told him my favourite line from the slightly less exhaustive world of cricket writing. Pinter wrote it himself in that essay about Hutton and the past. Recalling his days at RADA, when he would bunk off to watch cricket at Lord's, he described arriving one afternoon for the final session of play. 'That beautiful evening Compton made 70.'

It is a simple sentence, like Aguecheek's, and it has a similar quality of time held in store. We all know what Lord's looks like at five o'clock on a summer's day, as the shadows lengthen on the outfield. There is no ground like it. We think we know, those of us who never saw him, what a dazzling maker of strokes Compton was. Those who did see him have told us hundreds of times.

Pinter's pleasure is enhanced by the snatched nature of the visit. He had gone to drama school that morning, expecting to be there all day. Instead he took an early cut, and was rewarded with a glimpse of a master batsman in midsummer form. Rather like Hutton, whose years of plenty he celebrated in that short poem Simon Gray said he hadn't finished reading.

> I saw Len Hutton in his prime.
> Another time, another time.*

There was one final lunch before Pinter's declining health restricted him to home. In October 2007 Willis, Billington and

---

* 'I saw Len Hutton in his prime' by Harold Pinter

myself took him to a favourite restaurant in Notting Hill, where we were joined by Michael Atherton, the former England captain, and Michael Simkins, the actor and writer. By then he was a Nobel laureate, though the human spark was going. Not altogether. 'I've received letters of congratulation from all over the world,' he said of his Nobel Prize.

Did Philip Roth send one? I asked, knowing the pair had fallen out years before.

'Yes.'

He dispatched a note after that lunch, saying how glad he was to have met Atherton. 'As you say, quite a guy.'

The tributes when he died in December 2008 matched his reputation, and most recognised his love of cricket. The following September there was a memorial match at Lord's, on the nursery ground. Afterwards we filled the Long Room, that 'greatest room in the world', for a celebration in words and music. Billington and Peter Hall spoke of the man and dramatist, Janie Dee sang Gershwin, and Mike Brearley declaimed from *The Caretaker* to Mike Gatting.

He was an awkward man, who could be confrontational. Rowley Leigh, the chef who ran Kensington Place, remembered meeting Pinter in his restaurant, and being told to 'get out of my fucking way'. Simon Gray, on the other hand, who dined at Kensington Place every week, 'was utterly charming'. Ronnie Harwood, one of Pinter's closest friends, was appalled by his behaviour towards waiting staff and others he considered to be below the salt.

We are all compounded of different elements, and Pinter's clay was mixed more thickly than most. He was a man of the

left, though not the humourless, tub-thumping left. In literature, as in life, he looked outwards. He fell in love at an early
age with James Joyce, and befriended Samuel Beckett. He wrote
a screenplay of Proust for Joe Losey, which was never filmed.
'Every day, for a year, reading Proust, I learned something.'
Above all, however, he was an Englishman, and never more
English than in his love of poetry and cricket.

Lord's was his personal Eden. He was enchanted by that
meadow, where, one beautiful evening, he saw Compton make
70 for Middlesex.

Every year, when the Gaieties had played their last fixture,
the players would gather in a pub, usually the Windsor Castle
in Kensington, to say farewell to summer. Pinter would read
Francis Thompson's nostalgic poem, 'At Lord's', with its
evocation of the 'run-stealers' flickering to and fro, and 'my
Hornby and my Barlow long ago'.

Lord's is a repository of outmoded tradition, some say.
When the agents of social reform take over, and we are sent
away for re-education, they might turn it into a detention
centre for wrong thinkers. Harold Pinter's lifelong love of the
ground, and what it meant to people like him, suggests there is
a different story to tell.

The Lord's Test was traditionally played in the third week of
June. It was part of 'the season', that social merry-go-round
which picks up passengers at the Chelsea Flower Show in May
and drops them at the Henley Regatta in July, making stops at
Royal Ascot and Wimbledon.

Lord's is also royal. Her Majesty the Queen pops in on the Friday of the Test, to meet the teams at lunchtime. An MCC member who woke up from a prandial nap to peep through the glass once exclaimed, 'Heavens above, there's a woman in the committee room!' adding, 'And she's talking to Swanton!' E. W. Swanton, the grand old man of the *Daily Telegraph* and the BBC, might have judged that meeting as one between equals.

As the international calendar has expanded, to take in as many as seven Test matches in a summer that used to be happy with five, 'Lord's' has become a moveable feast. This year's Test starts on a Wednesday in August, two days after the 'Glorious Twelfth'. It is the sort of adjustment that used to denote the stirring of a social revolution. Drums in the foothills.

There is a drummer in the ground today. Paul Cook of Shepherd's Bush, who smashed the cymbals for the Sex Pistols, is coming along for a day at the cricket. He's a football man, Cookie, a fan of 'the Chelsea', so this is a bit of an adventure. Witty and wise, in an undemonstrative way, he has seen a bit on his travels and is not easily fooled.

On a previous visit to Lord's two years ago, he was responsible for an observation of 'Friday etiquette' that may never be bettered. Casting an eye over members lunching in mid-afternoon on the Coronation Garden, ties and tongues loosened, he said, 'The last time I saw so many people in this state we were playing the 100 Club in 1976!' I would nominate P. T. Cook to bat for my life, whoever was bowling.

If you play a Test at Lord's on a Wednesday in August it is bound to rain, and it does. The skies weep buckets, and not only because England come here from a thrashing at Edgbaston, where Steve Smith, restored to the Australian team, made a century in each innings. The outfield is flooded by lunchtime, and spectators make alternative plans for the day.

Cookie and myself are lucky. We are quartered in a box hosted by Tim Rice, one of cricket's great benefactors, who has a knack of bringing together interesting people, not just well-known pals. Soon we are nattering to Barry Mason, who wrote 'Delilah' for Tom Jones, and – a real feather in his cap – 'Here It Comes Again' for the Fortunes.

He was also responsible for 'Love Grows', a number-one smash, as disc jockeys like to say, for Edison Lighthouse in the spring of 1970. 'She ain't got no money . . .' O wolves of memory! 'Love Grows' is one of those songs, like 'When You Are a King' by the White Plains, that reels in the years. Never trust a person who sneers at the music of their youth.

Tim, who knows more about pop songs than anybody except possibly his brother Jo, is recalling his salad days. On a trip to the States to promote *Jesus Christ Superstar,* when he was no' but a lad, he hitched a ride through Colorado with a driver who insisted on playing tapes of the Grateful Dead.

'Do you have any other tapes?'

'Sure, they're in the back.'

They were. Dozens, all by the Dead. It was a long journey.

There are only so many tales to swap before the rain persuades people to find alternative billets. After lunch, with no prospect of play, we head back to W6, for the home comforts of the Anglesea Arms, and pints of Landlord.

The next two days are patchy. Saturday dawns bright. For

one young man it was the brightest day of his life. Jofra Archer, newly qualified as English, was promoted to the one-day team, where he bowled England's 'super over' in the final last month. He has subsequently joined the Test team, making his debut in the debacle at Edgbaston, where James Anderson limped out of the attack with a torn calf after bowling four exploratory overs. England had Australia by the throat at 122 for eight, yet lost by 251 runs.

This Saturday will be remembered for years. Archer gave it to them like one of his kinsmen at Agincourt, taking five wickets with bowling that was fast and fearsome. He also hit Smith, the relentless run maker, on the head with a bouncer that laid him out cold. On this evidence he is a bowler comparable, in pace if not talent, with anybody who has worn the England crest.

Only Charles Kortright, Tom Richardson, Harold Larwood and Frank Tyson regularly exceeded 95 mph. It was thrilling to watch, and disconcerting. When Smith returned to the crease, clearly concussed, the cricket became dangerous, and it was a relief to all when he departed eight runs short of a century, lbw to a ball from Chris Woakes he did not pick up.

So many great days come back unbidden during a Lord's Test, memory feeding memory in forget-me-not lane. That first Test in 1975, with Bruce Knight, my oldest friend from Foremarke. The Centenary Test of 1980, when Dickie Bird was heckled in the familiar manner for fussing over bowlers' run-ups when the sun came out: 'Get on with it, Bird!' Allan Border's century in 1985, when Ian Botham slipped himself, and bowled as fast as Archer did today.

Three Saturdays stand out, and Indian batsmen were the stars of two. In 1990 Mohammad Azharuddin, the visiting captain, put England in, and had plenty of time to reflect on his folly. Graham Gooch built a monument, brick by brick: 333, out of England's declaration total of 654 for five. When it was finally Azharuddin's turn to bat on Saturday the eyes of the world were upon him.

What a time, therefore, to play the innings of his life. Where Gooch built a monument, he scattered jewels. He made more runs on other occasions. Indeed, he made a bigger score in the Test that followed, at Old Trafford, a match remembered now for the first of Sachin Tendulkar's 51 Test hundreds. But Azharuddin never batted more gracefully than he did that Saturday, when he cast a spell over Lord's. Monuments may inspire awe. Jewels dazzle.

The facts will tell you he made 121, and 88 of those runs came from strokes that reached the boundary. They do not indicate the mesmerising quality of his strokeplay. Time and again he turned balls of good length on the line of off stump past square leg with a whip of his wrists. Gooch could have placed four guards on the rope, with fierce dogs, and Azharuddin would still have found a way to confound them. Only a master of the bat could have played as he did.

There were 1603 runs scored in that match, and Gooch, who followed up his triple century with a single in the second innings, notched 456 of them. England won by 247 runs. Many spectators, fully acquainted with the facts, will still recall it as the game in which Azharuddin played like a prince. Statistics are dry bones. Players provide the flesh that makes sport enthralling.

'Talent is plentiful,' Laurence Olivier once said. 'Skill is much rarer.' Rahul Dravid offered proof every time he went to the crease. He was sometimes called 'the wall', a *nom de plume* that suggested the ball bounced off him. Dravid did defend his stumps. It is the first rule of batting, from which everything else follows. But his cricket was never an exercise in self-preservation. He could bat in any position, and always shaped his innings to the team's requirements.

Dravid introduced himself to England in the Lord's Test of 1996, going in at number seven, and making 95. In 2002 he made three successive centuries in England, though not at Lord's. When he returned in 2011 he was 38, waiting for an old rocking chair. India lost that series feebly, though Dravid's skill was unimpaired; the skill of an indentured craftsman.

On another great Lord's Saturday he made 103 not out, the first of three more centuries in a series. England didn't give him the runs. Anderson and Stuart Broad bowled superbly after lunch, at Dravid and Tendulkar. It was a contest within a contest, between four men of contrasting skills. If the bowlers prevailed it was not at Dravid's expense.

Anderson bowled as well as he ever did on the final day; well enough to take the edge of Dravid's bat. That was the wicket England needed to unlock the innings. As with Azharuddin 21 years before, England won the match. As with Azharuddin, an Indian batsman left the spectators with a vase of memories worth polishing.

It was the third Saturday, in 2000, that showed Lord's in its brightest colours. It was the third day of the second Test against West Indies. The tourists were not then the force they had been.

They still had some formidable players, led by Brian Lara, Curtly Ambrose and Courtney Walsh. In the first Test, at Edgbaston, they had won comfortably. When they took the field that morning they expected to increase that lead. Although England had dismissed them for 54 in two riotous hours the previous evening, Ambrose and Walsh would surely prevent England making the 188 runs they needed to win.

That Friday was unique. For the first time in Test history a single day contained all four innings, two in their entirety and two in fragments. Andrew Caddick led the way with five for 16 when England ran through the West Indies after tea. He owed the first to his fellow fast bowler, Darren Gough, who held a remarkable catch at third man to dismiss Sherwin Campbell. It gave England heart after they had been bowled out for 134, and prompted sceptics, of whom there were many thousands, to think 'something strange might happen here'.

The Michaels, Atherton and Vaughan, batted with scrupulous care on that Saturday morning. Atherton was coming to the end of his career, cognisant of the discipline required. Vaughan, more expansive by temperament but fairly new to the team, was playing a vigilant role for the first time. They were tested every ball by the great West Indian opening pair. Ambrose went past the bat with such regularity there were titters of embarrassment in the crowd, which watched intently.

This was Test match cricket at its most demanding, and the batsmen accepted their responsibilities. If one or both went in that first session, before England had secured a foothold, the jig was up. They would be two matches down, with little hope of clawing their way back. England had not beaten the West

Indies in a series since 1969. In six series between 1976 and 1988 they did not win a single Test. Atherton and Vaughan held firm, making 92 for the second wicket. In the context of the match, they were riches.

Lord's was seen at its best that day, and *heard* at its best. The famous murmur, unique to this place, supplied the soundtrack before lunch, as all eyes were drawn to the cricket. In the afternoon, as the match was pushed forward by the batsmen and pulled back by the bowlers, the spectators became more lively. Finally, as Dominic Cork bashed the strokes that took England closer to an improbable triumph, there was the kind of authentic noise that comes only when an event has developed naturally, without manipulation. It was for the most part a slow day's play. It was also the most exciting I have ever witnessed.

When Cork pulled Franklyn Rose for six, and the match was won, delight and relief competed for primacy. The acclaim was genuine, for both teams. Walsh, bowling heroically, had taken six wickets in the innings, and ten in the match, and finished on the losing side. Ambrose had bowled 22 overs, for 22 runs. Few victories are so hard won.

England went on to win the series 3–1. A team that had grown used to losing became familiar with winning. They won in Pakistan that winter, and in Sri Lanka the following spring. When Nasser Hussain handed over the captaincy to Vaughan in 2003 the new leader inherited a team tweaked with sufficient vigour to beat the Australians, at long last, in 2005. And it all began on that Saturday at Lord's.

On such days Lord's is supreme. There are bigger grounds, and there are 'better' grounds. But cricket is not played in a void. History counts for something. It is 'a pattern of timeless moments', as Eliot wrote, and nowhere does past and present conjoin so beautifully as at the home of cricket. That is why people fly in for the Lord's Test from all over the world, and why players of all nations and denominations want to excel there. Lord's is a ground where spectators are neither customers nor cheerleaders. They are witnesses.

There are two revealing faces in the president's box. Anthony Wreford (Charterhouse and Oxford) has already burnished his year in office by appointing the great Sangakkara as his successor. There have been far too many insiders in recent years. Good men, to be sure, but too close to the club. Sangakkara's nomination as the first foreign president is a proper rabbit from the hat.

Wreford has invited an authentic outsider into his box for the last day of the Test. Pavel Florin, a bodyguard from Cluj, in Romania, makes an unlikely cricketer. Having watched the game a few years ago on television he wanted to get involved and now does so every week, with such enthusiasm that his unusual bowling action has made him a hit on social media. He looks trim in his casual clothes, and is clearly touched to be here, as a guest of the club.

Cluj is deep in the mountains of Transylvania, where Miklós Bánffy set the evocative novels that make up the *Transylvanian Trilogy*. Does he know of Bánffy?

'Oh yes. His family had famous castle.'

It sounds lovely. Villagers in traditional garb, old craftsmen at work, deep forests. Are there bears?

'Many bears, yes. They come to the villages.'

Aren't you frightened?

'No. Friendly bears.'

Jason Roy misses a catch at slip, and spectators groan. 'Not easy catch,' says the eagle-eyed visitor. 'Not high, not low. Hard.'

Another Test is over, and people slip away, carrying memories of Archer's explosive bowling and Ben Stokes's century. England could not quite force the win, but the tide may have turned in their favour. The teams now go to Headingley, where odd things have been known to happen.

For some spectators it will be their last visit, though they do not know it. Ken Tynan, writing in his diaries, suspected his time was up during the West Indies Test of June 1980. He died within the month. At least he caught Richards in the midsummer of his career. King Viv made a century that day, treating even Derek Underwood with disdain, and prompting John Arlott to wonder what words could do justice to the majesty of his batting.

On the last day of the Australia Test in 2013 I was sitting with some actor friends in front of the old Tavern. Behind us, a few rows away, was Peter O'Toole. He loved Lord's so much that, years before, he moved from Hampstead to Brondesbury so he could be closer to the indoor school, where he liked to knock up in the winter. The MCC head coach at the time was his friend Don Wilson, who used to bowl slow left arm for Yorkshire, where O'Toole was born. A few corks popped when they were together, in London and Ampleforth, where the actor sent his son Lorcan.

It was touching to observe him sitting there, content in his solitude, taking one last look at the ground in July sunshine.

Within five months he too had gone. There was something of that melancholy in Pinter's farewell, on the day of 'the five playwrights'. In their own ways these men of the theatre wanted to say goodbye to their favourite stage.

Lord's is a reason for living in London. It is a pendant to the Royal Parks. It also offers a pretty good reason for being alive.

VIII

Places, Loved Ones

Canterbury, Old Trafford

There have been many Canterbury tales. The most significant remains the first, that of Augustine, the Benedictine
monk, dispatched from Rome in 595 by Pope Gregory the
Great to make Christians of the Anglo-Saxons. His ordination
two years later as the first archbishop was a signal moment in
our island story.

Another archbishop, Thomas à Becket, was the victim of a
macabre tale. Slain on 29 December 1170 by four knights, who
had interpreted Henry II's exasperated cry about a 'turbulent
priest' as a call to arms, his martyrdom has been told many
times, in many tongues. Modern historians doubt the veracity
of the monarch's plea, but the legend has persisted. Becket's
tragedy inspired T. S. Eliot's best-known play, *Murder in the
Cathedral*, as well as the drama by Jean Anouilh, which was
turned into a film starring Peter O'Toole.

In the fourteenth century Geoffrey Chaucer added another layer to the legend with his tales of 30 pilgrims, representatives of all the crafts, walking from Southwark to Canterbury to visit Becket's shrine. *The Canterbury Tales*, the first 'English' masterpiece, gave readers the style of bawdy that has become a national comic trait, and served as the bridge between Middle English and the language we speak today. Chaucer, our linguistic midwife, was the first writer to be interred in Poets' Corner in Westminster Abbey.

The Elizabethan age brought Christopher Marlowe, who lends his name to the city's theatre. Kit Marlowe, born, like Shakespeare, in 1564, lived in the shadow of his great contemporary. His plays, which include *Doctor Faustus* and *Tamburlaine the Great*, mark him as a major figure in his own hand. Infamously, he breathed his last in a Deptford pothouse.

Imagined characters also feature in the city's history. David Copperfield, the eponymous character in the most famous *Bildungsroman* in English literature, roamed here from London, and was educated at the King's School. It was in Canterbury that young David, barely out of short trousers, met the unctuous schemer Uriah Heep, who was never as 'umble as he liked to boast.

Somerset Maugham published his own novel of youthful identity in the twentieth century. *Of Human Bondage*, with Philip Carey taking Maugham's part, begins in Canterbury, where the author had been brought up. Like Marlowe in real life and Copperfield in Dickens's imagination, Maugham had also gone to the King's School. A big success when it was published in 1915, *Of Human Bondage* has fallen from favour in the past generation, along with its author. It is ripe for rediscovery.

The most interesting tale of twentieth-century Canterbury was written for the big screen by Michael Powell, who was born in Bekesbourne, just outside the city, in 1905, and educated, like Marlowe, Maugham and Copperfield, at King's. Powell may not be the greatest English film-maker. Alfred Hitchcock, David Lean and Carol Reed made movies that are classics. What cannot be gainsaid is that this son of a hop farmer was the greatest maker of *English* films.

Hitchcock went to America in 1939, conquered Hollywood with *Rebecca*, and stayed. Lean left behind *Brief Encounter* to become a master of the epic: *The Bridge on the River Kwai*, *Lawrence of Arabia*, *Doctor Zhivago*, *A Passage to India*. Reed's best film, *The Third Man*, was an Anglo-American collaboration, set in post-war Vienna. Powell concentrated on films that revealed the quirkiness, and off-centre romanticism, of the English character.

Having opened his innings in the 1930s, he lengthened his stride when Alexander Korda, the producer, introduced him to his fellow Hungarian, the screenwriter Emeric Pressburger, in 1938. There followed a decade of abundance: *49th Parallel*, *One of Our Aircraft Is Missing*, *The Life and Death of Colonel Blimp*, *I Know Where I'm Going!*, *A Matter of Life and Death*, *Black Narcissus* and *The Red Shoes*.

The missing film in that sequence, released in 1944, between *Blimp* and *I Know Where I'm Going!*, is *A Canterbury Tale*. It wasn't a commercial hit at the time, and remained undervalued until 1978, when the British Film Institute screened a revised cut, and a younger generation learned to see it with fresh eyes. The praise of Martin Scorsese, a long-time Powell admirer, assisted the reformation. Powell repaid him by marrying Thelma Schoonmaker, Scorsese's film editor, and dedicating his memoir, *Million Dollar Movie*, to the younger man, who had grown up watching Powell's films in New York.

It was that partnership with Pressburger, the Jewish émigré from the old Habsburg Empire, which gave these movies their unique character, fusing Powell's Englishness with a seasoning of paprika. 'The Archers', as they called themselves, were a real partnership. Each man assumed joint responsibility for the film's script, direction and production, and their visual affirmation of ownership, an arrow scoring a bull's eye, opened each of their movies like the parting of a cinema curtain.

In Kent, the garden of England, there are flowers aplenty, and a few thorns. Powell's films contain both. When Winston Churchill expressed his displeasure at *Colonel Blimp*, released in 1943, one of the film's leading men supplied an answer on behalf of director and company. Only the English, said Anton Walbrook, the Austrian-born actor who shared the film's honours with Roger Livesey, 'would have had the courage, in the midst of war, to tell people such unvarnished truth'. Thank goodness Powell and Pressburger prevailed: *Colonel Blimp* is one of the masterpieces of cinema in any language.

Pressburger was one of those gifted émigrés from Hungary and Germany, many Jewish, who added lustre to the cultural life of his adopted country. English was his fourth language, but you wouldn't have known it from the screenplays he wrote with Powell. He ended his days in Suffolk, near George Clare, another Jewish exile from the European catastrophe. Clare, born Georg Klaar, wrote *Last Waltz in Vienna*, a memoir in the tradition of Stefan Zweig's *The World of Yesterday*. Zweig was another man to become British, before he took himself off to Brazil with his wife to fulfil a suicide pact, exhausted beyond endurance by what had happened to the Europe he loved.

A Hungarian, it used to be said, was somebody 'who gets into a revolving door behind you, and comes out in front of you'. British life in the mid-twentieth century appeared to confirm the truth of that joke. Korda was the film producer who introduced Pressburger to Powell. George Mikes achieved literary fame with his book, *How to Be an Alien*. Georg Solti, music director of the Royal Opera for ten years from 1961, made his home in Hampstead even when he left Covent Garden for the Chicago Symphony Orchestra. András Schiff, the pianist, remains with us, knighted, like Solti; a British subject very proud of his honour.

The intellectual life of England has been flavoured by these men, and others, from middle Europe. Isaiah Berlin (born in Riga), Claus Moser (Berlin), Nikolaus Pevsner (Leipzig), Karl Popper and Ernst Gombrich (both Vienna) added significant chapters to British philosophy, political thought, music, architecture and the history of ideas.

George Weidenfeld (Vienna), along with Paul Hamlyn (Berlin) and André Deutsch (Budapest), transformed British publishing. Fritz Busch, Carl Ebert and Rudolf Bing, exiles from National Socialism, were brought in by Sir John Christie to run Glyndebourne Opera, which swiftly became a shrine to

Mozart in Sussex, and a highlight of the English summer. Tom Stoppard, Lucian Freud, Leon Kossoff and Frank Auerbach were either born overseas or the sons of parents who sought refuge in this country. Stoppard, talking of his adopted identity, said he 'put on a coat of Englishness' and found out that it suited him. William Davis, the editor of *Punch*, that repository of English humour, was another German.

The finest modern novel about the English landscape, *The Enigma of Arrival*, was written by Vidia Naipaul, born in Trinidad. Set in Wiltshire, where Naipaul went to live in 1970, it is a hypnotic book, rooted in the cyclical life of the natural world, and brings to mind Eliot's lines from *Little Gidding*: 'history is now and England'. Naipaul, like Pressburger, saw England refracted through the lens of a foreigner who felt both assimilated and detached.

A Canterbury Tale is a gripping, ultimately moving film, but it is easy to see what perplexed so many viewers when it was released. It is the story of a 'glueman' played by Eric Portman, so-called because he pounces on girls in the blackout and drops glue in their hair. One of his victims, a land girl played by Sheila Sim, is a modern 'pilgrim' bound for war-ravaged Canterbury. The other pilgrims, who join her in the course of the film, are a British soldier (Dennis Price) and an American sergeant (John Sweet, a real combatant).

The film is a tribute to Powell's native county, which bore the brunt of the Nazi assault, and an attempt to link the past with the present. Powell achieves this in the opening sequence with a superb image. A falcon hovering in the sky above Chaucer's pilgrims is transformed into a Spitfire, defending

England from German aggressors. To add piquancy the cinematographer, Erwin Hillier, was German. It is a touch of magic that never palls.

At the film's climax the forces of past and present converge as Sim and Sweet approach Canterbury Cathedral, under the watchful eye of Portman. She is reunited with the man she thought was dead. He discovers his fiancée is in Australia. Price, a cinema organist in civilian life, is offered the chance to pull out all the stops, as it were, on the cathedral's instrument before leaving with his battalion for active service. The blessings conferred upon these pilgrims give this odd tale a moving climax. It is an unusual film, which baffled the first audiences, but it is a masterpiece.

While Powell and Pressburger were making it in the autumn of 1943, another Englishman had just completed one of his greatest works. Ralph Vaughan Williams was a famous composer by the time war broke out. He had written many of the pieces for which he is known, including *A Lark Ascending* and *Fantasia on a Theme of Thomas Tallis*, as well as four symphonies.

When he started work in 1938 on a fifth symphony, which he eventually dedicated 'without permission' to Jean Sibelius, the old world was in turmoil. Music lovers could be forgiven for expecting to hear a sombre work, in accordance with the brutal times. Instead the symphony is Vaughan Williams's most serene. The radiance, which confounded those who heard the first performance in July 1943, is characterised by a ravishing solo for cor anglais in the third movement, and it remains the composer's best-loved symphony.

What does it say about the English character that, at the height of war, with ultimate victory by no means assured, two giants should create works not of anger and recrimination but mercy and forgiveness? Nowhere else in Europe did artists of their standing respond to war with such restraint. Powell and Vaughan Williams were saying, softly yet insistently, 'this is the land we were born into, and these are the qualities we are fighting to preserve'. It is a very English romanticism, tempered by stoicism.

It is sometimes said that artists respond to the perils of the age. That isn't always the case. Matisse and Bonnard lived through two world wars, and left no evidence in their work. They are not diminished. They were painters of genius, who did what they wanted. Matisse painted still lifes in his sitting room, Bonnard almond trees in his garden. Those who like looking at great paintings are richer for it.

'I believe,' said Vaughan Williams, 'that one's own community, one's own language, customs and religion are essential to our spiritual health ... without local loyalty there can be nothing for the wider issues to build on.' His fifth symphony, like *A Canterbury Tale*, dignifies us all. These works are not just thoroughly English. They have an emotional charge that should make every one of us feel English, and happy to be so.

My own Canterbury tale unfolded not in Kent but Berlin. In November 1987, two years before the Wall came down, I went to 'Faust's Metropolis' when Simon Rattle conducted the city's great orchestra, the Berliner Philharmoniker, for the first time.

Rattle, then 32, had made a name for himself with the City of Birmingham Symphony Orchestra and done a fair bit of guest conducting, particularly in America, but he had waited for the right moment to work with the Berliners. That orchestra tests a conductor more than any other, and some talented baton-wielders have gone away feeling daunted. Rattle, despite entreaties from Herbert von Karajan, the Berliners' dominant music director, put off his debut until he felt he was properly prepared.

It proved to be a significant weekend. Rattle scored such a triumph with Mahler's sixth symphony that one member of the orchestra said on leaving the stage: 'I am going to have to take this young man very seriously.' That man was my friend, Peter Steiner, appointed to the cello desk in 1948 by Karajan's predecessor, Wilhelm Furtwängler. Through Peter, who retired in 1995 after spending 47 years with the Berliners, I established a lifelong friendship with several members of an orchestra I have heard more than a hundred times.

The youngest member of 'the musical family Steiner', as they were known in the early years of the last century, when they toured the grand hotels of Europe, was the orchestra's unofficial archivist. One evening at his house in Grunewald Peter produced leather-bound volumes that contained details of every concert the orchestra had ever played: the programmes, the soloists, the conductors. He then showed me photographs of some of the great men with whom they had worked.

'That's you with Shostakovich.'

'Yes, we played his tenth symphony in Moscow with Karajan. It was a great success.'

'And that's Stravinsky.'

'Yes, he came to Berlin often.'

On his wall was a photograph of Furtwängler, the great conductor of Bruckner and Wagner, sitting on top of a camel, looking self-conscious in a fez.

'We were in Egypt,' said Peter.

That night, after some gentle prodding, he listed the great conductors he had played for, not merely the very good ones. There were eight, led by Furtwängler and Karajan. 'I loved him,' Peter said of Karajan, which is something to bear in mind when people seek to belittle that great musician. In 1988, to honour Peter's fortieth anniversary with the orchestra, Karajan wrote a letter to mark 'the great days we have known'. Another letter, sent to Peter by Lorin Maazel after the American conductor had failed in his attempt to succeed Karajan, as he had expected to, was a curio. 'I shall now return to the great orchestra I am proud to lead in Pittsburgh,' wrote Maazel. A fine orchestra, certainly. Just not Berlin.

The other great conductors, in Peter's estimation, were Otto Klemperer, Sergiu Celibidache, Dimitri Mitropoulos, Pierre Boulez, Sir John Barbirolli and Carlos Kleiber. Shortly before Karajan died, in July 1989, Peter was asked to approach Kleiber during the Salzburg Festival, and ask him on the orchestra's behalf to succeed his friend as music director. 'I told him after von Bülow, Nikisch, Furtwängler and Karajan, the next conductor of our orchestra should be Kleiber. That is the tradition. He told me he only conducted when he looked in his fridge and found nothing to eat.'

In 1996, invited by Frank Johnson, editor of the *Spectator*, to write a piece about a 'Composers XI' in the manner of a cricket team, I obliged out of duty. It was an opportunity to rebuke Cardus, who had written a book on the subject and found room for César Franck! A fine composer, Franck, but in cricketing terms he was a second-change bowler. In my XI Haydn and Beethoven opened the batting, Verdi and Wagner the bowling. The following summer at Lord's, Peter Jonas, the intendant at the great opera house in Munich, told me the cricket-loving Kleiber had read the article and said: 'Perhaps he will now select a team of conductors.'

These are not conversations one often hears in the press box at Grace Road.

I heard Kleiber only once, at a gala evening at the Vienna State Opera in March 1994. Felicity Lott, Anne Sofie von Otter and Barbara Bonney were the singers – and what singers! – in *Der Rosenkavalier*, Richard Strauss's 'Viennese masquerade'. Once was a feast. As Bernard Haitink, another great conductor, said to Rattle after hearing Kleiber conduct Verdi's *Otello* at Covent Garden: 'You know, Simon, I think my studies are only just beginning.' Rattle paid his own tribute years later, when he said that 'all conductors, when they talk to each other, know that Carlos is the greatest'.

That day in 1987, at the final rehearsal of Mahler Six in the Philharmonie, near Potsdamerplatz, I found myself talking to Rattle's father Denis, who asked the usual questions. He was delighted by one answer. 'A cricket writer? Another Cardus!' After the concert that night, as people queued to greet his son in the green room, he took me to one side and said, 'Let me tell you a story.'

It was quite a tale. Rattle senior had been schooled at Chatham House in Ramsgate, where Edward Heath was a contemporary – and later, a fellow student at Oxford. Denis loved his cricket, and when Kent sent a full-strength county team to play the school he found himself facing A. P. 'Tich' Freeman, the famous leg-spin bowler, with Les Ames, the only wicketkeeper to make a century of centuries, behind the stumps. In those days the stars turned out, happy to lend a hand.

'I was sitting next to Ames at lunch,' he said, 'and I told him how petrified I was. So he volunteered to tell me what to expect. "First ball, leg break. Second ball, top spinner. Third ball, googly. The fourth ball will bowl you." And it did, though I'm not sure how. It seemed to be a wide but it turned at least 45 degrees to hit the leg stump.

'Didn't they play well tonight? Though the trombones aren't a patch on Birmingham. Now come and meet Simon.'

Rattle junior, who has no interest in sport, nevertheless signed my programme 'caught in the slips again'. In June 2018, when he gave his final concert as the orchestra's principal conductor, a position he held for 16 years, he squared the circle by performing Mahler Six again. Afterwards, at a reception attended by Angela Merkel, I presented him with the programme he had signed 31 years before.

Another Canterbury tale, of sorts.

Denis Rattle had no need to feel abashed. Freeman was one of the great figures of English cricket, taking ten wickets in a match for Kent 128 times. His career haul of 3340 wickets for the county is exceeded only by Wilfred Rhodes of Yorkshire.

At the same time Frank Woolley was making 47,868 runs for Kent, another county record.

The modern St Lawrence Ground is very different to the meadow where Freeman wove his web, and Woolley stroked centuries of careless rapture. For a start it is no longer called the St Lawrence Ground. The Spitfire Ground it is now, which retains local honour. The Spitfire ales, named after the fighter aircraft that helped to win the Battle of Britain, fought in Kentish skies, come from Shepherd Neame of Faversham, the oldest brewers in the land.

By the entrance on Old Dover Road, where cars used to park on the grass, there is a supermarket. The famous lime tree, which stood inside the boundary at midwicket, was blown down by gales in January 2005. Behind the sapling, planted by way of remembrance, there is sheltered accommodation, which looks rather agreeable. Not all retired folk can watch county cricket from their balconies. For Kent, as for so many clubs, this is the way of the world. They sold the land because they needed the money.

The match against Essex marks the 168th 'Canterbury Week', making it the longest-established festival in the world. The first week was in 1842, when the great Peel of Bury was prime minister, and the kingdom was torn apart by reform of the Corn Laws. There was no championship in those days, and Kent had not been constituted as a club. There were, however, Gentlemen of Kent and Kentish Gentlemen.

Today the ground welcomes Herren von Deutschland. The German cricket team are present, as part of an English tour, though it is not exactly *echt Deutsch* as none of them are speaking German. They are speaking English, loudly, as they drink to the fixture back in the beer tent at the Nackington Road end.

There is also a group of French schoolchildren, for whom the beer tent is out of bounds. Their presence is not surprising, because Canterbury is full of French tourists, and French citizens. Perhaps one day the son of a French family will play for England, as Joe Denly has done this summer. The first cricketer born in the city, it may be noted, to represent his country. Another Canterbury tale, and a surprising one, for Kent has never been short of great cricketers.

Alfred Mynn, 'the Lion of Kent', is the first name in the pageant. Mynn, a hop farmer who stood six feet tall and weighed 20 stone, was the finest 'round arm' bowler of his day, between 1832 and 1859. He is followed by Ivo Bligh, the 11th Earl of Darnley, who was the England captain presented with the Ashes urn after he had led England to victory in Australia in 1883. Percy Chapman, another man of Kent, was the victorious captain when England beat Australia at The Oval in 1926.

The stands at Canterbury honour the county's great ones. Ames and Woolley are there, by right, and Colin Cowdrey, Baron Cowdrey of Tonbridge, forms the bridge that leads to Kent's two finest players of the more recent past. Derek Underwood and Alan Knott share a stand, which is named correctly if imprecisely. It should really be called the Knott Underwood Stand, in that order, as in 'caught Knott, bowled Underwood'.

'Stumped Knott, bowled Underwood' was another dismissal regularly inked into the scorebook. They were one of the greatest pairs, never more effective than at Headingley in

1972 when Underwood lived up to his pet name 'Deadly' by bowling out Ian Chappell's strong Australian side on a pitch infected by fusarium. 'Knotty never missed a ball,' Chappell said three decades later. 'Whether it leapt off the pitch, or crept, it stuck in his gloves.' The opposing captain that day, Raymond Illingworth, was the successful skipper when England had won in Australia two winters before. 'I do not believe,' he said, 'it is possible to keep wicket better than Alan Knott did on that tour.'

Those supreme cricketers came from the north of the county; Knott from Erith, and Underwood from Bromley. In the 1960s and 1970s, when they were stars of the Test team, Kent took their White Horse flag to Blackheath and Dartford, as well as Maidstone, Dover and Folkestone. Now the only outgrounds are Tunbridge Wells and Beckenham, towns that reveal the two facets of Kentishness.

Tunbridge Wells, as Noël Coward warbled, is where 'you can hear the yells of the woebegone bourgeoisie'. Beckenham is where Kent is sucked into south London. Town and gown in this county of oasthouses and Medway encampments are woven through contrasting strands of cricket, represented in their highest moments by Cowdrey on the one hand and Knott on the other.

Cricket's most affecting Canterbury tale was told on canvas by Albert Chevallier Tayler. The painting, known as *Kent v Lancashire at Canterbury 1906*, now hangs at Lord's, an inappropriate home for a work that captures the mood of a game, and a time. Lord Harris, the chairman of Kent, commissioned it from Tayler, an artist of the Newlyn school, to celebrate the county's first championship title. What it also celebrates, viewed through the filter of history, is cricket in the Golden Age.

Standing at the Nackington Road end, to the left of the tent bulging with those Germans of all nationalities, you can make out some of the details that Tayler painted. The tents and flags he saw are missing, and the cathedral's Bell Harry Tower is only there in the imagination, as it was in his. But you can feel the ground as it was, and hear the murmurs of the past.

Harris insisted that Tayler found room in his painting for every member of the side that beat Lancashire in August 1906, by an innings and 195 runs. They are all present and correct, some in improbable fielding positions, as Colin Blythe, the great left-arm spinner, bowls to J. T. Tyldesley. Tayler catches his arm high, as he prepares to release the ball.

Blythe, reckoned by batsmen who faced him to be second only to Rhodes of Yorkshire, took eight wickets in the match. Johnny Tyldesley, who had plundered 295 undefeated runs from the Kent bowlers two months before at Old Trafford, was a strokeplayer who 'took the senses by assault', in the words of Cardus. Here were men who stood on equal ground. The batsman at the non-striker's end, Harry Makepeace (unavailable to sit for Tayler, and represented in the painting by another Lancashire player, William Findlay) was another sportsman of distinction. Earlier that year he had played on the winning side for Everton in the FA Cup final.

From our perspective the spirit of *The Go-Between* haunts the painting, so apposite are the opening words of Hartley's novel: 'the past is a foreign country'. In 1906, the year after

Michael Powell was born, Edward VII was in the fifth year of his reign. The Boer War had ended four years earlier, and imperial rule continued confidently, if not altogether serenely. The Liberals, led by Sir Henry Campbell-Bannerman, routed the Conservatives in the general election that February. The Labour Party awaited its formation.

John Galsworthy published *The Man of Property*, the first novel in a sequence of books that would become known as *The Forsyte Saga*. By the time Galsworthy was awarded the Nobel Prize in Literature in 1932 the world he described had been blown to smithereens. The great Larkin, writing half a century later, caught the mood in 'MCMXIV': 'never such innocence again'.

Blythe was a casualty of the Great War, the one that was supposed to end them all. He joined the Kent Fortress Engineers in 1914, was posted to the King's Own Yorkshire Light Infantry, and was killed by a shell at Passchendaele on 8 November 1917. He was 38. On 8 November each year, three days before the Armistice, Kent honour his memory, and those of others who perished in war, at the St Lawrence Ground's memorial fountain.

Lord Harris died, 'with all his honours on', in 1932. The year before, on his eightieth birthday, he sent a letter to *The Times* that has become part of cricket's folklore. Cricket, he wrote, was 'more free from anything sordid, anything dishonourable, than any game in the world'.

We laugh at such attitudes now because we imagine we are wiser than those who came before. But people a century on will laugh at our follies, and wonder how certain we could be of our beliefs. The views that Harris expressed are old-fashioned, and therefore unfashionable. The hopes invested in them are not. That is the conundrum of the Golden Age, which oscillates in the retelling between fact and mythology.

Blythe was an important figure in that age. He helped bowl Kent to three further championship titles, in 1909, 1910 and 1913. In 1914 he played a few matches alongside the young Freeman. After the war he had intended to coach at Eton. He lives on in Tayler's painting, which fetched £600,000 when Sotheby's sold it at auction in 2006 to Andrew Brownsword, who loaned it to MCC. A copy, painted by Barrington Bramley, hangs at Canterbury.

In the fragmented modern programme the 'week' is not what it was. When the Hundred arrives there may be no week at all. But it is good to stroll around this famous plot of earth, where Woolley and Cowdrey charmed the birds from that lime tree, and W. G. Grace scored the first triple century recorded in first-class cricket.

On the grassy mound Tony Sanders has set up his bookstall. He takes his collection to Tunbridge Wells and Beckenham, too, and to Cheltenham, for old times' sake. It seems rude not to slip something into my bag so I pick up a hardback edition of *The Best Loved Game* by Geoffrey Moorhouse, originally published in 1979, when Kerry Packer's World Series Cricket threatened to rupture the game beyond restoration. The young Moorhouse worked for the *Bolton Evening News*, shortly after my father left the staff, and his *tour d'horizon* of English cricket is a wonderful book. Three quid, it costs. Less than a pint.

In the tent next to the bookstall John Shepherd, the Barbadian all-rounder who was one of the most popular men to wear the Kent colours, is recalling his first Test wicket, at Old Trafford in 1969. It was Geoffrey Boycott, a scalp worth having. Boycott had made a century, and was looking for a hundred more when Shepherd struck his front leg, and Charlie Elliott's finger went up. As he left the crease he told the umpire what he thought of the decision.

'Close enough,' Elliott told him. 'And besides, Shep's a good lad.'

Paul Baldwin and Ian Blackwell, the umpires in our match, are awarding the bowlers plenty of wickets to lbw decisions as Essex close in on a victory that will strengthen their position at the top of the table. When the match concludes on the third afternoon, Essex scraping home by three wickets, 15 batsmen have been adjudged leg before, a record for any match involving Kent.

Three of the wickets went in Essex's first innings to Darren Stevens, whose autumnal flowering as an opening bowler furnishes one of the most unlikely Canterbury tales. The young Stevens spent the first eight years of his career at Leicestershire as a batsman, playing handsome strokes in the middle order. When he joined Kent in 2005, at the age of 29, he had taken only six first-class wickets.

Behold the transformation! The wicket of Alastair Cook, the newly dubbed knight, on the second morning took his tally to 494. At 43 Stevens takes the new ball by right, not some dispensation for senior pros. Kent, looking to the future, would rather he didn't. There is talk that this season will be his last, but the balding Stevens is having none of it. When he took his sweater on that second day he had bowled nine overs for 11 runs and three wickets, including England's leading run-scorer in Tests.

The third day brought one of those astonishing reversals of fortune that make this the most bewildering of games. Essex were bowled out for 114, and conceded a first innings lead of 112. They then ran through Kent in an hour and a half. Sam Cook took seven wickets, making it 12 in the match, as the batsmen fell in a heap: 40 all out, with nobody reaching double figures. It was one of those bells that now and then rings.

Set 152 for victory, Essex had problems of their own and were rocking at 84 for six. Adam Wheater and Simon Harmer steadied the Buffs with 57 runs for the seventh wicket, and Wheater was there at the end. The cheers from the Essex dressing room were not so much a roar of triumph as a mighty exhalation of relief.

When 26 wickets fall in a day, something remarkable has happened. Essex, hunting their second title in three years, will recall this barmy frolic with favour, because they were on the right side of events. It was one more Canterbury tale.

There is another pilgrimage to undertake before the autumn weather turns the leaves to flame. Old Trafford awaits, and Lancashire's championship match with Derbyshire. This is where I came in half a century ago, when Peter Eyre's 'syrup' fell off, as he ran up to bowl, and John Eyre (no relation) made a century.

I take a seat close to where I sat in June 1967, to the left of the pavilion. Spectators were situated at midwicket in those days. Now that the pitch has been turned round, to run north–south rather than east–west, they watch from mid-off, underneath a newly constructed hotel. On the other side of the pavilion, where the ladies' stand used to be, there is a slightly older construction, the Point, where the corporate entertaining all year long rakes in millions for the club.

Derbyshire, who have just qualified for the T20 finals day for the first time, bat after Billy Godleman wins the toss, and the captain goes into lunch with 53 runs to his name. Had Wayne Madsen not been lbw to Richard Gleeson in the over before the interval Derbyshire would have tucked into their grub happy to lose only one wicket in the morning session.

Gleeson's success proves to be a warning that goes unheeded. When play resumes Derbyshire are soon five down, and it takes Godleman's century to push the score to 244. Gleeson finishes with five wickets, and there are three for Saqib Mahmood, a lively bowler closer to fast than medium pace.

Born in Birmingham, Mahmood was brought up in Rochdale, and is one of eight local lads in the team. Six are Lancastrians by birth (Barrow, Liam Livingstone's birthplace, was always in the County Palatine), Mahmood is a Lancastrian by residence, and Rob Jones comes from Warrington, on the Cheshire side of the Manchester Ship Canal. Members of all counties take pleasure in seeing their team represented by young men who have come through the local schools and leagues. Even the infamous pit of hate, which made Old Trafford such an unwelcoming place, may raise two cheers for Lancashire's imminent promotion to the top division with a side of players from Blackpool, Bolton, Darwen and Preston.

One local lad isn't here. Haseeb Hameed, the opening batsman who impressed when he came into the team at the back end of the 2015 season, as an 18-year-old straight out of Bolton School, has been told he can leave Old Trafford at the end of the season. It's a sad story, yet the outcome wasn't hard to predict. After making 1200 runs in 2016, and winning a place in the England team on the tour of India that winter, his regression has been alarming.

Upon his return from India with a broken finger, he had a thin time. Second season blues, some said, trying to be kind. Last summer his form deserted him completely, and he was dropped. When he began this year with a century in the first match at Lord's everybody hoped the penny had dropped. He had taken on a strong Middlesex attack, and prospered. It turned out to be a mirage. Nine more championship matches brought only 211 runs, and Lancashire announced last month he could leave with their blessing, and make a fresh start.

Lancashire have known this before. In 1975 the left-handed opener, Andy Kennedy, was named Young Cricketer of the Year, which has usually proved to be a stepping stone towards stardom. His career promptly withered on the vine, and he ended up playing Minor Counties cricket for Dorset.

Hameed's fall from grace has been different. People invested such hope in him partly because he is a Muslim, and could be presented to the wider public as a blazer of trails. Their intentions were good, if misplaced. Any sportsman who is appointed representative of a religion or a race carries a burden that might unnerve even the most balanced soul.

When Hameed returned from India, where he had his picture taken 'at home' with Sachin Tendulkar, newspapers were knocking on the door. It was too much, too soon, and the gap that separates hope from hyperbole was soon crossed. A careful batsman whose success in that first full year was grounded in a sound technique allied to a placid temperament, not a palette of colourful strokes, was never the chap others wanted him to be. After three years, waiting patiently for signs of recovery, Lancashire realised they could offer him no more time.

Unlike many young batsmen, who have grown up in the fizz-bang world of instant cricket, Hameed is temperamentally suited to the longer form. For two months in midsummer he must kick his heels, as team-mates don coloured clothes for T20. We are now in the second week of September, and there has been no championship cricket at Old Trafford since 15 July.

It is another Boltonian many Lancastrians are thinking of as autumn begins to nip. Jack Bond, captain of the club between 1968 and 1972, died in July at the age of 87, and there was more than the usual sadness at his passing. He was not a great cricketer. A record of 14 first-class centuries in 18 seasons is not that of a first-rate batsman. A career average of 25 reveals a modest player.

Modest players may be remarkable men, whatever the figures suggest. He was also, as all have testified, a thoroughly good man. Lancashire were a terrible side when Bond was asked to lead them out. When he retired they were the outstanding one-day team of their era, playing to full houses at Old Trafford, and winning three successive Gillette Cup finals at Lord's. Those are the players I remember today, through the mists of Septembers past, wearing the traditional caps with red roses, clad in sweaters fringed by red, blue and green.

In the pavilion a board lists the capped players who have contributed to the story. For the life of me I can't remember Andrew Symonds and Brad Hodge wearing the red rose. They left no trace. I can just about recall V. V. S. Laxman, the Indian charmer. Yet the mind's eye clearly sees Harry Pilling driving through midwicket, right foot hovering above the turf at 45 degrees. He seemed to play that stroke all summer, every summer, throughout my childhood.

A meat and potato pie can release early memories as sweetly as any tea-soaked madeleine. Ken Snellgrove and John Sullivan, like Pilling, were not stars, but I see them too: Sully with the hunched shoulders of the boxer as he was heaving sixes into the Wilson stand; Snellgrove pushing his cover drives to the boundary with the grace, we thought, of Tom Graveney. Ken Shuttleworth, a fast bowler brimming with the vigour of youth, running in from the sightscreen; Peter Lever hitting Farokh Engineer's gloves from the boundary with hard, flat throws from the strongest right arm in cricket.

Michael Kennedy knew the ground in earlier days. Northern editor of the *Daily Telegraph*, a paper he served for 71 years, having started as an errand boy at the age of 15, and a critic known throughout the world of music, Michael enjoyed a professional life of distinction. There was sadness, too, and tragedy. His father walked out on the family when he was young ('we just got on with it, that's what you did'), and he nursed his first wife, Eslyn, who was afflicted with MS, for 50 years before her merciful release enabled him to marry Joyce Bourne, a fellow music lover.

Michael had the good fortune of befriending a great

composer, Ralph Vaughan Williams, and a great conductor, Sir John Barbirolli, the man dubbed 'Glorious John' by Vaughan Williams and known to Michael as J. B. He wrote fine books about both men. Indeed, Vaughan Williams stipulated that he write his biography. That was the measure of their friendship.

It was while serving with the Royal Navy as a teenager that Michael wrote a letter to the composer, praising the fifth symphony, which he had just heard. 'To my great surprise I received a reply, addressed to "Commander" Kennedy, which raised a few eyebrows on deck, as I was only a coder.' Back in England he met Vaughan Williams, who was then in his seventy-fourth year, and impressed him so much that the composer took him into his confidence.

Barbirolli he got to know after the war, when J. B. was the principal conductor of the Halle, Manchester's great orchestra. Giovanni Battista Barbirolli, born in Holborn to an Italian father and a French mother, was a great English patriot. 'On Nelson's birthday, he used to cook a great banquet, with the courses named after naval victories.'

Alarmed by the European war, and appalled by American indifference, Barbirolli returned from the United States to England by boat in 1943. He had gone there seven years earlier, as Toscanini's successor at the New York Philharmonic, an appointment that strengthened a family connection. Barbirolli's father had played violin when Toscanini conducted the first performance of *Otello* at La Scala, Milan, in 1887. When the chance came to come back to England, at the helm of the Halle, he took it, and stayed in Manchester until his death in 1970.

Loved for his warmth as much as his musicianship, Barbirolli was an important influence on the young Daniel Barenboim, when that prodigious young pianist began to conduct. It was Barbirolli who conducted the London Symphony Orchestra in the celebrated recording of Elgar's cello concerto by Barenboim's wife, Jacqueline du Pré, in 1965; an interpretation that reveals as much about Barbirolli as the cellist.

They loved him in Berlin. When the Philharmonie, the hexagonal concert hall, opened in 1963 the opening concerts were shared by Herbert von Karajan, Karl Bohm and Barbirolli. Peter Steiner told me of the day in 1964 when the orchestra recorded Mahler's ninth symphony with him in the Jesus-Christus-Kirche in Dahlem. 'We didn't know it very well. Mahler was not so popular then. Barbirolli joined the cellists in the first movement to show us how it went.' After his death Barenboim conducted the Berliners in a performance of Bruckner's seventh symphony dedicated to his memory.

Barbirolli also loved his cricket, often sitting with Kennedy beneath the scoreboard by the railway line. 'He didn't really want to go in the pavilion. He thought that members would buttonhole him, and demand to know what the Halle were playing next season. Sitting in the cheap seats, so to speak, he felt free to watch cricket in his own way.'

Michael's first great experience as a cricket watcher came at Horsham, during his days at prep school in Sussex, when he saw Wally Hammond make a century for Gloucestershire. His favourite batsman as he grew up was not Cyril Washbrook, the Lancashire opener, as one might imagine, but D. C. S. Compton.

'Denis never let me down. I never saw Bradman get runs, he never made a Test century in Manchester, but Denis never failed. In 1948, I was there when Ray Lindwall hit him on the head. All the papers said Lindwall went easy on him when he came out to bat again. Never! He ran in just the same, trying to knock him over! But Denis came through, 148 not out.'

After Denis came 'Ian'. Michael saw in the young Botham the fearlessness that Arlott noticed when the commentator first met him at Taunton. 'What a cricketer he was!' Never greater than that summer of 1981, when he walloped the Australians all over Old Trafford, making 118 in two hours of splendour. It was the innings of his lifetime, and of all who were witnesses.

It is often forgotten just how murky it was on that Saturday, and how crabby the cricket was in the morning, as Geoffrey Boycott and Chris Tavaré plodded like horses under the plough. When Tavaré came in at lunchtime a member in the pit of hate stepped forward to denounce him as 'a bloody disgrace'.

Botham entered to the cheers of a crowd that recognised his heroics in the two previous Tests at Leeds and Birmingham. The skies remained gloomy. Metaphorically, however, Manchester was soon bathed in celestial light. Australia took the new ball, Botham lined up his sights after a restrained start, and the following hour was all gold. Tavaré occupied the crease for seven hours, and found the boundary three times. Botham was in the middle for two hours, and cleared the boundary six times. It is impossible to tire of that innings.

The finest stroke landed slightly to the left of where I am sitting today, between midwicket and mid-on in the ground's old arrangement. Terry Alderman, that skilful swinger, bowled a ball that was not particularly short, and Botham swivelled to pull it with a bat that sounded like the crack of a whip. Flat and far it flew, into the brick wall at the back of the bleachers.

Old Trafford was giddy with excitement, real excitement, not the kind that can be whipped up today whenever the ball crosses the boundary. Standing by the bell, at the bottom of the steps that led to the dressing rooms, a privilege that seems inconceivable from this distance, I spent the afternoon with my old school friend, Jeremy Ogden, overwhelmed. We all were.

This is the day I place above all, for the generosity of a great player sharing the bounty of his gift with spectators who could hardly believe their fortune. Randall Jarrell, the American writer, thought that old men would recall lines of early Auden in their last hour. Many people at Old Trafford on that sepulchral day may recall Botham's innings, thrown off in the heat of a Test match against Australia like a country boy scrumping apples. It was the sense of fun that made it unforgettable. 'A cricketer,' as John Arlott said, 'is showing you his character all the time.' That innings will be his memorial.

His deeds that summer, after he had resigned the captaincy at Lord's, are as familiar as the five times table. Within four matches the broken man became the king of England, and the coronation was at Old Trafford. The century at Headingley was an inspired slog. His bowling at Edgbaston punished some palsied Australian batting. Old Trafford saw Botham at his height, with the bat and at second slip, where he held a storming catch to dismiss Dennis Lillee.

At The Oval, in the final Test, when the other bowlers had gone lame, this titan bowled 47 overs. Little wonder his teammates loved him as much as the rest of us. Without question Botham is the greatest English cricketer of my lifetime. His knighthood for services to cricket and leukaemia research speaks on his behalf but, really, he should have been awarded a baronetcy.

Greatness cannot be measured by facts alone. An outline of Botham's career shows that he averaged 'only' 34 in Tests. Those who saw him fully robed will disregard that statistic. He changed the course of Test matches, with bat and ball, when the outcome lay in the balance. That is the measure of greatness. To do it with such playfulness, smiling between sixes, made spectators love him even more. He brought, as Mike Brearley said, a touch of the village green to the most demanding stage.

'What a player he was,' Michael Kennedy liked to say. 'One of the pleasure givers, like Denis.' And there's no law against that.

Michael died on the last day of 2014, at the age of 88. He had known tragedy in his life, and the lives of others. On duty with the Royal Navy he witnessed the aftermath of Hiroshima. He had known greatness, too, and the great ones responded to him, understanding he would never write anything he would not say to their face. Knowing that I was to go to Chicago, where Barenboim was conducting his final week of concerts with that city's magnificent orchestra in June 2006, Michael offered to write a letter of introduction. Barenboim took one look, and beckoned me into the green room, where he lent me an hour of time he did not have to surrender.

At Michael's funeral, where I helped to carry the coffin, Sir Mark Elder, who now stands before the Halle as Barbirolli once did, gave an address that chimed the grace notes. Conducting the orchestra's next concert in Bridgewater Hall, he began with the *Tallis Fantasia* by Vaughan Williams. Later that year, at a memorial concert at the Royal Northern College of Music, musicians and singers came from all over the world to pay tribute to a man whose life had touched so many.

He wrote many books about music, including biographies of Britten and Mahler, and an outstanding portrait of Richard Strauss. Sometimes Michael claimed to be the only person in England who understood that prickly genius. There were books about the Halle, *natürlich*, and the city of Manchester, where he was born in 1926, and never left after he had returned from wartime service.

I was born here, too, but Manchester is no longer mine. The city of political liberalism, free trade and cultural breadth has shifted on its axis. What Alan Bennett wrote of Liverpool, that the people have acquired a cockiness that comes from being told too often they are special, has come to pass here. No, I am an Englishman, from Lancashire. Birth is merely an accident of geography.

The mills and burning chimneys have gone, and we can all celebrate that. The soot-encrusted buildings have been cleaned. 'Cottonopolis', the world's first industrial city, considered by Disraeli to be 'as great a human exploit as Athens', is now full of fashionable hotels, bars and restaurants. There is a gay village, where the local television news programmes seem to interview people every week. There's progress there, too.

It's not long since Alan Turing, the so-called father of the computer, lived and died in Manchester when homosexuality was a crime that led to imprisonment and, in his case, chemical castration.

And yet.

There's a hole in the modern city. The Manchester which enticed Hans Richter from Vienna to run the Halle, where Annie Horniman established the first provincial repertory theatre, and aesthetes-in-waiting such as Neville Cardus and Anthony Burgess educated themselves, has changed colour. There are great libraries here, the Portico, the John Rylands, the Central, yet the modern city prefers its representatives to act dumb. Its symbol is a pop group, Oasis, who, lacking high talent, degenerated into a 1960s tribute band. Much was made of their admiration for the Beatles. Angels and ministers of grace defend us! Where the Fab Four were original and witty, and possessed a melodic gift that bordered on the supernatural, Oasis specialised in rancid stupidity.

The Mancunian youth culture's regimental goat was a Cambridge-educated television presenter called Tony Wilson, who cultivated a self-image as some latter-day Diaghilev. The Russian impresario, he neglected to note, had Stravinsky and Nijinsky to do his bidding. He lived in Paris in the early decades of the twentieth century, when men of genius lived on every street.

Modern Manchester could never be mistaken for Paris, however much Wilson gilded the lily. It is the city of *Shameless*, a television drama in which David Threlfall, a superlative actor, played an alcoholic slob who had never done a hand's turn.

The show was amusing, up to a point, as was *The Royle Family*, another drama about Mancunian idlers.

In real life those people are never funny. One, a drug-addled pop singer, was held up by Wilson as a poet in the tradition of Yeats. Perhaps he meant Yates, as in Eddie, the man who emptied the bins on *Coronation Street*. A letter writer to the *Daily Telegraph* in 2002, when Manchester staged the Commonwealth Games, said any person seen publicly reading a book in Denton, where *Shameless* was set, ran the risk of assault.

Nor is Old Trafford, where I spent so many enchanted hours in my childhood, the place it was. The ground was never pretty, and before its restoration it was falling to pieces, but it was at least a cricket ground. Now it is a stadium without a soul, and without a sense of history. It exists to stage pop concerts and conferences, and cater for the supporters who attend the other Old Trafford, half a mile up the road.

Had the ground not been gutted in 2011, there would be no cricket here at all. That must be acknowledged. Full marks to Jim Cumbes, the chief executive during some stormy years, when Lancashire nearly folded. He saw the job through when others might have given up.

Close to ruination a decade ago, Lancashire are in clover. The ground can cram in 26,000 spectators for Test matches, 8000 of them in the temporary stand, which serves as the stage at the pop concerts – and cram is the appropriate verb. At the Test match last month there was hardly room to breathe, still less move, in the alleys beneath the stands.

The red-brick Victorian pavilion, the only feature of architectural distinction, has become a functional block of glass and steel, and gained an extra floor for the benefit for executive clubbers, without whom no sporting event may proceed. It holds hands with the Point and the new hotel, which resemble Fafner and Fasolt, the giants in Wagner's *Ring* cycle. Oh for a newly forged Nothung, the sword of destiny, to cut them down, and return the ring to the flat-capped Rhinemaidens in the Ship Canal!

That pavilion was the focal point of Old Trafford. The players walked out through its gates, and returning batsmen who had conquered were greeted by an ovation which spread round the ground. It was part of the game's ritual. Now the players are quartered in an ugly three-storey building directly opposite, by the railway line. There is no sense of theatre when they come in or go out.

Members have become customers. They mooch about the spruced-up pavilion like survivors of a tornado, unable to understand what has happened. The refreshment hall on the ground floor is like a canteen at a motorway service station. The library, where those odd folk who come to watch the cricket like to spend idle hours reflecting on those who have gone before, is no more. The temple has been sacked.

There are no blessings on this pilgrimage. The ground that meant everything to me has been cleared. The feelings I thought would last for ever have evaporated. There are only echoes of the golden years, and ghosts, like those of the 'run stealers' Francis Thompson glimpsed in his famous poem about Hornby and Barlow. The poem that Harold Pinter liked to read to his Gaieties team-mates at the end of each summer, as a benediction.

It's gone. That was clear during the Test, when I suddenly felt like a stranger in a place I had known all my life. I take one last look and leave, through the door marked nevermore that wasn't there before.

IX

At Grass

Taunton

'Keep silence now, for singing time is over.'
Swinburne is a perfumed scent few modern readers want to wear. He batted at the fag end of the Romantic age, after the famed middle order of Keats, Shelley and Byron had hogged the bowling, and sometimes didn't get to the crease at all. Even scholars find him recherché, and his manners would have shamed a pig. But he wrote one of the most plangent leave takings in our language, the one that chimed: 'though we sang as angels in her ear, she would not hear'.

Singing time is never over. The balladeers will always be with us and in 1975, when hippies were starting to clip their beards, Roy Harper took another kind of leave. Harper was a folkie who rode the electric wave in the early 1970s, when he became fashionable for about half an hour. That was the length, if memory serves, of one of the songs he played at Repton in 1972.

He enjoyed his cricket, as did many of those minstrels, and his song of farewell was prompted by memories of players of his youth. 'When an Old Cricketer Leaves the Crease' appears simple enough but the feelings it releases are more tangled. During its seven minutes the listener is nudged, though not in a manipulative way, towards a gentler world.

The song begins with bare, almost provisional chords on a 12-string guitar, as Harper sings words of completion, though his projection is really speech on the brink of song, like a slow bowler leaping into the crease at the point of release:

> When the day is done
> And the ball has spun
> In the umpire's pocket away

It is autumn, and the shadows are lengthening. A season has run its course, and the players are putting away their bats, some for the last time. The verse, descriptive and wistful, leads to a declamatory chorus, sung in a higher pitch, as the singer raises the emotional temperature:

> When an old cricketer leaves the crease
> Well you never know whether he's gone.
> If sometimes you catch a fleeting glimpse
> Of a twelfth man at silly mid-on.

Unlike Larkin he is not lamenting the alteration of a cherished landscape. He is reflecting on the biblical adage: all things must pass. Then, to make the general particular, he invokes the names of two contemporary cricketers.

It could be Geoff, and it could be John.

In 1975 those names were familiar to all. They still resonate. 'Geoff' is Boycott of Yorkshire, the most famous batsman in the land when the song was recorded, though he had chosen to absent himself from Test cricket the year before, and did not return to the colours until 1977. 'John' is Snow of Sussex, who bowled beautifully at Lord's that summer against Australia. Both men were held to be members of the awkward squad, which may have tickled Harper, who dedicated the song to them.

Batsman and bowler; north and south; the son of a miner and the son of a clergyman. Boycott and Snow represent both sides of cricket's coin. One was intense, and only felt alive when he gripped a bat and told opponents 'get past that'. The other slipped happily into normal life, and wrote poetry. But the song was really about all those men who, in John Arlott's phrase, are 'cricketers of the heart'. It is a song for Everyman.

> It could be me, and it could be thee,
> Or it could be the sting in the ale.

What crowns it is the appearance of the Grimethorpe Colliery Band after the first chorus, in an arrangement by David Bedford. Their cornets evoke the world of yesterday, filtered through the golden haze of communal memory. Snow and Boycott join Trueman and Statham, from the songwriter's youth, in a round dance led by Grace and Fry. 'Those fabled men', Harper says, in the song's clinching line, 'are more than just yarns of their day'. 'Those fabled men': only three words, yet they suggest a life of recollection and yearning. Like Pinter's 'beautiful evening' at Lord's, the memories of favoured players merge in ways that send an emotional tremor through the bones of all cricket-lovers. They live on, through embroidered tales, to be remembered whenever people reminisce about days of friendship and great feats.

Harper forms another link with the past. He was born in Rusholme, like Cardus, and brought up in Lytham St Annes on the Fylde coast, a dozen miles from Preston, the birthplace of Francis Thompson, author of that famous poem about Hornby, Barlow and 'the flickering ghosts'. The hippie and the opium-addicted Catholic mystic, who wrote *The Hound of Heaven*, found common ground in recalling cricketers from the past. Three quirky Lancastrians, yoked together by a love of bat and ball. Invisible bonds permeate the game like bees in a comb.

In October 1992, when the few remaining pits in Yorkshire were closed, I went to Grimethorpe, to hear the famous colliery band play at Nostell Priory, near Wakefield. The next day I accompanied the bandsmen on the coach to London. That weekend they were named champion brass band of Great Britain at the national championship in the Royal Albert Hall. The story was told on screen a few years later in *Brassed Off*, a film that took a few liberties. The men I met in Yorkshire were solid types, who did not swear. They called their conductor 'Mr Howarth' out of respect, not fawning. The film, entertaining as it was, diminished them.

Ian Bousfield, who grew up in York, was a bandsman in his youth. He played trombone in the National Youth Orchestra, before he joined the Halle in Manchester and then the London

Symphony Orchestra. Eventually he reached Vienna, and the city's great Philharmonic, where he spent a decade before he retired to Switzerland, where he teaches, collects good wine, and follows Yorkshire cricket from afar.

One night, in Carnegie Hall, Pierre Boulez was conducting the Vienna Philharmonic in *Boléro*, the piece that Maurice Ravel, its composer, said was a masterpiece without music. 'It was bloody slow,' said Ian. 'I thought it would go on for ever. Suddenly I remembered Ian Botham's innings against Australia at Headingley. New York is going to get a surprise, I said to myself. When the trombone comes in, I didn't half give it some umpty! The wind players turned round to see what was going on, and Boulez looked pretty startled.'

Botham was a Somerset man, as well as the hero of all England. Like Arthur Wellard, the great six-hitter of the county's past, he could fit snugly into Harper's elegiac world of country folk taking their pleasure on the green. There is no need to keep silence. It is September, the end of summer, when we sing our goodbyes.

An old cricketer is leaving the crease at Taunton. Marcus Trescothick is 43, which puts him among the ancients, and has made 26,234 runs in first-class cricket, starting in 1993. That's 27 years of service. He scored 5825 of those runs for England in 76 Tests, before he called time on his life as an international sportsman. Here is another of those fabled men. In Somerset he stands almost as tall as Botham and Vivian Richards.

Trescothick, it is clear, has played one year too many. He has made only five championship appearances this season, and contributed 86 runs. He is not playing in the final match, against Essex, though everybody wants him to enjoy a taste of honey before he goes. To claim the championship for the first time in the club's history Somerset must win. But Essex, 11 points ahead, are in no mood to yield. While Somerset were losing last week at Hampshire, dismissed twice by Kyle Abbott, who ended up with 17 wickets, they were thumping Surrey at Chelmsford. The weather forecast is unpromising. It will rain for much of the week, and every session lost suits the visitors.

Four times this century Somerset have finished second. They thought they were champions in 2010, only to be denied when Nottinghamshire's bowlers snatched a bonus point in the last session of the season. Six years later, having wrapped up proceedings with a victory that put them on top of the table with two hours left, they watched aghast as Yorkshire collapsed at Lord's, and a hat-trick by Toby Roland-Jones gave Middlesex the championship.

They feel left out in Taunton. For most of their history they have been the club 'down there', beyond the Somerset Levels, to be patronised or ignored altogether. Even when Botham joined forces with two of the great modern players, 'King Viv' and Joel 'Big Bird' Garner, the championship title proved as illusory as Camelot.

Those stars, supported by an able cast of locals including Peter 'Dasher' Denning, Vic Marks, Peter Roebuck and Brian Rose, won five one-day trophies between 1979 and 1983, but they could never boast of being the best team in the land. The years of glory did not bring the trophy that would have settled the argument. In the end that failure led to a schism in the

autumn of 1986, which separated one half of the dressing room
from the other. There followed the departure of the three men
who had done most to make Somerset a strong team for the
first time in the club's history.

They have been excluded in other ways. When the Hundred
starts in 2020 there will be no Somerset team based at Taunton.
Instead the county has been lumped in with Glamorgan at
Cardiff, and their players will represent 'Welsh Fire'. They are
not happy about it, and it is easy to lend a sympathetic ear. But
Somerset are not an influential club, and Glamorgan's Welsh
identity is more useful to an England and Wales Cricket Board
that wants a geographical balance when they unveil the new
tournament.

Taunton, in the west of the county, is cut off. The Somerset
of legend is found further east, between Glastonbury and Bath,
the Roman city that John Arlott thought was his favourite in
the world. There are hills in the west. Many cricketers, led by
Jack 'Farmer' White, the county's record wicket-taker, have
wandered down from the Quantocks. But the low-lying acres
as you cross the Levels make for an incomplete landscape.

This is a land of mist and water, soaked in a melancholy that
can feel oppressive. As Auden wrote of Brussels in winter, it has
lost 'the certainty that constitutes a thing'. Much of Somerset
resembles an unfinished watercolour. The towns lack interest.
The villages, named after every saint in the calendar, are dull.
The people look fearful. The atmosphere is spooky.

Perhaps, when considering how this mood is rooted in native
soil, we should start with Geoffrey of Monmouth, who put King
Arthur and the Isle of Avalon at the heart of our island story in

the early years of the twelfth century. By 1485, when Sir Thomas Malory published *Le Morte d'Arthur*, the Knights of the Round Table were international stars. Through that infallible sieve of history they have slipped. Arthur, 'the once and future king'; Guinevere and Lancelot, the lovers; Merlin, the magician. Excalibur, the famous 'sword in the stone', the Holy Grail, the Fisher King, courtly love and knightly chivalry have found their way into other cultures, hymned by writers and musicians from Purcell to Roxy Music by way of Wagner, Lerner and Loewe, and Crosby, Stills and Nash. *Parsifal* and Monty Python, Tennyson and *Camelot*. What a long, strange trip it's been.

Mark Twain, that intrepid traveller, was not the only American writer to use the Arthurian legend as quarry. In 1959 John Steinbeck of Salinas, California, lived for six months near Bruton, with a view of Glastonbury Tor. In this retreat he prepared an updating of the Arthurian legend he never, alas, completed. His publisher, thinking the novelist had taken leave of his senses, showed little interest. Yet Steinbeck counted the half year in Somerset among the happiest days he had known.

John Cowper Powys did complete a book, a whacking big one, about the Grail legend. *A Glastonbury Romance*, published in 1932, takes 1100 pages to unfold. One chapter describes the west wind blowing through the town at night. Another, at the heart of the book, shows the townsfolk going about their business on Midsummer Day. It's as if the *Oberammergau Passion Play* has come to Somerset.

Powys, the eldest of 12 children born to an Anglican clergyman, is one of the most unusual, not to say forbidding, figures in English literature. He has often been compared with Dostoevsky.

George Steiner, the cultural critic, thought Powys was the only English novelist comparable with the Russian. Other points of reference are Proust, Blake, D. H. Lawrence and Nietzsche.

Brought up in the rectory at Montacute, near Yeovil, Powys was educated at Sherborne School, and *Wolf Solent*, his best-known novel, is set nearby. He spent the first three decades of the twentieth century in America, where he wrote the longest of his six novels, which, taken together, form a West Country legend of their own. In his later years he decamped to Wales, where he lived as a latter-day Merlin without the magical powers.

Influenced initially by Hardy, to whom he dedicated his first novel, Powys should not be regarded as Hardy's heir. Nature, in the younger man's imagination, is seen through a filter of magic, mystery and sexual perversion. Hardy's universe may be dark. Powys paints in colours that verge on the supernatural. It's a strange world, which repels more readers than it attracts. Those readers who are drawn in find it intoxicating, if distasteful. The characters he brings to life are not always wholesome.

Some part of this sadness and mystery may be found in Somerset cricket. Harold Gimblett, the club's leading run-maker, and Peter Roebuck, the captain who led the revolt against the stars in 1986, both took their own lives. So did R. C. Robertson-Glasgow, the bowler and writer known as 'Crusoe'. Although he was not a Somerset man by birth he was thoroughly assimilated, playing for the county between 1920 and 1935.

Gimblett was a countryman, from Bicknoller in the Quantocks. Roebuck, the son of teachers, attended Millfield and Cambridge. Opposites in terms of class, temperament and style at the crease, they were united across the decades by their deep personal unease.

Few batsmen have introduced themselves with such directness as Gimblett, who played his first match in 1935, against Essex at Frome. Entering on the fall of the sixth wicket, he clobbered 123 runs in an hour and 20 minutes, an innings that did much to win the match. Feted as the great hope of Somerset cricket (although the club had originally told him he wasn't good enough), he played the first of three Test matches next summer, against India. He made runs, too, but international cricket was not his thing. 'Thank goodness that's over,' he said, when he was allowed to shuffle off back to Taunton, where he felt comfy among people who understood him.

He suffered a breakdown in 1953 and, after retiring the following summer, never adjusted to life after cricket. David Foot, in one of the most sympathetic biographies ever written of a sportsman, followed Gimblett's decline to his self-willed death by an overdose of pills in 1978. The poor man never felt good enough. Those he left behind held a higher view of his talent. The county ground has created Gimblett's Hill, by the churchyard of St James's, whose tower stands watch at long-off.

If Gimblett belonged in Hardy's world of men damned by Fate, Roebuck could have stepped from the pages of Powys. He was an intelligent, contrary man of enthusiasms, hastily acquired and just as easily dropped. He travelled far, to Australia and southern Africa, and could never throw off the shackles of a profound unhappiness. Loner is not a sufficient term. He belonged in a world where he heard only one voice, and ultimately it drove him mad.

The early days held exceptional promise. He played for Somerset seconds at 13, and made runs all the way through school and university, where he took a degree in Law. A dogged opening batsman, completely different to Gimblett the basher, Roebuck never dragged drinkers away from the bar.

When he joined the county's first team in 1974 he enjoyed the great advantage of being captained by Brian Close, whose leadership made men of the talented, if callow, youngsters who were growing up at Taunton. He also enjoyed the good fortune of playing his cricket alongside Botham, Richards and Garner, which made the eventual enforced parting so painful.

Unlike Gimblett, Roebuck never played Test cricket. He wasn't quite good enough, even in a thin year, and England knew a few of those in the 1980s. The lack of international recognition did not wound him, for he understood he wasn't equipped for the highest level. Instead he moved into journalism and made a lively impression as an essayist of firm views, and became an author. One of his books was a history of Somerset cricket.

He could never, however, suppress his urges. In 2001 he was convicted at Taunton Crown Court on three counts of actual bodily harm, and given a four-month jail sentence on each, suspended for two years. Roebuck, who had spent much of his adult life in Australia, moved to Sydney permanently, and became an Australian citizen, heaping praise on his adopted country and rarely missing a chance to belittle the land of his birth.

On radio, as a summariser for the ABC, he put on a faux Aussie voice, which fooled few listeners. It was an act of conscious rejection, a sad one in the ears of British visitors, who found his ventriloquism unconvincing. They had known him in his earlier life, and although they were not privy to his secrets, they understood there was more to his sculpted personality than many Australians, for whom he was an exotic fruit in a straw hat.

The court case was a humiliation. Roebuck was a didact in the manner of Narziss, the instructor in Hermann Hesse's *Narcissus and Goldmund*, his great novel of master and pupil. He had done some teaching in Sydney, and throughout his life he took young men under his protection, to educate them through word and deed, hoping that one might turn out to be Goldmund.

At Taunton the Cambridge graduate who had captained Somerset, and led the fight against Richards and Garner in 1986, was exposed as a pervert. The court heard how he had beaten three South African teenagers, who were spending an English summer in his house, for failing to live up to the standards he expected. Passing sentence, the judge noted how he had ordered one boy 'to fetch the cane'. He had behaved in a manner, he said, 'to satisfy some need in you, whatever that may have been'.

He might have followed the example of Dennis Silk, another Somerset man, who played cricket for Cambridge and the county before becoming a schoolmaster. Silk, who died in June 2019, ended up as Warden of Radley College and president of MCC. On his watch Radley was widely thought to be one of England's finest public schools. That was the life Roebuck could have had.

Alternating between Sydney and Pietermaritzburg in South Africa, Roebuck continued to tutor adolescents in matters intellectual and physical. He used his own money to set up a fund that helped young South Africans and Zimbabweans get to university. It was a noble gesture. Yet rumours abounded.

In November 2011, when police officers entered his hotel room in Cape Town, where he was covering a Test match between South Africa and Australia, he leaped from a window on the sixth floor. Aware that some of his 'boys' were prepared to give evidence against him in a court of law, he decided he had lived long enough. He was 55.

One of the obituaries carried a revealing photograph taken in those starry-eyed days at Somerset. It showed Botham at the crease, giving the impression he had not a care in the world. Watching from the boundary was Roebuck, regarding his team-mate with an envy the camera could not disguise.

That shot told the story of two lives, shared for so long, so differently. Botham lived freely; if not without doubt, then certainly with no self-doubt. Roebuck, suspicious of people, withdrew from life in case it should be noised abroad that he liked it. The talents he wanted so desperately to possess, for cricket, friendship and ease in his own skin, had been granted to a man he admired and then turned against with a ferocity that undid him.

In retirement he was a bitter man. He would tell anybody within earshot that Botham, assisted by unnamed 'friends', was determined to bring him down. It was fantasy. Botham never gave him a moment's thought. Roebuck brought himself down, through obsessive behaviour that crossed the line into criminality, and a self-loathing he tried to pass off as independent thought. In Australia it worked, for a while. In England, where people knew him better, he was regarded with pity.

For a man who was deliberately unclubbable he could be jolly company when he lowered his guard. In February 1996 we travelled in an old-fashioned Morris Minor from Bombay to Pune for the World Cup match between West Indies and Kenya. The journey took five hours there, and another five back the following day, after Kenya had pulled off one of the great shocks, beating Richie Richardson's team by 73 runs.

Roebuck didn't watch the game, opting to catch up on the local culture. His match report for the *Sydney Morning Herald*, assembled from the verbal accounts of witnesses, was nevertheless one of his best. He was good fun during that World Cup, and his writing matched his mood. If only he had presented that face to the world more often.

When he retired from county cricket in 1991 his place at the top of the Somerset order was taken by Mark Lathwell, a Devonian who made such a startling impression that England called him up in 1993 to open the batting against Australia. Here was a player who owed more to Gimblett than Roebuck; a strokemaker of exceptional gifts. Those two Tests he played as a 21-year-old were his first and last. By 2001, exhausted by pressures he found intolerable, he went back to Braunton.

It was a loss for club and country. The young Lathwell looked set to take on the world. Sadly, although he didn't find it at all sad, the professional game held few attractions for this withdrawn man. If he could have played all his cricket at

Taunton he might have prospered. But the world does not adjust to the whims of the wilful, however cleanly they may strike a ball. Another solitary Somerset cricketer left the stage, leaving observers to ponder anew.

Trescothick's early career simmered on a low flame. Although he made his debut in 1993, as a 17-year-old, it took seven years to reach the Test team when Duncan Fletcher, newly installed as coach, took a punt on his potential rather than his record, which was modest. Fletcher was proved right, from the first ball. Trescothick was one of those batsmen, such as Michael Vaughan, who came alive in Test cricket.

He made runs everywhere, against all types of bowling. In Sri Lanka in 2001, on a spiteful pitch at Galle, and in searing heat, he made a magnificent maiden Test century. England lost the match, but won the series. By the time he made 219 against South Africa at The Oval in the summer of 2003, turning round an unpromising position so that England went on to claim an improbable victory, he was a batsman of true Test class.

One of his finest innings came in the second Test against Australia in that extraordinary summer of 2005. Australia had vanquished England in the first match, at Lord's, which marked Kevin Pietersen's Test debut. When England batted at Birmingham, after Ricky Ponting told them to have first go, Trescothick set the innings on a roar by hitting Brett Lee's first ball for four. He made bigger scores but the 90 runs he scored that morning from 102 balls helped to shape the game, which England won narrowly. They went on to take the series, after winning at Trent Bridge, and holding out at The Oval in a day that has gone down in the annals.

All this is well-known, as is the barking of the black dog that brought Trescothick's Test career to a premature end. He returned from the tour of India in February 2006, seeking the sanctuary of home. Hoping the skies would clear he went to Australia that autumn, played two matches, and returned again, broken. A book published two years later, *Coming Back to Me*, opened a few eyes about the nature of depression. It won awards, and admiration for a man who was not scared to share his story with a wider public.

A thread of solitariness runs through the fabric of Somerset cricket. Occasionally, as with Gimblett and Trescothick, it translates into a depression no amount of runs will overcome.

Alan Gibson, another Somerset man, was yet another sufferer. A fine writer, and for many years a courtly presence on *Test Match Special*, Gibson had glimpsed the glittering prizes. He took a First in History at Oxford, where he served as President of the Union. He was a poet, an all-round broadcaster and a writer on many subjects, with an enviably light touch.

His cricket reporting in *The Times* earned him a fan club. It was Gibson who dubbed Colin Dredge, the Somerset medium-pace bowler, 'the Demon of Frome' and he conferred upon John Woodcock, the great *Times* cricket correspondent, a title that has stuck: 'the sage of Longparish'. For many summers Gibson entertained readers with tales of changing trains at Didcot. One morning, arriving late at Southampton to find that Somerset were five wickets down, he asked a gateman what had happened, and the answer gave him his 'intro' the next day: 'Lost toss. Green seamer. Marshall.'

The drink got to him, and the big black dog pounced. The

Liberal parliamentary candidate and Baptist lay preacher died an unhappy man. How deeply this West Country melancholy seeps into the soul, like water through the boots. Gibson and Roebuck were men of intellectual resources. Gimblett and Trescothick were, it seemed, less complicated. You don't need to read Powys to understand there's something unsettling about this porous county.

Oh, that rain. For two days Taunton is under water, and the players spend more time in their dressing-rooms than the middle. Not a ball is bowled on the third day. On the final morning of the season the weather relents, and the umpires agree that play can resume at noon but after two overs they're off again. If you expect to play county cricket in the last week of September, an angry Somerset member tells anybody who will listen, this is what you'll get.

They get on again, though, and the Somerset spinners take advantage of a bare pitch, which is spinning like a top. Three times an over the fielders throw up their arms as Jack Leach, Roelof van der Merwe and Dom Bess, two left armers and an off-spinner, tie the Essex batsmen in knots. In the pavilion, on Gimblett's Hill, and in the new Somerset pavilion, the partisan hopes of witnessing something astonishing have not been extinguished.

After lunch there is a reversal of fortune. Alastair Cook and Tom Westley take the score to 102, batting watchfully. Westley, in particular, makes no attempt to score runs, content to block it out until the cows come down from the Quantocks. When he and Cook are out, though, there is a mighty rush of wickets. Somerset take the last nine for 39 runs, and Essex are all out for 141. Leach, one of England's men of the summer, takes five for 32, and there are four for van der Merwe.

What now? Is there time for Somerset to pull one last rabbit from this summer of peculiar hats? They forgo their second innings, and challenge Essex to make 63 runs for victory in an hour and six minutes. To the third ball, bowled by Leach, Nick Browne offers a chance to Vijay, the squarer of two leg slips, but he puts the ball down, to the dismay of spectators who have convinced themselves a miracle is about to happen.

At half past four, as the umpires indicate the last hour is upon us, the sun comes out for the first time since Monday morning. Somerset have 16 overs to achieve their fondest wish. Cook and Browne, who have wishes of their own, stand resolute. The overs slip by.

To warm applause, and a few cheers, Trescothick trots on to the field at 12 minutes past five, to perform his last deed as a professional cricketer, as substitute fielder. Two balls later Browne is caught at slip, and Bess takes the final wicket of the season. At 5.22, with Essex 18 runs short of victory, the players shake hands. A draw leaves honour on both sides, and Trescothick is accorded a guard of honour as he walks into his new life as an ex-cricketer.

Before he goes, Cook gives him a warm embrace. There is feeling, and meaning, in this exchange. Cook, the leading English run scorer in Tests, won the first of his 161 caps, another England record, as a replacement for Trescothick in Nagpur after the Somerset man had flown home. He opened his account with a century in the second innings, and added another 31 hundreds before he retired from Test cricket last autumn.

'Those are my runs he's making,' a more selfish man might have thought. Had he been granted a clearer mind Trescothick might well have established the batting records that stand next to Cook's name in *Wisden*. He was the fastest batsman to 5000 runs in Tests, and had the world at his feet. He was 30 when the fog of depression descended; a batsman of high talent in the prime of life.

The Essex players return from the pavilion to receive the championship trophy, for the second time in three years. There is the usual horseplay, and spraying of champagne, acclaimed by perhaps a hundred of their members, who have spent four sodden days awaiting this moment.

A season that began on 5 April, two weeks before Easter, ends with a misty view of the Quantocks, towards Combe Florey, where Evelyn Waugh spent the last decade of his life. Sydney Smith, the great wit, lived there in the nineteenth century, as Rector of the Church of St Peter and St Paul. His idea of Heaven, he said, was eating foie gras to the sound of trumpets.

There are no trumpets to be heard this evening, only a few muted cornets in the ears of those who recall Harper's lament. A cricketer has left the crease for the last time. Those who watch him go wait awhile, hoping to glimpse a twelfth man at silly mid-on.

'Credences of summer,' Wallace Stevens called them. Those 'fidgets of remembrance' that call us back to days when the sun shone and the hammock swung.

Talking once to Stephen Sondheim, another master of language, I confessed that although I warmed to Stevens I didn't understand his poetry. 'Neither do I,' he replied, 'and I studied him at college!' There's rather more of that trickery where poets are concerned than interpreters are prepared to admit. Auden in his whimsical moods used to pluck lines out of one poem and stick them in another. Take that, you scholars.

What credences shall we carry from this summer, before cricket shatters into a thousand fragments?

England's one-day cricketers won the World Cup for the first time. There's no arguing with that. The Test team shared a series 2–2 with Australia, twice coming from behind. The link was Ben Stokes, whose 84 unbeaten runs in the World Cup final enabled England to force a tie, with the scores level at 241, and prevail after the first-ever 'super over' when he was again at the crease. He then made an extraordinary century at Headingley, 135 not out, as England won the nerve-jangling third Test by one wicket.

In 2019 Stokes was granted a boon offered to few sportsmen: the permission to write his own reviews. The man whose career lay in the balance when he was suspended by the ECB after violent incidents outside a Bristol bar in September 2017 was ordained as a world champion. He had been suspended by the ECB, and missed a tour of Australia, before prosecutors failed to win a conviction on the charge of affray. Now he was a free man, and how. His reversal of fortune had people humming one of Sondheim's best-known songs: 'Good times and bum times, I've known them all and, my dear, I'm still here'. This summer Stokes was everywhere.

Headingley turned out to be the summer's main course, as it was in 1981. When Jack Leach, the last man, joined Stokes England still needed 73, six runs more than the team had managed in their pitiful first innings. Blocking the balls that Stokes trusted him to face, wiping his spectacles between overs, Leach became the summer's most unlikely hero. One run he contributed, but what a run. Stokes bashed away at the other end, striking eight sixes, to claim one of the great victories. No England team had ever reached a target of 359 in the fourth innings of a Test. As in 1981, when Botham and Bob Willis turned round the match that had passed them by, the country seemed to stand still. Only Test cricket, which has five acts, can do that.

Stokes, born in New Zealand to a father who played rugby league, came to England as a 12-year-old. He learned his cricket at school in Cockermouth, the Cumbrian town where the young Wordsworth wandered lonely as a cloud. Nobody doubted his identity, or his loyalty to Durham and England. National identity, however, remained an ideological battle-ground all year long.

The first shots were heard in May when Jonathan Agnew, the BBC's experienced cricket correspondent, pondered on the wisdom of selecting Jofra Archer, the Sussex fast bowler, for England's 50-over team. Archer, born in Barbados to an English father, had played for the West Indies under-19 team, and just completed a qualifying period reduced from seven years to the three he had spent in England.

Agnew did not prosecute his case on the player's biography. As a fast bowler for Leicestershire and England, who learned a thing or two about the human chemistry of a dressing-room in his own career, he wondered whether Archer's promotion within a month of serving his qualification period might affect the balance of a team that had been carefully prepared for the World Cup over the previous four years. Chris Woakes, one of England's regulars, made a similar point in a radio interview. Archer's selection meant that a player would miss out, and late demotions have been known to disturb a side's equilibrium.

It was a reasonable question, which did not receive a universally reasonable response. In some quarters Agnew was portrayed as a backwoodsman. The overwhelming majority of cricket lovers, who find him a reassuring presence on the radio, did not support that view. Yet some people did, and the summer began on a peevish note.

Archer presented his argument with the ball, bowling quickly and well. In the World Cup final he was trusted by Eoin Morgan, the England captain, to bowl the 'super over' that determined the match. It cost 15 runs, perhaps the least expensive 15 runs a bowler has ever conceded in six balls, as England were deemed to be winners on a count-back of boundaries struck during the two regular innings. The new boy was a hero; if not of all England, then certainly for a joyous hour at Lord's as MCC members swatted aside decades of prudence to swell the scenes of madness.

In the days after that victory, which put a spring in the step of all English cricketers, Morgan received much praise for the way he had forged a winning team from the ashes of the previous campaign, four years before, when England were humbled by Bangladesh. 'Team spirit' was passed off as an elixir, as if it could be bottled at will and sold to anybody who had a prescription.

Sport is never so straightforward. England did not cover themselves in glory in the opening round of World Cup matches when Pakistan, Sri Lanka and Australia beat them. In any of the previous 11 finals they would not have been judged winners, as New Zealand lost fewer wickets in their innings. How thin the margins are, and how tender the budding rose of team spirit. Had England not collected four runs from overthrows in the final over of their innings there would have been no retrospective talk of team spirit at all. They would have been judged either as plucky losers or, in the unlovely language of the day, 'chokers'.

Ultimate victory banishes all doubts, heals all rifts, and bathes the victorious in light eternal. It was still a bit of a surprise to read the day after England had turned Lord's into a playground that they had been 'destined' to win the tournament. Yet that is the verb Moeen Ali used to explain their success. After they had lost to Australia he told his team-mates they were bound to come through. Like the conquest of the West it was manifest destiny!

Morgan, asked whether England had enjoyed the luck of the Irish, replied gently that Allah had been on their side. One Muslim, Adil Rashid, played in the final. Another, Moeen, had appeared in some of the matches. It was meant to be an amusing response but it enabled some observers to set loose a few multi-cultural hares. England had won, apparently, because their team represented a diverse nation.

It didn't take long to unravel the premise of that proposal.

Four members of the winning team were born overseas: Morgan, Stokes, Archer and Jason Roy. Adil Rashid was born in England to Pakistani parents. In 1992, when England lost a World Cup final to Pakistan, they fielded six foreign-born players: Derek Pringle, Gladstone Small, Phillip DeFreitas, Dermot Reeve, Allan Lamb and Robin Smith. There was no talk of multi-culturalism then. There was no need. When you are selected to play for your country the only thing that counts is talent.

Moeen unwittingly let the cat out of the bag in his news-paper column. 'It doesn't matter where you come from,' he wrote, 'or what you believe in.' Quite right. A sportsman should be judged on his performance, not on the way he votes or prays. His personal background, while it may be interesting, ought never to get in the way of disinterested judgement. To be fair to Moeen and Rashid, who have made the most of their talent, they are less culpable than some who like to speak on their behalf, as though cricket was part of a social experiment designed to separate the virtuous from the damned.

Identity has often had more than one distinguishing feature. Exile and emigration, whether optional or enforced, introduce a dimension that is not present at birth. Henry James and T. S. Eliot, born in America, became British. Wystan Auden and P. G. Wodehouse took American citizenship. Józef Korzeniowski of Berdyczów in Polish Ukraine transformed himself into Joseph Conrad of Sussex. Wassily Kandinsky, Russian as a samovar, adopted first German and then French nationality. Thomas Mann, who spent the Second World War in America and then retired to Switzerland, was proud to say 'wherever I am, is Germany'. A person may have multiple identities. A team has only one.

In that newspaper column Moeen highlighted the England team's motto of 'courage, unity and respect', like Gene Kelly in *Singin' in the Rain* spelling out 'dignity, always dignity'. Uniting the country, he said, trying not to sound too solemn, 'was always the bigger cause for us'.

Those players discovered, like so many sportsmen before them, that people associate with winning teams, irrespective of their social composition. It is a human trait to rally round the triumphant, and if victory makes a nation feel good about itself then so much the better. Moeen's heart was in the right place, even if his bat increasingly wasn't.

The best game in the World Cup, other than the final, came at Trent Bridge on the first Monday of June when Pakistan beat England by 14 runs. Moeen's bat did not come down courageously or respectfully that day. After Joe Root and Jos Buttler had made centuries to lead the team's pursuit of Pakistan's 313 for seven, they looked towards him as a senior player to see the job through. The responsibility proved beyond him. He lost his place in the side, and his team-mates found a way to win the tournament without him.

That was a happy day for the Pakistanis who had gone to Nottingham wondering what kind of dish their team would set before them. It turned out to be a banquet, and their rejoicing was understandable. It was also a good day for the English spectators, who saw a well-contested match played in what appeared to be a good atmosphere.

Certainly the spectators around us, who were mainly

Pakistan followers, behaved with an even-handedness that was warming. Although they wanted their side to win, many clearly identified as British. It was a day of amity and apparent unity, so it was a bit unsettling to read the next day of how some England players had been abused by flag-waving Pakistanis as they fielded by the boundary.

Better to hold to the view formed on the day. It was a happy occasion, and the right outcome. There will always be a few birdbrains. Anyway, nothing should be allowed to take the edge off a day at Trent Bridge, a ground where unpleasant thoughts should be forbidden by statute.

If only Root could turn the clock back to 3 June, and have another go. The century he made at Trent Bridge was the first of only two three-figure scores in a summer that began to curdle on the opening day of the series against Australia, the rubber he had to win to prove he was a leader and not just captain in title. That first afternoon at Edgbaston the Australians were on the ropes at 122 for eight as the bowlers made light of James Anderson's withdrawal from the fray with a calf injury. It was then that Steve Smith, restored to the national side after serving a year-long ban for ball-tampering, and reduced from Hauptmann to other ranks, showed the world who was the real leader. He made a century, and added another in the second innings as Australia plundered victory by 247 runs.

In the second Test it was only Archer's heat-seeking bouncer that denied him a third successive century. He was fully primed again at Old Trafford in the fourth Test, to the giddy tune of 220 runs in Australia's first innings, which put them 2–1 ahead and retained the Ashes. Smith made 774 runs in seven innings, confirming his status as a member of international cricket's top table where he bangs bumpers of mead with Virat Kohli and Kane Williamson.

Root's aggregate of 325 runs from ten innings represented the scraps fed to minions. There were no centuries, and many blunders. Far too often he got himself out when he appeared to be set, and the harder he tried the more desperate his failure. This was a '*Kaiser und König*' summer for Root, a double-headed eagle. He could show everybody he was a great player, and lead England to victory against Australia in sport's oldest rivalry. On both counts he was weighed in the balance and found wanting. By September his mood had gone beyond careworn. He looked a troubled soul.

Many times the mind went back to the Lord's Test of 2013 when Root made 180 in England's second innings, going in first. He was 22, and batted like a prince as England overwhelmed the Australians by 347 runs. They could do no wrong that summer, and Root's century was interpreted as a harbinger of things to come. Here was a batsman of distinction, and a captain in waiting.

Smith batted at number seven in that match, making one and two, and bowled a few overs of leg spin. Not a few spectators wondered what a bits-and-pieces player was doing in their team. Now the whole world knows. After that year of disgrace the man who blubbed before the cameras on losing the captaincy of Australia returned in glory. Like Stokes, he wrote his own notices.

Credences are beliefs, and those beliefs feed into the way we see the game. The statistics reveal that Smith has achieved greatness. An average of 62 after 70 Tests, with 26 centuries in his pouch, leaves little room for doubt. From an aesthetic point of view, however, he will never be mistaken for Mr Wonderful. This was a summer of personal triumph. It was not a summer of delight.

Does it matter? For the bread-and-water materialists who insist sport is about how many, not how, it matters not a bit. But if sport does not fire the imagination it is not worth a fig. Facts are the mere bones of a game. They tell us what happened. True glory comes from the way players make things happen.

Nobody of a romantic disposition would ever rank Rafael Nadal above Roger Federer. Both are great men of the tennis court but one stands apart because he plays as we do in our dreams. The same powers of imagination separate Lionel Messi from Cristiano Ronaldo. The Portuguese is a phenomenon of muscularity. The Argentine belongs to a guild of craftsmen numbering only a dozen in the history of the game. Severiano Ballesteros had the same capacity to inspire devotion. Other golfers struck the ball further, and putted with more skill. He had some quality that cannot be acquired by rote, only recognised as the touch of the elect.

Facts, Mr Nickleby! Up to a point, Mr Squeers, and no further. The imagination also has its uses. It may help us see the world more truthfully.

Jacques Kallis was undeniably a great batsman. He made 55 runs every time he batted for South Africa. There were 46 centuries in Tests, hewn out of granite. Yet few people purr with pleasure at the mention of his name. He was relentless, and relentlessness rarely stirs the spirit. David Gower's Test average was 11 runs lighter, and those who saw him bat will never forget the grace of his strokeplay.

Colin Cowdrey, another man who would fit snugly into a Charmers' XI, thought it was possible to assess a batsman, in part, by the way he picked up the willow. Ken Tynan spoke for many when he said he would rather watch Neil Harvey make 20 than Winston Place of Lancashire plod all day for a century.

It was Tynan, in his day job as a theatre critic, who identified 'the high definition performer'. He was thinking of actors such as Laurence Olivier and John Gielgud, who in their different ways defined the nature of great acting. Olivier was earth, thought Tynan; Gielgud, air. What united them was a command that came from years of stagecraft allied to an imagination that made the words fly. Andrés Segovia and Rudolf Nureyev were high definition performers, as were Judy Garland and Lester Young. Dear old Doddy, too.

A personal inventory of 'credences' would always place Brian Lara ahead of Sachin Tendulkar. Lara won matches through brilliance and daring, often against daunting odds. Give me Mark Waugh any day to some cold-eyed accumulator; or that dashing opener Michael Slater, who took on the best bowlers at their freshest and, by defeating them, achieved glory. On the pleasure principle the romantic vote goes to the Sri Lankan trio of Aravinda de Silva, Mahela Jayawardene and Kumar Sangakkara. Occasionally pleasure translates into majesty. Barry Richards and Greg Chappell offered evidence every time they walked to the crease; Warne as he prepared to bowl. And Garry, of course, with bat or ball.

Smith may be excused. For all his runs he makes a

displeasing sight, twitching after each ball, rearranging every part of his armour as part of a tiresome ritual. It's like watching a one-man band who has attached coconuts to his ankles, cymbals to his knees, a horn to his mouth and bells to his cap. He has also acquired a smugness that suggests he alone is the judge of his work. After every boundary he seems to mull over the execution of the stroke, and award himself marks out of ten.

To some eyes his batting may be a thing of beauty. Not a romantic's eyes. Be gone, worthy Smith, back to your forge.

There were happier memories to take from this last summer of county cricket. They were supplied by a man of 43, and a greenhorn 22 years junior. Darren Stevens of Kent showed everybody, not least the folk at Kent who thought they could do without him, that he was still a cricketer of substance. Ollie Pope of Surrey revealed touches of a talent that should burn for years to come.

Few players have ended a season in the manner that Stevens chose. Going in to bat at Headingley when the score stood at 39 for five he caned the Yorkshire bowling for a career-best 237, with nine sixes. He then took five for 20 as Kent won by 433 runs.

In the final match, against woebegone Nottinghamshire, he helped his team win by 227 runs. His share was 88 when Kent batted and ten wickets, distributed equally between the innings. Here was a cricketer content to carry on until they take his bat away, out of love for the game. As for Notts, relegated after losing 10 matches out of 14, and winning none, how far it seemed from that day in April when Joe Clarke's century suggested the summer was full of possibility.

Pope missed most of the season after dislocating his left shoulder in May. When he returned to the Surrey team in August he made an unbeaten 221 against Hampshire, which helped make up for lost time. In his seven hours at the crease at least one mind went back to Malvern and recalled Elgar's thoughts on his first symphony, 'a massive hope for the future'. As English cricket prepares for its Year Zero we have to hold on to something.

Postlude

After a summer of cricket, it's time for an autumn restorative in Munich and a cleansing week of paintings.

The Flemish and German masters dominate the Alte Pinakothek. Kandinsky, Klee and Gabriele Münter hold court in the Lenbachhaus, home of the Blue Rider group, which made such a charge in the momentous year of 1911. The Pinakothek der Moderne outclasses Tate Modern by the length of Maximilianstrasse. The Neue Pinakothek, alas, is closed for repairs. No matter. There are riches, by the score, and not enough hours in the day.

Munich is Bavarian, German and, befitting its reputation as 'the most Italian city north of the Alps', European. It feels comfortable in all three faces it presents to the world, and the world feels comfortable here. All year round thousands of visitors may be found in Marienplatz, waiting for the glockenspiel chimes, or strolling in the Englischer Garten. Everywhere you look people are revelling in the riches of a confident metropolis.

Some of those visitors occasionally play cricket in the Englischer Garten. In July 1996 I was one of them, turning out for a London XI against MCC (Munich Cricket Club) on a matting pitch inside a running track on the southern fringe of the park. The next day I drove across the Austrian border with Daniel Harding, the young English conductor, to hear Simon Rattle direct the Vienna Philharmonic Orchestra at the Salzburg Festival.

Eleven years later Danny and I returned to the festival. He was now conducting that great orchestra himself, in *The Marriage of Figaro* no less, and I was listening at quarters that could not have been closer. 'Sit in the pit,' he said. 'Wear something dark, and don't stand up to peer at the audience.' Shades of Noël Coward's instructions to his actors!

I did as I was bid, perched on a chair so near the violins I could have turned the pages of the score. It felt like fielding at third slip in a Test match, invisible to all except the players. Not even Cardus, who spent almost as many hours at Salzburg as at Lord's, ever got quite so close to the Vienna Philharmonic.

There is an ease about these cities that puts our crowded, increasingly grubby towns to shame. How well they dress. How well they eat and drink. How content they appear. Too content, possibly. Many Germans regard Bavarians with a detachment bordering on distaste. But there is no doubt that Munich works in ways that should make Britons envious.

Yet even here the serpent lurks.

For 25 years I have feasted on hearty peasant food at Andechser am Dom, situated directly behind the high altar of the twin-domed cathedral, and drained the superb beers brewed for the restaurant by the monks at the monastery in Andechs, 15 miles south-west of the city. It is a Munich landmark, or was, for now it has gone. The block was excised last year, like a troublesome tooth, and will be replaced by offices and – where that convivial meeting place stood – a Bayern München fan shop. As if this city needed one more.

They have re-created 'Andechser' 80 yards away. The beer is still magnificent, the black pudding the best in the world, and the serving lads and lasses wear their traditional clobber. They are putting on a brave face but it is not the same. On the principle of 'excuses that make them all needs', another of life's small pleasures has been lost. And those pleasures are never quite as small as the modernisers imagine.

At Lord's, meanwhile, the Hundred auction came round at last, and had cricket's modernisers drooling into their porridge. Televised live by Sky, and conducted in a spirit of general bafflement, presenters encouraged to 'make every ball an event' welcomed viewers to the self-willed world of a sport happy to proclaim it knows the cost of everything and the value of nothing. That Sunday evening it was another of Wilde's lines that resonated, the one about each man killing the thing he loves.

The identity of the eight teams was officially declared, though 'identity' is *le mot faux*. There can be no sense of belonging when decades of tradition have been ripped up to create cosy amalgamations for the benefit of the ECB's marketing department. How pleased they must be with their work: Birmingham Phoenix, London Spirit, Manchester Originals, Northern Superchargers, Oval Invincibles, Southern Brave, Trent Rockets and Welsh Fire. Is this not progress?

Each franchise was permitted a centrally contracted England player, and the Superchargers, representing Durham and Yorkshire, opted for Ben Stokes, hero of the summer. That meant Joe Root, the Test captain, was packed off to Trent Rockets and another Yorkshireman, Jonny Bairstow, was dispatched to Welsh Fire.

A three-course dinner for dogs.

Then the real fun began. The selectors had 100 seconds to choose players in salary bands between £30,000 and £125,000. Liam Livingstone of Lancashire went to Birmingham, and Ben Foakes of Surrey was snapped up by those eagle-eyed Superchargers. Another Surrey man, Ollie Pope, was collared by the mob at Southampton. They may just as well have thrown all the names in the air, like confetti.

Rashid Khan, the Rockets-bound Afghani wrist spinner, led the procession of overseas players, three to each team. There were also two 'local icons', which in the case of Tom Banton proved a faulty signifier on both counts. The Somerset batsman, all of 20, and yet to make a century in first-class cricket, will play as a 'Fireman' at Cardiff. As Paul McCartney sang of another fireman, in 'Penny Lane': 'Very strange'.

Publicity photographs showed representatives of the eight franchises, four men and four women, looking sheepish in their new kit. Six, uncertain of what pose to adopt, reflexively thrust their hands into their pockets. It was a group portrait of awkward teenagers; an entirely appropriate snapshot, as that is the audience the ECB longs to conquer.

The eight coaches, naturally, all came from other lands. Five were Australians, supported by a New Zealander, a South African and a Sri Lankan. By such means are the game's governors determined to revive the spirits of all involved with the game in England.

After a year of guesswork nobody was wiser. The general view seemed to be that although it is unlikely to succeed, in any meaningful sense, the Hundred, with its ten-ball overs and time-outs, will not be allowed to fail. Its sponsors have invested too much money in the enterprise, and will carry on prodding the naysayers until they give in. The process of re-education will not end until they can plant a pole on some snow-capped summit and say, 'We've done it!'

Cardus the myth-maker has finally been disproved. From now on there will be high summer in England without county cricket. It turns no wheels, bakes no bread, and therefore serves no purpose. Without a county championship worthy of the name Test cricket may also fall in time, and that really will be England gone.

The boat heading for the new world awaits, rigged and masted. All we can do is hand the game on, and hope those eager to remake it in a manner of their choosing acknowledge we did our best. If we promise to be good they may even wave at us.

Valete

All glory, laud and honour to those friends who brightened the days and made the nights merry. A 'double excellent' to Andreas Campomar, who persuaded me to write this book over breakfast at Clarke's in Kensington Church Street. Thanks also to Claire Chesser, Howard Watson and Kate Truman. Chapeaux to my 'readers': Malcolm Ashton, Michael Billington, Boynton of Bulawayo, Philip Collins, Neil Hallam, Duncan Hamilton, Rowley Leigh, Colin Shindler, Mark Semmence and Sue Wakefield, whose advice was rigorous and precise.

The book is dedicated to Giles Phillips, who ran a tight ship for three decades at Albertine in Shepherd's Bush, even if a few matelots had occasionally to be fished out of the briny. And it honours the memory of Bob Willis, a great servant of English cricket and an imperishable friend. How we miss you, Bobby.

Others played a part, whether they knew it or not: Andrew Arends, Michael Atherton, Ed Atkinson, Philippe Auclair, Mark Baldwin, John Billington, Keith Blackmore, Henry Blofeld, Ian Bousfield, Jo Bridgeman, Martin Campbell-White, David Chappell, Paul Thomas Cook, Tom Courtenay, Jonathan Coy, Al Denham, James Denham, Charles Dent, Mike Dickson, Marina Dudley Williams, Sebastian Faulks, Charlie Feather, Angus Fraser, Nigel Gardner, Craig Goldsack, Simon Haggas, Richard Harding, Jamie Hayes, Don Hewitson, Huw Humphreys, Barry Kernon, Bruce Knight, Robert Madge, Jonathan Marland, 'The Marshalls', Jeremy Martin, Paul Matcham, Professor Michael Morley, Graham and Diana Morris, Patrick Murphy, Jeremy Ogden, Michael Parkinson, Tim Rice, James Ross, Sybil Ruscoe, Mike Selvey, David Shepherd, Michael Simkins, John Snow, Mark Stimpfig, John Tomlinson, Stan Townsend, Francis Wheen, Richard Williams, John Woodcock, Anthony Wreford and Roger Wright.

Some friends no longer with us added a verse or two: Barrie Atherton, Brian Bearshaw, Stephen Fay, David Green, Geoff Hartley, Ronnie Harwood, Michael Kennedy, Alan Lee, Geoff McMillan, C. M.-J., Robert Mills, Gerald Mortimer, Barry Norman, Tony Reeve, Martin Searby, Chris Travers, Alan Tweedale and David Welch.

The summer was illuminated by some great musicians: Julian Adderley, Bill Evans, Johnny Hodges, Paul Lewis, Hank Mobley, the Takacs Quartet, Ben Webster and Lester Young. Astaire, Bennett, Ella and Sinatra are always there. Neil Hallam replenished the table in September with prime cuts of Dexter Gordon. He also shared the most toothsome ale I drank, in the best pub: Timothy Taylor Landlord at the Holly Bush in Makeney. English classics, both.

It is only fair to acknowledge P. L., who would have been as rude about the Hundred as he was about John 'Honker' Coltrane. He had the first word and will have the last: 'We should be kind, while there is still time.'